RAISING WEST POINT

THE UNMASKING OF A HERO

CHRISTINA HUNTER

ISBN 978-1-0980-8104-1 (paperback)
ISBN 978-1-0980-9325-9 (hardcover)
ISBN 978-1-0980-8105-8 (digital)

Christian Faith Publishing, Inc.
832 Park Avenue
Meadville, PA 16335
www.christianfaithpublishing.com

Printed in the United States of America

PRELUDE

I believe everyone's story in life has been written already, and God has a brilliant plan for our lives before we are born. I also believe that how we choose to go through that journey changes and molds us into who we ultimately become as humans. A big problem in our society today is that too many people, especially parents, are largely focused on their goals to be comfortable in life, whatever that source of comfort is to them. Too many people in society are okay with status quo. They are okay with being typical and simple and just going through the motions on the day-to-day routine. They expect to just get through this life making a little money, having fun, retiring, and then dying. Having passionate fire and determination for greatness is not in the hearts of people I meet. If I do see someone who is goal-oriented and passionate about life, it is usually connected to selfish ambition in such that they are on a journey to be intelligent, be rich, and have a big beautiful house with an impressive bio, which ultimately leads to a big ego to go with it. Where are those people whose ultimate desire is to love their neighbor? Where are the people who climb that mountain of greatness and become something bigger than themselves for the sake of others? This book is a story about my experiences in life and why I believe God's love in us can change the world. It's my journey through a scary beautiful world. It's my testimony of God's unconditional love toward me and how I learned how to channel that love as I searched for inner joy and peace.

When I was a little girl, my dad told me I could do anything I wanted in life and that nothing could stop me from becoming a vessel of honor for God. This intrigued me as a young child; but as I got older and life's challenges seemed too difficult to over-come, I lost some hope and felt very lonely in my seemingly mun-dane existence, trapped by my own fear of failure, and unable to break the chains of anxiety stemming from feelings of self-doubt. I never forgot the words and teachings my dad instilled in me, and as I continue to journey through life, I cling to the idea that, even through my failures, God still loves me and has a good plan for my life. As I am a now, a married mom of six and a registered nurse, I am thirty-eight years old but still feel like a child since I am constantly learning of weaknesses I never knew I had. I have to tell of what I learned on this beautifully chaotic journey we call life as I struggled to overcome obstacles and conquered adversity while working to raise my kids to be more than just survivors of this life but kids who have a passion to succeed and grow to become the best possible version of themselves.

It's become my mission to teach my kids to be more than just common clay used by the potter but to be well trained, ready, and willing to grow into instruments useful for noble purposes and honorable vessels for God. God has never left my side; and as I was faced with the ultimate battle of supporting my oldest child, Sabria, on her journey to West Point Military Academy to become an officer in the army and play Division 1 basketball, I found that I needed God's strength, love, power, and guidance more than ever. I will tell of the struggle I had becoming an advocate for my kids in school, sports, and then with Sabria after she was injured at the academy. I was faced with being that parent on the sideline as my son Quintin was carried off the football field after a serious injury. This is a story of how I witnessed a true miracle in my life as I learned that one can have complete joy and peace while staring in the face of fear and opposition at every angle. When three of my kids needed surgeries in a four-month span, I learned that while every day brings suffering and storms, it also brings opportunity to be that light at the end of someone's tunnel, proof that, even while going through our own struggles, we should be loving our neighbor, and how this unconditional love is what brings us peace. I learned that by raising your kids up to know and love God, they can be sent out like flaming arrows on a passionate mission, spreading Gods love to the world.

CHAPTER 1

LEADING UP TO R DAY

O n the days leading up to R Day, which was the day we would drop Sabria off at West Point and she would begin in-processing, I found myself looking at who I was and trying to let God prepare me for what was to come. I knew Sabria was choosing the path of most resistance, as was the opposite of most people these days. I always told the kids that if they were ever in a situation that required them to make a choice between two roads, the harder one was most likely the best choice. Just go the harder route because the results will always be worth the efforts. The road to greatness is narrow, and not all will choose that route. Most athletes who are being recruited will choose the most popular school. The best-rated program for their particular sport of choice. They want to be a hero somewhere or want to at least wear a jersey that represents the idea of heroism. Many don't care intently on the latter part of their life when they are eighteen. Their priority is to get into a top-ranked school. The more popular view is to get more bang for their buck. Work hard now, and rest easy forever more. Sabria had a different view. She gave so much of herself and lived so passionately up to this point that as she looked at her options (she had a box full of college offers), she just couldn't get away from the desire that burned inside her to want more. It seems like such a cliché nowadays.

Kids are pushing themselves hard into the doors of a paid education. We've all known "that kid" who tells the whole world what school they've been recruited to. Since seventh grade, they'd been sought out by a particular impressive college. Meanwhile, no one talks about how they have an uncle or some family member in the sports arena who has paved the way for them the whole time. They're not a tremendous athlete, especially at seventh grade. They may have a lot of potential at that age. In fact, Sabria was told in seventh grade that she had the potential to play Division 1 basketball if she worked hard and continued to improve. No one should ever just assume they have a full ride to college at a young age. This way of thinking opens the door to so much negativity including self-entitlement, unmerited boldness, lack of commitment, and lack of desire to persevere. They will not reach their full potential but are used to being treated as superior athletes. So when they are passed by a runner in a conditioning class or they make a mistake on the field or court, they can't own the fail. They will quickly make some cheap excuse for the display of weakness when it could be just a simple mistake anyone could have made or just that they simply couldn't keep up with the well-conditioned athlete next to them who will never get that chance to play in college but who just showed them up in the gym because they dare to dream and have passion with the belief that anything is possible. These "self-entitled" kids may, in fact, go on and play well in their sport in college, but good character never develops. It's a true shame. I've worked very closely with athletes of this nature, and it isn't a pretty sight. Sabria had little patience or respect for these athletes because they only cared about the superficial. They wanted the look of a good athlete on the outside, but everything inside was fake, always looking for the opportunity to boast or brag of their big plans for the future. She hadn't initially even looked at West Point, but when the topic came up, her curiosity drove her to investigate. A college that wants you to strive to live for something bigger than yourself? That was the phrase Sabria had heard from me many times going into a game. "Remember to play for something bigger than yourself." The phrase really hit home when there was a dad at one of the school events in our township who told Sabria something that she never forgot. He said that his little daughter, who was in grade school at the time, ran around the living room at home with her little basketball pretending not to be Michael Jordan or Lebron James but to be Sabria Hunter. Sabria was intrigued, and this fueled the fire within her to strive to extend the ceiling of her potential. To be even better than she could imagine but not for her own sake, for the sake of the little ones who watched her so they could know that their own potential was yet to be known but the possibilities were endless.

If we all tried to max out our potential only to push our own ceiling of limits higher and higher, what kind of world would we live in? We would break the chains of self-doubt for ourselves and encourage our kids to do the same. Everyone would say to Sabria that with a degree from West Point, she could go anywhere and she would be set for life. Sabria appreciated the compliment, but it was not seen that way to her. She would put everything aside for the completion of this program. She would lose many freedoms she once had and would be willing to die for her country if that was necessary. She would commit to give 100 percent of herself, leave her close-knit family, and be forced to love her siblings from four hundred miles away. She knew this program would have the potential to change her but in an amazing way. The price she was paying to learn to a high degree the way of living a life of service and a commitment to duty, honor, and country was too costly to just have the reputation of being a West Point grad. She was humble enough to understand that it would be eleven years by the time this process of getting "set for life" was completed. By then, many things would have changed at home. These would be years not just spent studying, doing roll call, surviving SAMI, working and thinking well under extreme conditions, sleeping with her rifle at her side, learning to put the anxieties of soldier life aside to appreciate the simple game of basketball, and, of course, playing at the Division 1 level. This would all be at the cost of losing her spot at her five younger siblings' birthday parties, basketball games, family outings at the lake, and all the little joys of living as the oldest of six kids, and leaving a community where she'd grown to love and had loved her. I knew Sabria understood the true struggle she was going to experience, but in the months leading up to her leaving, we were all very connected to what we had as a close-knit family, and we truly engaged in the opportunities to spend quality time together.

One particular evening, I went rummaging through Sabria's room looking for a cube to charge my phone and was distracted by the beautiful presence of my sleeping kid. She was wrapped in my special decorative blanket, which was an illegal act in our house, but that night, I didn't care. I did not ignore the tremendous urge to put everything aside and seize the opportunity to embrace the moment. I gently crawled into Sabria's bed and cuddled my friend. I wrapped my arm around her being careful not to wake her. I lay there feeling her back push up against my chest and move rhythmically in and out as she slept. I was overwhelmed with the gratefulness I was feeling for that moment in time—thankful that I could see my sweetie, feel her skin, and hear her breath next to me. My eyes filled with tears as I realized how precious that moment was. In a few short months, I'd say goodbye to her and see her off to West Point, where she'd stay about four hundred miles away from me. Suddenly, I heard the wind blowing outside and the rickety windows shaking against the walls in our old house, reminding me of how I'd once hoped I'd be able to replace those old windows with new ones and how it no longer mattered to me. *Who cares about those old lousy windows when my baby is leaving?* I thought. I began to lose control of my building emotions. I didn't want her to hear my sniffling or feel my body trembling with sadness. So I tried to contain myself, calming myself as my tears moistened the pillow beneath my head, thinking of how my family will be destroyed after Sabria left but understanding this destruction would lead to a new construction of our family that was better and stronger than the unit it was before. I didn't know how we would deal with this. I did know that our hearts would need to be healed because part of our hearts would go to New York with Sabria, never to be put back into our chest. The healing we would need after, that could only be done by God. The wound would heal, and a scar would take shape, reminding us of the piece that was once there but was now gone. Sabria leaving our home in such a big way would leave a mark. As that chapter in our books closed, we would have to tell our hearts to beat again and to a new rhythm. We would have to adapt. Sabria was my best friend and a second mother to her siblings. Her dreams were our dreams, and our dreams were hers. We as a family spent our days adjusting and bending to each other to face battles of everyday life as a team, a special unit, celebrating in each other's victories and suffering together in times of trouble or defeat. I lay there hoping that she didn't forget about me. I could picture her in her uniform, at the academy adapting, thriving. But I hoped she would remember her tools back home. Those who had her back no matter what. Those who would hear her cries for help even when she made no noise and would know what she needed without her even asking. We would remain by her side, and the scars on our hearts would invest us further in the love and respect we had for our girl and would always remind us of the connection we have as a family and that God placed us together on this earth for a big reason. So wherever she was, whatever she was experiencing, we would remain by her side. I hoped she never forgot her roots and that the thought of us at home would not induce sadness but that with every heartbeat in her chest, she would feel her family there with her. That as she breathed in the fresh mountain air, the smell would remind her of home, of us—the ones she left behind but who also followed her in spirit and heart. Then we would never be far apart. I lay there next to her, embracing the freedom of being in her presence. A freedom I would soon no longer have. The freedom to smell her hair and wonder why I could use the same shampoo as her but my hair never smelled quite as good as hers. That moment was a gift, and I was so grateful for it. My grandma had told me when I was young to be careful to stop and smell the roses. This was a moment that I had the chance to stop what I was doing and smell the most beautiful flower. To inhale the aroma of Sabria. These are the moments of great opportunity. To see God's gift of grace in life and to take a moment to come away from the busyness of life's responsibilities and to find rest in the beauty and splendor of his creation.

Sometimes, as I was preparing for Sabria to leave, I'd be walking down the halls at work becoming overwhelmed with sadness. I'd pray, "God, I love that girl so much. How am I ever going to let her go?" The tears would come, and I'd have to go to a room alone to refocus and collect myself. It brought me back to the story about Jesus preparing to leave his disciples as the Crucifixion was approaching. He explained that the reason he was leaving them was it was in their best interest, that his leaving would allow the coming of the Holy Spirit. I knew that supporting Sabria to go on her journey was good, but I was struggling as I tried to understand how it would be good for me and the kids to let our friend go away. I thought, *There must be something really great in exchange for Sabria going away, but what is it? The one who teaches me how to detox and exfoliate and helps me find time to smell the roses. The one who tells me I look skinny when I least expect it and helps me with laundry when it's consuming me, who calls me on her way home to ask if I want a "coffee from Dunkin?"* I prayed, "Please God tell me how

I will survive without my best friend." I was struggling sending my daughter to West Point. Everyone thought I was so strong. I would hold back my tears until I was in my car driving home from work. This is when I would find myself becoming emotional, when I was alone with God and my thoughts. When people asked how I felt about Sabria going, I would say I was proud of her, which I was very proud of her. The truth was, I let her go a long time ago when I made the decision to be her mom, *when* I made the decision against abortion or adoption but to be what God asked me to be, her mom. As her mom and a teenager, myself at the time, I did the best thing I knew to do: turn her over to God and put her in his hands. This is where I left her eighteen years ago and this is where she'll remain. I knew back then as a young single mom that I wasn't good enough to have the beautiful gift of a child. I wasn't worthy to be a mom. No one really is. But I knew God wouldn't call me to do something that he wouldn't equip me to do. I knew I didn't have what it took to raise a kid on my own; but with God's grace, strength, wisdom, and guidance, I could do it. That was how I could take on such an honorable task. This is God's child. If he called her to the military academy, that's where she's going. I, as her mom, am honored to assist her in this opportunity. This is how I responded to her decision to go. I believed that no one including family and friends could understand or imagine how I was feeling at that time. It really is unexplainable. From the outside, I appeared to have it all together, but I was hurting and sorting this all out. I was continuously depending on God for direction to lead me as he remained my shelter, refuge, deliverer, and friend. He's the only one who truly knows how I was feeling. He taught me that all that love Sabria had shown me from day one, as a daughter, she can show to the world as an army officer and basketball player. That's my answer! *That's why I need to let her go*, I thought. Because God knit her in my womb for this very purpose. This is what all the work was for. All the sacrifices in life and all the struggles that as a mother caused me to love her more and more over the years, this was the reward. She has learned love and wants to give it to the world. I'm not losing her. I'm gaining. She's doing what I've been asking her to do all along. She's prospering, living in the hope and in the future of God's promises. She's not leaving me... She's loving me. Even being the living proof of God's love for me. She's my window to heaven. I thought, *If she can be that for me, how many others can she show God's love to? She's become the fruit of my labor, and now she has given me the opportunity to look forward to hearing her stories of how she loves others in her time in West Point as she learns to be an officer in the United States Army.* I asked for understanding, and God gave me more than that. He gave me a new perspective. That's when I began to really get excited for what the future would bring concerning Sabria leaving for West Point. This understanding allowed the sadness that held me captive to be overpowered, breaking the chains of fear and doubt about her leaving.

CHAPTER 2

THE FIVE-MINUTE CALL

I was at work in a patient's room. I will remember the time and place forever as it's ingrained in my heart and mind. It was 1700 (5:00 p.m.). My phone was ringing. I quickly looked down to see it was a number I didn't recognize. Up to this point, Sabria had been in basic training for almost two weeks. No communication was allowed with anyone outside of West Point. No TV, phone, or radio. Cell phones got taken during in-processing and put in a locked box. The days leading up to this phone call were very taxing. I faced many challenges after leaving my oldest child, Sabria, at West Point including anxiety, sadness, and sheer exhaustion. I would dream about West Point in my sleep. Sabria was my last thought before bed probably because this was mostly when I finally had time to write her letters. She was also my first thought in the morning when I woke up, and I would dream about her in my sleep. I worked swing shifts so if I had the chance to sleep in, I would. Then I would feel guilty because I knew Sabria wouldn't get to sleep in. Her day started at 5:00 a.m. and ended at 10:00 p.m., and she was working even harder than me and getting very few breaks in between. I even felt bad eating because Sabria ate when she was told to eat and ate what she was told to eat and how she was to eat, so why, as her mother, do I get to eat whenever, whatever, and however I want? I lost my appetite even getting nauseous at the thought of eating. I had a hard time doing simple things like going to Dunkin' Donuts for coffee because, number one, Sabria went there almost daily when she was home and I knew she couldn't continue that routine at the academy. Number two, I became so concerned about saving money to go see her that even a couple dollars for coffee was too much money spent. So I would pass Dunkin' Donuts and figure she and I would get coffee together when we met up again.

We came home from West Point after dropping Sabria off with only a few hundred bucks to our name. I had already emptied all of my savings except for maybe a hundred bucks to get Sabria squared away with admission fees over the last year and all needed supplies up to this point. I thought, *Well, I guess I'm going to skip that oil change on my car.* It was already four hundred miles over, but I planned to get it done when we got back from the trip. My brother added a quart of oil and checked out my other fluids and tires for me. I felt we could hold on till we got back on our feet financially. But then my next paycheck came, and as I was expecting some relief, I then remembered that I had gotten cancelled from work when they didn't need my help at the hospital, and once again I was faced with the reality that I could pay my bills but that only left me with $250 to get us through for two more weeks until we got paid again. I was really feeling defeated. All of this that Sabria was doing and all this my family was giving up to make a difference and I couldn't even afford to buy groceries. I knew this was going to be a very hard two weeks. I just prayed that the hospital would have work for me. Sure enough, that very day I was able to pick up four extra hours, which made my shift sixteen hours. The next day, the hospital was still busy, so I went into work even though I had RSVP'd to my family reunion at the lake. I figured it was a no-brainer since my family was so broke. But the sun was shining outside, and I knew everyone was going to eat, visit, play, and have fun, but the Hunters had to miss it. I was feeling really down, and there I was again, sixteen hours at work. I had about four hours of sleep in between those two doubles, but I always worked at max capacity. I don't cheat my patients or coworkers, because I'm tired or sad. I figured if my honey is suffering at West Point and striving to make a difference, so would I.

My attitude changed and I realized I was on a mission. I thanked God for putting me on a mission, a mission to take care of my family and get us out of the rut we were in. This is where I was, emotionally and spiritually when my "five-minute call" came. It's called that because as a cadet, Sabria is given five strict minutes to call home during basic training. Your cadet can call at any time, so you have to just be ready and have your phone available to answer so you don't miss it. I had no idea when this phone call was coming from Sabria, but I was given a heads-up two days in advance. I was told that within forty-eight hours, the call would be coming. The call came about ten hours into my first of two sixteen-hour shifts. I looked at my phone as it rang. Jacksonville Florida came up. I was told to answer for numbers I didn't recognize, so when I saw this unfamiliar number, I knew that it must be her! I politely excused myself from my patient's room and headed down the hall. I answered, "Hello... Hello? Hello?" before she answered, and I could tell she was emotional and could barely speak. She was choked up. She struggled to softly mutter that little word *hello*. My heart leaped! It was my girl! "Sabria! Hi, honey! How are you! Talk to me! Let me hear your voice!" Finally, she said in a weak weepy voice, "I wanna come home so bad, Mom. I gotta get outta here." I said, "Oh, honey, why! It'll be okay! I miss you so much. Everyone is thinking of you and misses you so much. We are all here for you rooting you on. You are not alone." My stomach was twisted up like a pretzel. *She hates it*, I thought. *My God, is she giving up?* The academy had prepared me to be ready for our cadet to need encouraged at this point and to be a listening ear. It was all part of the process of working the person down to see if they had what it took to be a soldier and an officer in the army. Part of me was happy. *She needs me*, I thought. *She really does miss me. All this time I've been thinking of her and praying for her and crying over her, she really was suffering!* I was thinking a mile a second, so I prayed God would help me to know what to say and to calm down. Out of all the people in the whole world, she had one five-minute phone call, and she chose to call me. What a humbling feeling. She told me to write her as many letters as I possibly could. That it meant everything to get a letter from home. I said, "I am writing every day, and I don't want it to be overkill." She said, "No, I need 'em. Write as many as you can." She talked about Acceptance Day, which was the day after graduating from basic training when you get accepted into the core. She was looking forward to this day, knowing her dad, Bobby, and I would be coming to see her. She listed some things she wanted to do with us on that day that she believed she would make it to. She let me know she was allowed to be as far as seventy miles from the base. This was encouraging to me because she was always thinking ahead and finding ways to keep her focus during hard times, and this meant she was still in the game, telling herself there is encouragement in what was to come and the struggle was temporary. Then she said, "Mom, I have twenty seconds left." I told her I loved her and that I missed her. She told me to tell Papa, Dad, and the kids hi and that she loved them. She said, "Ok, I have to go." We reluctantly said our good-byes, and that was that. It wasn't enough time, but no time would be enough. She ended the call. She hung up first. It reminded me of R Day when they called her away from us and her dad and I proudly watched as she never looked back. She was on a mission then, and she still was now. Nothing changed. She was still a leader and much stronger than me.

After I hung the phone up, I sat down and gasped. I crumbled. I ugly cried. As wonderful as it was to hear her voice, I missed it already. I wanted her to be okay. I walked away from that phone call confused because I expected her to say, "Mom, this is so hard, but I love it," not "I gotta get out of here. I wanna come home so bad." I pondered her words and had vented my frustrations to my sister and dad. They were really able to help me understand the situation. I prayed, and God really calmed me so I could gain perspective in this. Sabria used me as a tool that day. She vented to someone she could trust. Someone who could understand her position. Someone who knew where she was coming from and could take what she said with a grain of salt to grind off the extra and see her heart. That person was me. God allowed me to be used as a vent. A detoxifier. A cleansing agent. Sabria always loved to use detoxifying masks, soaps, and teas to cleanse herself and rid her body of impurities. She was always looking for new ways to exfoliate, even putting together her own formulas of natural ingredients to create the perfect serum to rejuvenate. This was her chance to do that, but instead of a five-minute exfoliant mask, it was a five-minute call to Mom. I knew she wasn't giving up or coming home, but she was being put through hell and wanted me to know. She wanted to come clean with her feelings of missing home. She wanted to put her toughness aside for that five minutes with no judgment from the one on the other end, exfoliating her anxieties and shedding unnecessary, negativity, stress, and sadness to expose her true feelings of love, determination to succeed, peace, and joy. I was able to be that exfoliant for her that day. I was honored to be used by God that day to be an outlet for my girl. I will forever be grateful that she gave me that opportunity and those precious five minutes.

As we sat for our briefing on R Day just a couple of weeks before this phone call, we were told about how the program at West Point was designed to provide the cadets with fundamental soldier skills along with building the physical and mental endurance needed to be an officer in the army. It was understood that this journey to building a leader of good character was no easy task as it was announced that out of 11,674 applicants, 1,219 were being accepted into the program on that day (R Day) and would report to the cadet in the red sash and begin taking orders. This day of leaving Sabria and watching her walk away from me into the unknown played over and over again in my mind, always leaving me with a sense of pride and shear amazement at the bravery and unrelenting perseverance of these cadets during the very grueling admissions process and then into the start of this terrifically challenging experience they were embarking on. I had faith that this same unrelenting attitude of grit would continue to bring Sabria through the whole process to completion. The process was designed to weed out those who just weren't a right fit; and there were many different avenues that led to that particular road, the road to not completing the program and instead giving up and going home. After all there are many, several hundred it's presumed, who will not make it through the four years of this program for one reason or another. I was so proud of Sabria for her efforts thus far, and I had nothing but respect and hope for her now and for her in the future. Later on, she had written me a letter expressing that it really wasn't *that* bad there but blamed her homesickness for her emotional display on the phone that day. I think she needed to explain herself to herself. She was trying to make sense of that phone call. We both were, in our own ways, as it applied to us. We were connecting on that level. Both figuring ourselves out together. We were becoming closer than ever through the struggle of being apart and going through such trials. She wanted to make sure I knew she was tougher than that girl that called home that day. Her pride took a little beating after revealing some vulnerability, and she felt the need to explain herself to me. She was learning that even through fierce training you must remain humble. Be a savage but also maintain softness of heart. It's a balance many cannot achieve. In explaining herself, she was also protecting me. She didn't want me to worry about her, although I had much reason to worry but only in my weakness. God would protect my daughter. He was there with her where I couldn't be, and that was enough to calm my anxieties. Even in her struggles she was loving me, as her mom. Not wanting me to lose sleep over her battles. During all this, she was, in fact, teaching me about how it is possible to love at all times and in all circumstances and that unconditional love is a powerful source we can use to overcome any obstacle that separates us from success. I had no worry about losing sleep, because, as my daughter, her battle was my battle and our battles were fought by God. Although the road would be hard and tiresome, I remained confident in the hope that we would both learn and grow through this and the gains we expected to eventually see were worth our efforts in the struggle to continue the process.

CHAPTER 3

MY PRECIOUS PEARLS

A lthough my first pregnancy was experienced through a time of desperation in my life, I held all of my six pregnancies with the same regard. Those babies were gifts of grace. No parent has the right to claim their children as their own. If a child was conceived by in vitro, it was only by God's power and permission for that baby to implant, grow, and flourish. If God decides to take a baby to heaven before it's even born, that's his right. If someone chooses abortion, they chose the action of aborting, but it is God's decision to take that baby's life. After all, there are many babies whose moms attempted to abort but who are alive and well today possibly having a missing limb or distorted face as a reminder of the hate and disregard for their life, but they are, in fact, alive. Some have grown up with no lasting effects from the attempted abortion, and some still did, in fact, lose their life as God chose to take it. People of all walks of life will take birth control or will claim they wanted to get pregnant on this month or that time of year, and it happened. They really believe they planned their own child's existence. What craziness to think we had really any part in the existence of another human being. If God does allow someone to get pregnant when they seem to think it's best, that's nice. But the only power we actually have in the situation of procreating is the power God gave us in being a vessel. We all need to understand our place in this world and work to fit the best we can in the life of the child we were asked to parent, *sometimes* even being asked to parent a child we didn't birth ourselves. Miracles happen every day, but, unfortunately, people have lost their humility or maybe never had it in the first place in regards to being a parent and, therefore, don't even realize that they were given an opportunity to have a gift they didn't deserve, that they didn't earn or could ever create on their own. Every child was planned and planned by the One who made us all. None of us can rightfully take credit for our kids, good or bad. I am brought back to a memory I have when I was sitting in the stands one day at my son's first playoff football game of the season, freshman year. We were losing in the last minutes by three points. A man from the other team stood up with his arms raised as to if to welcome the victory and to announce his siding with the winning team. I looked to my husband sitting next to me and asked the rhetorical question, "Who is that man in the stands with the salmon-colored shirt, and who is he feeling like?" My husband said, "Well, actually, he has a son who played football in high school and went on to play in the NFL, so he can stand like that if he wants." My husband knows me better than that. I said, "And who does that make him if his son plays in the NFL? What does it make you that your daughter is in the army?" I answered my own question by telling him, "It makes you nothing…" Too many times people want credit for things they didn't earn. Even if as a parent you expend all your efforts in raising your kids to the best of your abilities and spent every penny you made investing in their good fortune, you still only did maybe a portion of what was expected of you in the first place.

We as parents should be continuously praying that God protects and prospers our kids despite our own shortcomings as parents. We should, instead of bragging of our kid's successes, be careful to get out of the way of God's perfect plan for their lives. If our kids do anything good in life, it is through the grace of God. As those kids grow up, parents will need to continue to be an example of God's love to them and thank God for the honor of loving them every day and in every way possible. It is silly to believe our job of loving our kids and sacrificing for them ends when they turn a certain age. There are many kids in the world who need loved, and those kids turn into adults who need loved. No one child or adult is better than another, but I believe the Bible states it best when it talks about running the race as if it mattered. We will all get a crown when we get to heaven. So why try hard on earth? Because God says to. Faith without deeds is dead. Being faithful in raising your kids to love God will allow your faith in him to grow, resulting in the birth of humility, which is needed to continue loving them as adults knowing all along we never deserved the task of loving them in the first place. It is a privilege and honor to love those around us, and to live a life of service is a true gift of grace. If we can learn to change our attitudes toward our responsibility to our kids and to our daily tasks in life, in general, we can become new creatures and make a positive impact on those around us resulting in the spread of more positive change.

As a child, I feared death. As I grow up, I realize how amazing it will be to be in perfect peace in heaven to escape the ever-steady challenges of my life here on earth. But I am reminded every single day to trust in God's love for me. He has blessed me with six beautiful kids who he uses to teach me of this love; and I now realize that although I do still look forward to my life in heaven, God showed me through raising my kids that he doesn't hold back all of heaven from us while we're here on earth. He showed me that the best part of heaven is him, and he is here with us. Often the very answer we need to any problem we are facing in life is sitting inside someone next to us just waiting to be discovered. As expert divers search the sea to find those oyster shells that house the most delicate and beautiful pearls, we should be searching around us for those beautiful signs of God's love and existence in our life. One day, as I was struggling through my day already wishing I could throw the towel in on my efforts in this life, my attention was turned to one of my kids yelling from the kitchen, "Mom! The ceiling is leaking!" I raced downstairs to find that one of our old pipes must have broken in the bathroom, which was right on top of our kitchen. I freaked. I was overwhelmed. I had recently been painting that kitchen ceiling and working hard to make it nice, so I couldn't believe what I saw. My son Dylan, who was fourteen, had already heard the commotion and was already standing on a chair holding a bucket up to the leak to catch the water. I said, "Oh my God, just kill me now!" My son responded, "Really, Mom? It's just a leak. It's fine." Feeling ashamed, I immediately changed my attitude. I smiled up at him and said, "You're right." Realizing that although I would have to scrape and repaint that ceiling and do repairs I didn't want to do or have the time or money or even the knowledge to complete, God knew I could handle whatever was put on my plate. Dylan was that precious pearl that day reminding me that life is an adventure and we should treat it that way, never knowing exactly what's coming but knowing we have what it takes to conquer, succeed, and grow. It took me a few days, in between work, chores, and being a mom, to fix that ceiling and leak; but it got done. Sometimes as a maternity nurse, I send parents home with their new babies, and they are scared and wonder how they will know what to do when problems come up. I honestly tell people that kids will teach us more than we can teach them if we just listen. If more parents claimed to know nothing about raising kids and looked to God for knowledge and guidance, we'd really be a much more productive and progressive race. People have asked me why I have six kids and if I always wanted a big family. This is how I think of my kids. In the Bible, there is the inspirational story of David and Goliath. David was a young, small guy who was no match for Goliath, a big strong man. David was expected to take on this giant and take out this enemy despite the size and strength of his big and strong opponent. Many people were depending on him to save them from this giant who represented a whole city of enemies. David knew it was his duty and only he could defeat the giant. He bravely chose five smooth stones. He used one of these stones which he flung at his enemy and was able to defeat the giant and save a lot of people. I see my six kids as beautiful stones that God provided to me to smooth out so he could use them as resources to destroy strongholds, enemies, evil giants in this world to be a witness of him and his love. They are very useful tools for God; and it's my job, although I may be small and weak, to bravely, in hope and faith, live by grace preparing these kids every day to be used by God to make the world a better place. As I raise these kids, they, in turn, teach me about love as God reminds me that although I don't deserve this job of being a parent, I am given the necessary tools needed to smooth out my beautiful stones, roughing out every edge, revealing a most beautiful, unique stone—perfect in shape and form to perform the exact task it was lovingly designed to take on. I don't know all the tasks that are in the future for them, but I don't need to know all that to be a good parent, because as the kids are called day by day to respond to the world around them, I should be there ready to instruct and support them; and this is how they will be chiseled and sanded, eventually taking on their perfect shape. I could never plan to have a big family, because this was God's plan. I thank him for his blessings and never could have imagined how beautiful a life he had in store for me.

When our family had visited West Point, a well-respected colonel said something to me that I will never forget. She said that West Point is not designed to completely change those who attend there. It is designed to accept people as they are when they come in and to refine them to be the best version of themselves. This process is an art. Describing the process at West Point is like comparing the cadets to patches being used to create a beautiful quilt representing all the different types of people who make up America. This will be a most beautiful quilt, taking all the values taught at home that built the character of these already impressive individuals and enhancing them to a higher level by further impressing on them the passion of duty, honor, and country. I always encouraged the kids growing up to stay humble, but I told Sabria the day I dropped her off to remember to continue to stay humble because the more times you can be quiet and not claim to know things, the more you can learn. Don't worry or be afraid about all that you don't know. Believe that you know nothing, and this will enable you to learn everything, even things you already knew you may find you didn't truly understand. Gain perspective. One day, about four weeks after R Day, I woke up thinking about my mom. For the first time in a month, Sabria was not my first thought in the morning. It took me a minute to realize what was happening. I realized I was entering a new phase, closing the door on my old life and stepping into a new day. Up until now, Sabria was all I could think about. This made me wonder how I was going to function and live a normal life without her. Missing her, as much as I did, pushed my daily compass into a tailspin. Eighteen years of having her as part of my daily focus and now she was gone. My body, mind, and spirit had to readjust so I could love her this new way. I prayed for her, wrote to her, and soon would be allowed to talk on the phone with her again and eventually be able to visit her periodically. So the mechanical adjustments and restrictions took place instantly, but the adjustments my heart had to make would take some time. There was a song on the radio that I heard while Sabria was in basic training, and I knew she was struggling and feeling alone. The song was by Lauren Daigle called "Rescue." I sent Sabria the lyrics in a letter I wrote to her. It was about there being no distance between us and that I could hear her SOS, or her (silent) cry for help. I knew Sabria felt defenseless and maybe hopeless at times because I had a true connection with her. We were two separate people, but we shared the same spirit. I told her God could be her shelter and her armor against her fear and sadness. I prayed that God would be there right beside her as she struggled to succeed. He is our strong tower sheltering and protecting us. I told her if she needed me to, I would come to wherever she was and rescue her but that it wouldn't be necessary since I knew that God was already ahead of me, that he had promised her he would never leave her and he was there still to see her through and marching alongside of her every step of the way. Whenever my kids heard that song on the radio, we would all smile, and someone would say, "Aww, Sabria." That song always makes me emotional as I remember the hard times Sabria endured at the academy.

This new way of life I took on wasn't so bad. It just took some getting used to. It was a challenge, but we found ways to stay connected to Sabria while she was away. Before she left, she and I had gotten matching tattoos, both on our left arms. It read, "God is within her, she will not fall" (Psalm 46:5). I told her, in one of her letters I wrote, to run her fingers across those words on her arm sometime during the day and I would do the same. It would be like we were meeting up for coffee but only in our hearts. I told her if she ever missed me too much, she should just look up at the sky. We may be separated by many miles, but no matter how far apart we were, the same sky was over both of us, and it connected us. Sun, moon, rain, shine, snow, clouds… It was all good because looking at the sky gave me hope of God and thoughts of my sweet Sabria. While my girls and I were at the store, we decided to pick out a good scent of oil to bring home for our diffuser. The girls pulled me aside and whispered, "This one smells like Sabria." I said, "Really!" I smelled it. It was soft, flowery, fresh, and clean. "Then let's get that one!" I said. We looked at each other and smiled as the decision to pick out a good scent was now a no-brainer as nothing at that point in time could ever smell better than our Sabria. We put it in the buggy, and as soon as we got home, we put that oil in the diffuser next to a picture of Sabria, and it allowed us to feel close to her. I believed I was up for the task and could love Sabria the way God was asking me to and teaching the kids to do this too. I was now an "army mom." This, I would come to find, would be no easy task. I'm thankful that at the time I had no idea how tough I would have to become to take on the role as "army mom" because that may have been too much for me to process all at once. God has always had a way of giving me just enough direction and instruction to take that first step, in faith. As the situation or mission would build, my faith and trust in him continued to build, and that is how he can take me into bigger battles and situations I would, on my own, never pursue.

During Sabria's first year at the academy, my mom had been battling liver and kidney failure and had been in and out of the Cleveland Clinic awaiting a multiorgan transplant. Up until now, she wasn't my focus. She couldn't be. At that moment, I was feeling all my senses in high alert, and I was shocked that I could feel for someone other than Sabria. For a second, I felt guilty that Sabria wasn't my first thought of the morning, and it made me sad, but I quickly realized that this was part of the process and God was leading me to not ignore Sabria but to realize he was taking care of her and my heart was healing and the kids were adapting. Sometimes as human beings, we allow ourselves to become comfortable in a certain situation or frame of mind because it's familiar, not because we have a purpose in it. When it's time to move on from something, move on. Staying when it's time to go holds back blessings. I knew for my mom's sake, Sabria's sake, my family's sake, and my own sake, I needed to take hold of this opportunity to see the new life that was before me and to know it was good. I began to feel very raw and organic. I thought, *Is this the path I go down? Should I allow myself to actually live my life without being consumed by my thoughts of Sabria and missing her so much that it controlled my whole life, even my dreams? If I did go down this path, I would be admitting that it's time for change. I would be surrendering to the idea that she can survive in this world without me right next to her every day. She is growing up. If that is true, then I need to change because she doesn't need this mom anymore.* This was a scary thought to me. This was the only mom I knew how to be. I thought, *Now what do I do? I need to learn how to be this new mom—the mom Sabria needs now and the mom all my other kids need.* Suddenly, I felt very refreshed, pliable, and loose. I felt like I had a real purpose in life. I was still needed in Sabria's life, but the time for feeling sad was over. During the first month she was gone, I went on my first run through the neighborhood without her and cried much of the way, stopping at the school and watching the American flag wave in the wind, realizing it had a much bigger meaning to me now. I watched one of our favorite movies, *G.I. Jane*, crying through the parts that reminded me of Sabria. I made dinner for the kids missing Sabria giving me her requests. I went to our jump stretch workout at the downtown YMCA with my other kids (we went as a family every week) and was choked up as we started stretching without our Sabria next to us and seeing the empty spot on the floor next to us that no one else could fill. All this I had been through, and God was telling me that enough was enough. It was like he was saying, "Don't worry. I have more for you to do." I was excited for my next mission, *or many missions* as it would turn out. There is much for me to do in Sabria's life and in other's lives around me. There was no more time to heal or be sad. The scar had taken shape in my heart, and it was beating strong and ready to take on the tasks at hand. I was excited inside. I suddenly felt weightless, buoyant like I could just float away. I felt raw and organic like a piece of fresh salmon on the grill, ready to accept all the seasonings, becoming enriched with all the nutrients needed to result in a most desirable taste. I was ready to take on the tasks needed to prepare me to be this new mom. I didn't know what I needed to do, but God knew. He would enrich me to be able to fulfill these duties. Only then could I be thankful because I was embracing the challenges before me.

I became thankful that Sabria was transforming. I felt us disconnecting but only for the purpose of connecting on a new level. When she was in my womb, I connected with her, loving her as best I could. I looked forward to those little moments in the day when I had time lay on my bed, on my back, making my stomach as flat as possible and placing both my hands in perfect position so that my thumbs and first fingers touched, making it possible to feel the tiniest, slightest flutter of a movement from that tiny being. I was early on in my pregnancy and couldn't feel her movements until I looked for them. Sometimes it would take a couple of seconds before I'd feel anything, but as I lay there thinking of her, my heart would flutter at the thought of her tiny existence. She would move, ever so slightly, as she was so small at this point. This was her saying, "Hi, Mom! Here I am." I would smile and talk to her for a while as she floated and fluttered in my womb. Those moments spent with Sabria were so special to me because I couldn't see her or touch her but we had such a special connection. I didn't know she was a girl until she was born. I just knew she was my special friend with much to offer the world. At that time, I was still in high school, a child myself. I felt as though I had nothing to offer this child, but she didn't judge me. God reminded me daily to fight off the tears and the overwhelming desire to give up, quit school, and stay in bed. He said instead to rise to the challenge, that he would do the work in her and in me if I would just be willing to be the vessel. So I found confidence in the God who sustained me this far in life and decided to peel myself out of bed every morning and go to school. As the time finally came and I watched her being born from my body, I knew then I needed to love her in a new way. The old way was gone because, of course, she couldn't stay in my body forever. The umbilical cord was cut, and we were disconnected from each other. But after that, I could hold her in my arms and look into her face, and I realized I would love her in a new way. Now, years later, she is away at the army, the umbilical cord has been cut again, and we are disconnected from the life we once knew. Once again, God was calling me out of bed, and Sabria was not judging me even though I was not good enough for the task of being her mom. We were both putting our trust in the one who had always loved us and kept us connected from day one. The thought of her still makes my heart flutter, and I am still that one she wants to watch her as she flutters and moves in life. As we are physically apart, our spirits are connected. I feel close to her, and I can sense her strength as she never looks back, knowing for sure that I am right there behind her on her journey, cheering her on. I will indulge in the process to be molded, sanded, and smoothed out in order to be the mom I need to be now for my West Point cadet.

CHAPTER 4

HAPPINESS

We were prouder than ever as Sabria approached A Day. This was the day the cadets graduated from basic training and were accepted into the core. Six weeks had gone by, and we missed our girl. We made the plans to go see her for the march-out parade. Bobby had worked for twenty-one days in a row in order to be allowed the two days off from work to attend this event. Most of these shifts were twelve-hour shifts. I was able to work extra shifts and save just enough money to cover the hotel, gas, and food for the weekend. I booked a hotel that was nestled into Bear Mountain across the troll bridge and located only seven miles from West Point. Although it was listed as "outdated," the hotel boasted of its great view of the Hudson River that I had hoped Sabria would appreciate. She was allowed to relax there with us during the days of that weekend. I, of course, was booking last minute, scraping together every dollar available and couldn't be choosy with such a small budget, but this sounded like a good deal to me. We left the kids at home with their uncle Codey, who was always there to help us in a pinch. Bobby and I headed out from Ohio to New York on a Friday to see our girl. We made it seven hours later to the hotel, which was more like a motel. It reminded me of the cabin I camped in at Cook's Forest as a kid—old, rustic with the sweet smell of must. The fixtures on the walls were original, accented with dusty cobwebs. The balcony outside was garnished with spiders in webs, and after I enjoyed the nice view of the Hudson River from that balcony for a minute or two, I quickly went back in the room and kept the door closed tight. It wasn't exactly what I envisioned, but it was fine. It had a bed, a TV, and a bathroom. *It is clean…just old and a little dusty, but it will do*, I thought. I couldn't sleep that night. I was so excited to see Sabria in the morning, and to know that I was only a few miles from her was hard to believe. It brought me back to the night before Christmas when I was a young child. My heart was full, and my body overflowed with good emotions. This feeling was unfamiliar to me in my adult years, and there weren't many experiences I had that provided me this level of emotion. I wasn't used to this feeling of fantastic anticipation. I finally fell asleep and awoke easily the next morning. I thought, *Today is the day!* I prayed that nothing would come between Bobby and me seeing our girl. It had been forty-eight days since I'd seen Sabria, and this marked the longest we'd ever been apart. I don't think Bobby and I were ever as organized and aligned as we were that morning. We were ready so fast and in the car on our way there before we knew it. We just could not wait!

We decided to park in a familiar lot on base and just walk some of the way to release some nervous energy. When we got to the plain, our emotions were building. We waited in the stand with the other parents as we did on R Day but now with a different respect for our daughter. We could hardly believe how far we'd made it in the journey and knew that others around us understood what we had just been through with our kid. We started to see the cadets marching out onto the plain in perfect sync. As they were accepted into the core, I could feel this overwhelming sense of pride as a parent. *How was this possible!* I thought. All the sleepless nights, running on fumes, watching our bank account dwindle to literally a few bucks. Now it was all worth it to see our girl graduating boot camp and pressing forward into the academy. Her journey was a true miracle, and we watched it unfold. After the parade, Bobby and I made our way through the crowd to get to Sabria. We walked for what felt like forever watching as cadets were passing us to get to their families. Finally, from a distance, I spotted her tall, slim, and muscular body walking fast toward me in a mechanical fashion—as if on a mission. Our eyes met, and we smiled big. I rushed to her, and we embraced each other, indulging in the blessing of presence. To kiss her cheek and look at her in the flesh was a joy only my heart can truly know. It is unexplainable. I literally had never felt happiness on that level in my life before this moment. I smiled so big that it hurt. We spent a wonderful weekend with our girl. We took her shopping to get all the last-minute necessities to finish the move into her barracks. We went back to our hotel room, warning her not to expect much. When we walked in the door, Sabria said, "Mom, this is nice! It's cozy. There's a shower! And there's no millipedes! You know I had to shower with millipedes, right, Mom!" She sighed with relief and plopped her whole body on the empty queen-sized bed that was all for her. She had air-conditioning and a place to relax. As she lay on the bed, I told her to look under her hat. While she was in the bathroom, Bobby had hidden a brand-new yellow iPhone under her uniform hat. It was the cell phone and specific yellow color she wanted but never thought she would get. Her mouth dropped, and she stared at it for a long few seconds before opening the box and indulging in cell phone heaven, saying a million times, "Thank you." Then she laid her tired head down and told me lots of stories of her first few adventurous weeks in the army as she allowed herself to drift off into a rainless, rifle-less, stress-free, bug-free sleep. Bobby and I watched her sleep, realizing at that moment that we could finally relax. Our hearts were full. I found it intriguing that

I worked so hard at trying to pick the perfect hotel room but at that moment found that she was so easy to please and really could care less about the beautiful view of the Hudson that I neglected to realize she saw every day of her life at the academy. She appreciated its beauty, but that weekend she as not interested in its view but rather needed rest and family. She had a curfew that night, so we dropped her off at around midnight.

The next morning, we were back on base around 5:30 a.m. to pick her up, not willing to waste any time with her. She was annoyed that she was made to wear her uniform whenever she was out. She didn't like to stand out. So after we left the academy, she changed clothes, and we arrived at the mall. We began walking around, and I could tell she was nervous; she was looking around and fidgety. I asked what was wrong. She said, "I'm supposed to be wearing my uniform right now." I said, "Then why aren't you!" She explained how she didn't think it was necessary or important to be doing all that. Just then we had passed some cadets who were dressed in uniform along with other officers who were dressed as well in their uniforms. Sabria realized she had made a mistake and felt urged to change back into her uniform as she could get into trouble being out of uniform. We panicked and raced back to the car. We left Bobby in the mall with our items that we hadn't purchased yet and just dashed for the door. We didn't realize we walked out the doors at the other end of the mall. So by the time we walked to the car for the couple of miles in the ninety-degree heat, we were irritated and covered in sweat. Sabria didn't remember that I had brought the smaller car to New York because we tried to save money on gas. This was also the car that had no air-conditioning because we couldn't afford to get it fixed at that point in time. I watched her from outside the car as her legs were covered in beads of sweat. I cringed as she pulled those polyester pants over those sweaty legs and buttoned up that dress shirt. She got out of the car with her beautiful bunned-up hair and irritated mood. I looked at her and said, "You're amazing." I was proud of her for doing what she didn't want to do but going forward because it was right. She just wanted a minute to forget who she was, but that moment would come later for her. Right now was still the time to be tough and follow orders.

In her uniform, she had to watch for those who she needed to salute. She needed to pay attention as she should recognize those decorations on one's chest and know when to salute and whom to salute to. Bobby and I were just relaxing and walking around the mall, but in that uniform, Sabria had to continue to be on mission. She was representing the country and her academy in that uniform, and that meant responsibility. I could understand how she just wanted to be like everyone else and dress sloppy or be unaware of her surroundings, but she was being called to a higher standard, and it was difficult to be molded into this person. I had remembered her explaining to me that West Point had toyed with the idea of letting their cadets wear plain clothes while they are out and about off base. The school decided to maintain their long-held tradition of the plebe (freshman) cadets staying in uniform while off base until they reached their destination. Sabria didn't necessarily see the purpose behind this thinking. I explained to Sabria that she was a West Point cadet whether she wears the uniform or not. Learn to be who you say you are and stay who you are no matter the surroundings or influences. Wearing the uniform only helps you train to be who you say you are. It helps put actions to your motives. It doesn't make you who you are or not make you who you are, but it is of importance. As we were going into a store, a woman looked at Sabria and told her she looked beautiful. She thanked her for her service and asked her a little bit about herself. The woman said she loved seeing women in uniform and how it was just awesome what Sabria was doing. Sabria was intrigued and said, "I guess it isn't so bad to wear this uniform, after all." To Sabria, it's about doing the work, not about the recognition. Wearing the uniform seems like such a simple thing to her. It is nice, though, to gain understanding of others' view of you, whether good or bad. Sometimes you don't realize the encouragement your simple efforts bring to others. So rather than not wearing the uniform to stand out, wear the uniform to encourage and positively influence those who desire to do good and want to see others doing good. I'm sure there will be that person who will read this and say, "Not everyone who wears a uniform is good." That goes without saying. All the more reason to be a person who wears a uniform of honor and acts with honor as well. Sabria was changing and embracing the opportunities to learn about life and about herself. She learned the value of time, asking me if I realized how long ten minutes was and that there was so much you can actually get done in ten minutes. While the three of us were eating lunch before taking her back to the academy, she finished eating and went to the bathroom. She came back and was standing at the table. Bobby and I looked up at her, wondering why she didn't sit back down. She said, "Okay, come on. It's time to leave." I looked at Bobby, and he looked at me. We were still eating, close to being done but hadn't felt the need to rush through lunch until now. We thought we could relax, eat, and chat. Sabria was used to eating quickly and talking less. I looked up at her as she stood there with her hat in hand, and I said, "But we're not done eating." She pointed at her watch said, "Okay, but it's time to go, so let's go." Bobby and I looked at each other again and smiled and said, "Okay, let's go." We were learning that we were helping her change and she was helping us change too. We were all changing together to make this thing work.

We drove her back to West Point recognizing that very familiar knot in our stomach as we approached the sign leading to Bear Mountain. Then after driving up to the guarded entrance to the base and showing the guards our military visiting IDs, we said those words we hated saying, "We're here to drop off our cadet."

We were proud and sad at the same time driving her through the beautiful grounds to her barracks making sure our tears had time to be released, wiped, and soaked up. We got to our destination at her barracks for drop-off and forced our sweaty bodies out of that hot car. We hugged not knowing when we'd be allowed to see each other again. My heart broke at the thought of goodbye. I just couldn't let go, but I did. Then she walked away and, of course, never looked back. I, of course, watched until I couldn't see her anymore as she walked with perfect posture back into that beautiful stone building with cupped hands ready to take on anything that came her way, knowing we were behind her. She was and still is my hero. Bobby and I left New York and headed home. Every mile we drove farther away was sadly another mile from Sabria and yet closer to our other kids. That was the silver lining of it all, knowing the kids at home shared our feelings and love and the bond our family had was strong. It was around a hundred degrees that hot August day, and driving with no air-conditioning was horrible. We planned to only stop once or twice to get home quick so that Bobby could get to work in the morning. We finally made it to the gas station. I followed him in and noticed the whole back of his shirt was wet with sweat. I leaned over his shoulder and whispered, "Dude, the whole back of your shirt is full of sweat." I expected him to be embarrassed, and I would tell him it's okay and not to worry about it, but instead he looked at me and said, "I know. So is yours." This is an example of how Bobby is, as I see him: a base to my acid. He wasn't worried about what his shirt looked like. He was on a mission to get home, and that little thing of us looking like we just escaped the rainforest didn't seem to distract him. So I followed suit. *Onward and upward*, I thought. *Keep climbing.* It was a long ride home, but Bobby drove most of the way. I was exhausted and fell asleep sitting up. I got a second wind at about midnight, and it was a good thing too. Bobby was spent, and just as 2:00 a.m. rolled around, I had tunnel vision, and driving anymore seemed impossible. Just then the song "Almost Home" by Mercy Me came on, and I felt a jolt. The song talks about finishing the race in life and how heaven is cheering us on here on earth. Soon all our burdens will be gone, and we'll get that second wind. That was what I needed to hear on that dark highway to give me hope to keep driving and to get excited enough to stay awake. This was all I needed to make it the rest of the way. Finally, as we approached home, Bobby told me that letting him nap at the end of that trip is what got him through and what got him to be able to survive going in to work. We were back home—back on the Hunter grid, and God took care of us as usual. Although that trip was hard in every way, God made it possible for us to succeed.

CHAPTER 5

UNCONDITIONAL LOVE

Back home, new struggles were coming. I was able to get four hours of sleep before heading to the Cleveland Clinic with my sister to see my mom. She had been hospitalized for reasons associated with her chronic liver disease and had a failed attempt at a liver transplant. A few hours into the risky surgery, they were unable to proceed, because her body was in too poor of shape to handle such an extreme procedure. They made the decision four hours into prepping her for that surgery after they still were unable to get her to a physically promising state, and the surgeons figured that if they continued, she may not make it through. Her body was not ready yet to receive the liver, after all. They decided to postpone and to instead try to get her to a healthier state before trying again to give her a new liver. This was devastating to our family. My dad sat at the Cleveland Clinic holding that pager for four hours thinking my mom was getting a new lease on life. Another chance to be healthy and active. He expected an update to be that everything was going well. Instead, he was told no surgery had even begun. There wasn't much communication between the hospital and my dad, because it was always someone else's job to do that. The nurses weren't allowed to give information. The surgeons were too busy moving on to the next patient who could receive the liver. When my dad called me to tell me the news, I was expecting my mom to be well into the surgery, but then he told me the news. I had many questions. What do you mean they couldn't proceed! Where is the liver? Well, we had assumed it was going into the next recipient. We assumed the doctors couldn't talk to us because they were moving on to the next patient. So the visit my sister and I were making was to see my mom for the first time after the devastation of a lifetime. My sister and I left our husbands and kids home, and after we were both weary from working long hard hours, we drove to see our mom.

It was an interesting time. Many questions and concerns were rotating around in my head and stirring up my conscience. There was a certain battle going on inside me that my sister was also fighting. We had grown up in a Christian home with home-cooked meals prepared daily by my mom. She would often stay up late baking cookies for us for the next day and cleaning the house to no end. She was always seemingly unsettled in her spirit, never satisfied for long before finding something to be upset about. She was Betty Crocker but with an attitude. She was a pistol with an apron. I spent my days trying to please her and make her proud, never seeming to quite figure out how to do that. I longed to spend time with my mom as a young child but always feeling like her long hard days of taking care of the family were too much for her to bear. I began to feel like I was a burden to her, and as the years rolled on, I searched for the connection I needed, the reciprocation of tenderness and unconditional love I had for my mom as a child I wished to see from her toward me. I longed for that love that I received from Jesus to be mirrored in my mom as I grew older. There were things that would set her off, and once that happened, she had a hard time responding to me other than with very deliberate scorning and harshness. There was so much delicateness to her that I saw her as a beautiful flower, smelling of refinement, and the scent was refreshing to me as a child. The aroma that only she had. She always looked beautiful to me even on those hot sweaty days when she worked tirelessly to cook, clean, and plan events in that hot old house with no air-conditioning. This could explain the moods she would get into when she just had a hard time responding gently toward me when I had reckless moments in life. I wanted to impress her, but I was always making mistakes. I wanted her to be proud of me, but I gave her reason to long for me to do better. I began to sense some resentment as a young child, instead of striving to be better and to show and give my mom a better life and maybe take some of the burdens off her shoulders by helping her by doing chores without complaining and being more careful with the house, cars, and curfews. I began pushing into another direction. I became selfish and wanted to please myself. I chose to search for that love and affection outside the house instead of indulging in loving the family God gave me. I should never have been bored.

My dad worked as many as three jobs at a time, and my mom stayed home caring for the house and four kids. Surely, there were things I could have been doing to show love to my family. I'm not saying I was a bad kid. I was a good athlete, got good grades, was involved in NHS and student counsel, was crowned homecoming queen, and was president of my class. Surely, I was looking good to those around me. But where was my heart? I'm saying this now twenty years later because now I'm seeing that the things I allowed to steer me off path affected my mom as well. Although I can make excuses for my actions in life and I could've been named just a normal kid finding her way in life, those decisions to be selfish and leave my mom's needs in the background had consequences. I don't blame my childhood decisions for making my mom an alcoholic at the age of fifty, but I definitely take my place in the situation. I cannot and will not ignore the connection between myself and my mom as I allowed myself to do as a young person. I should be there to help her through the battle because God has taught me to leave no one behind. Alcoholism is a choice. It only becomes a disease to the body and mind as we allow it to be. Humans have the power to allow sin to take over our bodies and literally disease ourselves. On this trip to Cleveland with my sister, I forced myself to focus on the battle within me. I wanted to be what my mom needed, but I also had lots of questions. It brought me back to the days when my dad would call me. I would answer the phone, and he would say, "Hey, I need your help with mom." I'd rush over there to the house I grew up in, where I'd usually find my mom making a big dinner or baking a batch of cookies; but instead, I would find my mom lying down in the kitchen on the tile floor my dad laid with his own hands—the very tile my mom picked out herself. As I quickly assessed the scene, I was trapped in this place. I was like a young girl again seeing my beautiful, sweet-smelling precious Betty Crocker mom on the floor after a fall. Yet I had to be a grown person, a nurse being aware that what I was actually seeing was a sweaty, sticky, bruised, bloody body with a swollen face and disheveled hair, partially dressed with only underwear in a position that her body was forced into after a reckless alcohol binge—a body of someone who's aware that she would drink so much she would throw up in the house and attempt to stagger around finding the bathroom, wherever in her drunken stupor thought it might be and eliminating where and when it seemed right. My dad was always there to pick up the pieces, but some nights, he couldn't do it alone. I had to help him get her off the floor and into a chair to assess her wounds to see if she needed medical attention. Sometimes this was necessary, but many times, we just guessed and hoped we were making good decisions for her. I would pour my heart out to my mom and tell her she was worth more than she had become and she could change. She could have a better life. She would cry and tell me she loved me. Alcoholics have one drive. They find ways to get what they want, and they get it. They are amazing schemers. You can do everything in your power to help them, but they must make the decision to stop. You can't make this decision for them. As my dad would find alcohol in places my mom didn't think he'd look, he would dump it. She would buy more and drink it alone where we couldn't see her. She always found a way to keep the dysfunction going.

As I make this trip to Cleveland and my mom's poor health over the last year has forced her into a state of sobriety, I am faced with the decision. Will I love my mom unconditionally as I expect God to love me? Or will I harbor hate for what she has allowed to occur in our family? Are my sins any better than hers? Have I not hurt people over the years, and did I ignore opportunities to better love my mom and others in my life? Of course. And now as my sister and I struggle to find our way through the city, I am brought back in my mind to remember struggling to find my way through my young adulthood after my sister, the one sitting next to me in this car, ran off with a boyfriend soon after she turned eighteen. No one knew where she was, and my parents were frantic to find her. She had dropped out of college and just disappeared. I was fourteen at the time and couldn't understand why my sister didn't find me worth sticking around for. I missed her. I was confused. *What would it be like if my sister would have stuck around to help me through this life?* I thought. In my young lost mind, in my weak faith, I felt like my experiences could have been easier or more tolerable if she'd been there. The truth was, when I was young, I couldn't see the love and assistance I had right in front of me in my other siblings and my parents who were still around and wiling to love me. Eventually, we got a hold of my sister, and she did not want to come home but instead chose to live her own life where she was, which was about an hour form our home. She stayed in the reckless situation she chose for herself and grew comfortable in the disorder. We all just tried to make do with this new life without her as she gave into her own desires. My mom and dad were devastated, and it took them a while to recover from that situation. This was no reason for my mom to become an alcoholic or for me to harbor ill feelings for my sister. I love them both today. The past is in the past, and today my sister lives less than five minutes from my house. We have a good relationship, and we understand each other. She has been there for me through the toughest times of my life, and I know that in life we all go on journeys that may not be understood by others, but if we hold out hope, the sun eventually comes back out. So, on this car ride, I knew her battles were my battles, and we were both figuring out how to love our mom through all of this. We both had a past, but at that moment, we were loving each other and loving our mom—even without knowing how to do it. That is the power of God. We made it finally to the hospital and zigzagged our way to my mom's room. We walked into the ICU. She was in pretty bad shape. Unrecognizable. She was swollen from head to toe. Had a million IV's and all the mechanics keeping her alive. She was awake but had a hard time breathing and talking. My brothers also met us there. We were all together. Our whole family. The six of us. Grown, with our own lives and families, stopping everything to be there with our mom. We were doing what we didn't know how to do. We were loving our mom. Sometimes if we just follow, God will slow down the pace for us. He doesn't expect us to be running all the time. He knows sometimes we just need to go one step at a time. He gives us resources along the way to help us do that. We just need to look for these things and use them. My mom is still struggling through alcoholism because, although the drinking is gone, the selfishness and self-centered thinking are still there. This is the part that I will pray for and that I hope to change. You see, an alcoholic appears to be ignoring themselves as the drink takes over their lives, but this person who drinks is attempting to escape life and go to a place in their mind that is lonely and all for themselves. This is a self-centered way of thinking that needs to be extinguished. Instead, burn with a fire to learn to love yourself as God loves you, and then spread that love to others. This is where you find joy and contentment. I hope my mom can find this on earth, and I will live to show her love every chance I get. I do hope she can say she is proud of me, but this should not influence my actions or intentions to love her. My actions are measured by God.

God tells me to love at all times. When visiting my mom on a number of occasions, I would see that her nails were painted like she used to do them when I was young, but I knew she was too shaky to paint them herself. That's when she would tell me that my dad painted them. She would proudly say, "Oh, that color is called robin's egg." You see, my dad wouldn't just paint her nails. He would lift her up and put her in her wheelchair and take her to shop for her favorite colors at the beauty shop, and he would get to know the different names of the polish so he could always buy again the colors she enjoyed most. He didn't just paint her nails; he indulged in the opportunity to spend time with her. I found out that he studied her favorite hair dye, and he dyed her hair for her because it made her feel good and she was too weak to get to the hairstylist. Her hair always looked nice. One day, she had a nice fur vest on. I commented on it and told her it looked so pretty. She was always cold, and when they were at the clinic for one of her visits, my dad wheeled her into the gift shop to look around, and she pointed it out and said she liked it. It was expensive, but my dad later went back to that gift shop and bought the vest to surprise my mom. He did this all the time. He was her complete caregiver now as she was bound to a wheelchair. Her body was too weak to walk from all the abuse she put it through. He got her a wheelchair and took her everywhere he could. He made lists of her meds and managed all of them including her insulin. Her diabetes had gone full blown after her failed attempts at dieting and stay-ing away from the high-sugar alcohol drinks that she indulged in constantly. My dad cooked for her and moved her bedroom to the living room as it was more accessible for her. He even built a huge ramp onto the back of the house to get her out to the car once she stopped being able to walk. During one of her stays in the hospital, he built an entire second-level porch onto their house, which he completed in maybe a week. He put a new door up that went from her new room in the living room to the porch so he could push her right out of her room to the sunshine. This is the resource I was talking about that God had given me to teach me to love my mom. It wasn't all these things my dad was doing for her that I was most impressed with. I was impressed with that fact that all these times my mom chose to drink, my dad chose to pick her up off the floor. All the times she stole the bank card from him to buy alcohol, he still went to work to earn a living. After he begged her to try harder and she still found a way to drink, he would clean up her vomit from the carpet after cleaning her up and putting her to bed. Even now as she is sick from her own doing, he refuses to let her struggle alone. He won't put her in a nursing home. As long as he is able, he will love his wife. He lives to represent Christ in every way possible. He shows me how to love unconditionally. This is what we were made to do. My mom is worth the fight, and I believe that I will see a complete healing as she grows to under-stand God's love as she witnesses it on a daily basis from her hus-band and from God who has given her more time on earth. God tells us to love at all times, not just when it's easy or gives us some kind of pleasure. We are to labor in love, which is to work. My dad only sees opportunity. He doesn't dwell on the hardship but always keeps his eyes on the goal to love. He knows this love himself as he had a miraculous moment of meeting God as a young man in his early twenties. He was married to my mom, and they had one child at that point, my sister. Although my dad was blessed in life, he couldn't see it. He began doing drugs and contemplated killing himself. As he was at his lowest point in life, he happened to see a preacher on TV. Whatever was said caught his eyes and ears.

He just dropped to his knees and prayed. Something came over him as he gave Christ his life that day. He was changed forever. Never going back to his old ways. I was the next child born to my parents. I obviously didn't know the man my dad was before being changed by God. I only know the man after. I've never known an equal to my dad. As long as my memory will take me back, my dad has always been the most, gentle, loving, devoted, disciplined, faithful, hopeful, and God-fearing person. He never changes. He is consistent, even through hard times, never losing his anchor. My dad tells me not to look to him as an example but to look to the one who made him and me. He knows he is not perfect and doesn't want his flaws to cloud my view of Christ. I do know in my heart that the one who made me also made my dad as someone, a special friend, to help show me the way to heaven. I, in turn, want to be that person for my kids and anyone I meet so they can know the truth of God's love.

CHAPTER 6

SIGNS FROM GOD

After visiting my mom at Cleveland Clinic, my sister hit the jets to get us home in enough time for me to jump into my scrubs and get into my car to head to work for the night shift at the hospital. The next day, I was able to sleep for a whole hour before getting up to take one of my sons to football practice. I then was able to lay down for two more hours before taking my other son to his football game. After that, my girls decided to have one of their friend's over to spend the night. As the kids played outside, I heard screaming and commotion as I was coming out to the front porch. Their friend had gotten stung by a bee and was allergic! She was feeling all right at that moment, but her mom came with her EpiPen and took her to the hospital for observation. By the time I laid my head down for bed that night, I crashed. I slept fifteen hours straight. God always knows exactly how much I can handle and, for some reason, seems to take me to that very moment, the moment of collapse. Maybe it's because I'm willing to go the distance with him. I know that when I'm not sure what to do, he visits me in many forms to shed light on the path I should take. The day after the bee episode, I had taken the kids to jump stretch, trying to maintain some kind of organization and structure while Sabria was away. I was fighting my emotions as my everything was missing her. The girls asked me to take them to Barnes and Noble, which was one of their favorite stores. I agreed, not wanting to miss any opportunity to spend time with them. I had been thinking of writing a book for a while at this point but not believing I could do such a thing but was something God laid on my heart to do. I never liked reading, and I certainly didn't have time or energy for such a project, but as it was recently pressing my conscience, I decided to ask God for confirmation that this was him asking me to do this. If it was direction from him, I knew I couldn't fail at it even though it seemed an impossible task. So as we entered the store, I decided to stop at a table and leaf through a book. I thought, *If I do decide to ever take on this project, I'd better learn a little something. Hmm, how do does a book start? How does it end? How do you find a publisher? What's this lady writing about in here?* I knew nothing about writing. I really had no desire to write until God was calling me to do so. Why this, though? I know nothing about this or cared to know. Still it was a thing that wouldn't go away. It stayed on my heart as a constant reminder that God was asking me to do something.

As I stood there in my sweaty gym clothes hoping the girls would shop quickly, a man approached me. I could feel him about to start talking to me, and I thought, *Oh, God, not now.* I was not presentable, to say the least, to be talking to anyone right then, but this is always the way it happens. I always see people I know in the grocery store or meet new acquaintances while running errands when I look the absolute worst. If I do my hair and makeup and dress cute, rest assured, I'll see no one when I go out, and no one will see me. This moment was one of those moments when I wanted to hide or swiftly move to the next aisle. I knew there was nowhere to go, so I pushed my face deeper into this book that I pretended to care about and nervously pushed back my messy hair behind my ear, hoping to look intent in what I was reading.

Suddenly he spoke. He started by asking me what kind of material I liked to read. I couldn't lie. I looked up at him and shamefully responded, "Oh, I actually don't read books. I'm just here waiting for my kids to finish shopping." I thought he would just walk away after that. I mean, why would I be in Barnes and Noble leafing through a book if I didn't like to read? It was true, though, and he didn't know me at all, and I didn't expect him to care about talking to me after my statement. But instead, he continued on, asking me, if I did read, what kind of information or material would interest me? I thought, *Is he kidding me? Who is this guy?* I was sure wishing I had popped a piece of spearmint gum in my mouth before coming in this store, but I didn't expect to talk to anyone. My breath is in no condition to be having a full-blown conversation with this stranger. I kept on and responded. Hmm, well, I guess I'm more into real-life drama because that's what I relate to. He asked me why I felt like there was drama in my life. I thought, *Okay, is this guy some kind of counselor or something? Do I really look like I need help?* I was intrigued with his boldness, so I just decided to amuse him. Well, I have six kids... He stopped me right there, as most people do, and his eyes got big, and he said what everyone says when I tell them that, "Wow! You have six kids!" I told him my oldest was at West Point and my youngest was seven and we struggle every day. He asked, "Why?" I thought, *Is that a rhetorical question?* So I just decided to list him a few of my problems. I mean, he asked me, so I might as well be honest. I said, "We struggle through financial burden and lack of strong family support, and through life, we're trying to raise our kids well and be good people." He said, "Well, you must be doing good. Whatever you are doing is working. Other women are having the same struggle and the same desire you are talking about. They want to raise their kids right and be good people. They want to be successful through the struggle. Why don't you write a book about how you are doing it so you can speak to others?" I was completely perplexed. Was this a joke? I had just recently told God that I would write the book he put on my heart to write if he gave me a sure clear sign that is what he wanted me to do and if he would light the path and give me solid direction. I didn't mention this to the man, but I did listen as he talked. He told me he was an author and that he had tips on how to get started on writing a book and the steps to continue out the process. He also asked me about my marriage and how we had managed to stay together and raise the kids thus far as a unit and how this is what I should share with the world because people want to know. I knew for sure my marriage wasn't great. In fact, I started thinking about all the things in my life that weren't perfect. Even at that moment, my kitchen was still a mess from the ceiling that was leaking, my mom was chronically ill, I was insanely missing my daughter in the army, and our bills were stacked up. All these catastrophes and here I was, at Barnes and Noble with my kids after a good workout, talking to a nice guy. I was fine. I was doing good. I just needed to realize that this was life. God was telling me to embrace the moments that come into my life and on my journey with him and know that the storms were around me, not in me, but that he was in me and he was good.

After we talked a bit longer, he had told me he was not from this area but actually from Michigan, which is about three to four hours from Ohio and he was only in town for the weekend. I gave him my e-mail so he could send me the "ten tips to writing a book" that he told me of. I left the store thinking, *Wow, that was crazy.* But a few days later, I received the e-mail. I never saw the man again or heard from him. It was like he came into my life for a brief moment and then was gone. I thought it was also important that he wasn't from the area because in the Bible God talks about how God sets up time and place for us. I'm terrible with names, but I do remember this man's name was Richard. He was a middle-to-late-aged African American man, maybe my height or slightly shorter with a slim build and seemingly intelligent, well-dressed, and seemed generally well versed. I believe he was sent to me by God and was one of many angels I have met in my life on my journey with God. I had no doubts about writing this book after speaking with this man. In fact, when my girls and I got to the car, I called my dad and told him I was writing a book and explained what had just happened. My daughters marveled at the experience as I told them what happened in the store. Their mouths dropped open, and they smiled and gasped as they knew I had talked about writing a book. I hope to, one day, see this man again whether on earth or in heaven and tell him how much he helped get me on my way to writing a book and just living in a new light. Inspiration is a powerful tool, and that man gave that to me that day. I thanked God for his patience with me and for the confirmation I needed as I doubted and for continuing to give me opportunities to serve him and taking what little bit of faith I do have and magnifying it so I can experience greater glories with him.

CHAPTER 7

BEING AVERAGE

I recently heard a woman with many kids make a comment that sticks with me. She said that she just wanted her kids to live simple lives and be average. This comment rattled me like freshly cut Christmas trees that get fed through that little machine before getting wrapped up and taken home. Why would you be comfortable with your kid being simple or average? Even worse, why would this be your goal for them? God has so much to offer us, and it should be of greatest importance to not only be everything God calls us to be but to also encourage this attitude in our kids and grandkids. There is no excuse to do less than what God calls us to do. Even those with handicaps, health issues, mental, psychological, and developmental issues can take part in society to serve God and serve the country with 100 percent effort, and God adds power to that effort to accomplish goals. God says he has the power to demolish strongholds, so there is nothing holding us back from doing his work. The problem with consciously raising kids that don't see a reason to give full effort is the automatic encouragement of laziness that results in us as parents. I don't just mean laziness of the body but also laziness of heart, which allows one to ignore their conscience, and before long, the person has a hard time filtering out good and evil. I've seen people act so rudely and obviously ill-mannered, selfish ways, and they don't even see the negativity in themselves and can't even imagine any other way of living. Parents set their kids up to blend in with the world, but the Bible teaches to be set apart to do good work. This should be our goal. God tells us we are his workmanship to do things on earth that he prepared for us to do in advance. There are those who raise their kids to be average, pretty, with nice straight teeth that look good in all the family pictures. They can do chores, are easy friend makers, have good skin, and have grown up to land successful jobs. Those parents have helped to raise a kid who can fit into a high or middle social class of people on this earth and have then pulled their parents along, too, so they can continue then to vacation together and help each other search for the big expensive houses in the neighborhood that would tell of their "good" choices in life. But while they were busy teaching their kids to try hard to fit into society so they can enjoy the benefits of feeling good about their efforts as parents, they neglected to teach them that God tells us we are aliens here on earth and this is not our forever home. So why would anyone ever want to push their kids to become so comfortable in such a place? Do you wonder why your adult child is suffering with depression, anxiety, eating disorders, and drug addictions? As long as they look the part of a structured, self-maintained, and self-made successful part of society, they can just self-medicate as well until hopefully these problems go away.

There are those parents on the other side of the spectrum who raise their kids to be content with not ever finding a job but to enjoy the benefit of a government who will supplement their bank account when they don't feel like going to work. If you encourage this behavior, you may have been a parent who was content in allowing the government to supplement your own bank account as you raised your kids, since parenting is a hard job and certainly your body couldn't possibly handle the pressures of earning money and being a parent at the same time. Maybe you chose instead to live in a certain state of poverty, justifying your decision by your efforts of making your own soaps and planting your own garden to "work" yourself into believing you had an excuse to stay home, because at least you were trying. If everyone was racing to have that good life and fitting into that perfect version of life they envision for themselves, whether it's to sit around eating their favorite treats and watching movies, manning their garden, scheduling a trip to their favorite vacation spot every few months, or pushing to have that perfect yard or mansion of a house or camper, who is left to lead the country and serve others out of love for Christ? My point is that we all can fit into any of those areas I've listed at some point in our life—whether it was how we were raised, how we live now, or how we dream of living, always searching but never being content with our current state. Who doesn't struggle to get off the couch, off the boat, out of the pool, off the Xbox? It really disturbs me at how much we give into our own selfish desires and how much we and our kids are missing out on because we choose to believe that we've done good and that we deserve a break. Which is why we give ourselves the excuse to excessively indulge. Who is left to fight for our freedoms in America, whether in the military or just in society or at our workplaces in general, if most people are searching to fight for their own contentment?

Where does the passion come from that I see in Sabria—a person who wanted to go to West Point to become the best version of herself and live for a reason bigger than herself for the sole purpose of using these experiences and training tirelessly to love God first and then to love others? The choice she made to be humble and choose the harder, less-traveled path not in hopes to earn enough money to buy that great vacation home she could enjoy or that expensive car that others could envy but to instead see an opportunity to become better equip to serve her neighbor. She had many Division 1 offers to play basketball. She could have played close to home and been a local celebrity. With that would have come a lot of opportunities to sleep in, go to parties, and just goof around like any college kid would want to do. She would have been able to indulge in the game of basketball that she loved and would have gotten elite training in that sport. The truth is that there are people out there who do desire to work toward something more than just goofing off and selfishly pursuing those opportunities to self-indulge or become a celebrity. I'm speaking of intentions here. I'm not saying that all kids who choose to stay close to home or go to a popular school to strictly play a sport are wrong. I do not have the right or desire to judge one's intentions. Whatever route is chosen, it should be in hopes of how one could love others the most; and that may very well be at a local school or a popular school, or not choosing college at all.

This, what I'm writing, is an attempt to stir the hearts and minds of people to search your own selves. The Bible says you will know a person's heart by their fruit. Sabria knew she could help more people by learning more about self-discipline and the value of duty, honor, and country. She would not do this without struggle, because it is something that will feel unnatural. This became an opportunity to let God, who is supernatural, do a work in her life, and I want to share this experience as the gift is available to everyone everywhere to tap in to God's presence and love. I'm not talking about never indulging in things that make us happy but instead to always grind. God actually tells us to indulge but to indulge in the fruits of our labor. There is a healthy way to enjoy the blessings on this earth, but, first, one must learn the value of contentment in God's calling on their life and learn to have passion in the pursuit of reaching the finish line. That time only comes when God finally strokes that last and final mark on his masterpiece which is our personal tapestry in life that he designed just for us. Our goal should be to help God make a beautiful artwork out of our life on earth so that when he looks at his finished product, it brings him the greatest pleasure. This thinking is what brought Sabria comfort through boot camp, knowing that, through the hard work and struggle, God was proud of her efforts.

I'm proposing that it is quite possible to be content in hard situations. I've learned it is of much benefit to learn to be comfortable in uncomfortable situations. This is where growth happens. This is only possible through much discipline. As you push yourself to your limits over and over in life, you are able to withstand more and more. If you teach yourself to tap out, you learn to fail and will either stay in a state of failure or cheat your way to victory. Instead of cheating or staying in defeat, when you fall, humbly pick yourself up and try again. All the while, if you keep trying through the fails to trust God and you decide to not cheat or give up, you are becoming a more pliable material that God can mold into a beautiful creature. This is also how you can then trust God to demolish strongholds such as depression, drug addiction, anxiety, food addiction, and any other battle you face here on earth. Instead of having self-pity through those hard times and questioning why God allowed them to torture you, understand that by struggling through those battles, you are actually gaining the perspective needed to take on projects you would otherwise never imagine even attempting to take on. God is actually correcting your vision through those hard times so you can better see him in your life and in the lives of others around you. So, in fact, our storms are a gift from God. This is how I can destroy anyone's idea that God does not exist. I've seen him. Whenever I am brave and faithful on my journey with God, I will ask to grow closer to him. I am saying that I know that if I want to draw closer to God, a storm will come. So if you would ask if I do pray for storms to come into my life, the answer would be yes. We all do when we want to better ourselves. Yet still, in our weak faith, we will ask why God allowed the storm to come. There are those who live so safely that they never struggle. They also will not grow in faith. Start asking to see God, and be brave as the storms come. You can find God, but you must seek him with all your heart. This means to trust him through the storm and look for him in it.

CHAPTER 8

MOVING WITH VISION

S abria would face many battles, but one that lingered was missing home. After boot camp and our visit with her was over, the reality of her long journey was becoming clearer. It was September, and Labor Day allowed for the cadets to leave the base with their families if they chose to do so. Sabria could only leave West Point when it was permitted and when the four-hundred-mile trip was feasible for either her to come home or us to go to her. That particular September weekend, it was not feasible for us to meet up. Sabria felt sorry for herself as other cadets were able to have a long weekend with family and friends, but she did not get this opportunity. She found herself alone in her room at the barracks as all her roommates were able to leave. She and I had, of course, talked about the good use of time that she could take advantage of. She did some studying and took a ten-hour nap that day. I prayed for my daughter and felt concern for her knowing part of the reason she slept was to escape the reality of the pain in her heart from missing us; but I also knew that if God wanted us to have been together that weekend, it would have come to pass. I encouraged her much-needed nap and her study time as this was a good choice of action. I also told her the struggle she had was shared with us at home, and this meant we were connected even with many miles between us. Being the light you want to see in others will be hard work, but the more you get out of bed and try, the more you will see change. To be the light, you must know the light, and to know the light is to trust God. Find ways to continue the fight. Learn to see the good around you. If you can't see any good, let it come from you where God is.

Sabria's sponsor family invited her over that Sunday evening. All cadets were issued a sponsor family for this very type of situation. The academy could seem like a very lonely place especially under the harsh requirements expected on a daily basis from the cadets. The sponsor families live on base and serve as teachers, administrators, coaches, etc. They are available to be a listening ear, counselor, or a place to catch a nap outside the barracks or do a much-needed load of laundry. Sabria's issued family was a young Christian couple and their infant son. They also had a dog. It was good to know Sabria had a nice family to spend time with during this time away from home. She ate a good, healthy, home-cooked meal; and they had a bonfire. I thanked God for this family who took good care of my daughter that day when I couldn't be as close as I wanted to be. I had remembered celebrating Fourth of July as we celebrated at home right after our July 1 dropping off of Sabria. We had attempted a cookout; but as we sat down as a family, just the seven of us, we just looked around for a moment. That moment made me think of the movie *Signs*, starring Mel Gibson, specifically the scene where everyone chose their favorite meal and they were all sitting around the table as a family expecting to eat their last meal before the aliens took over. I looked around at my kids and husband, and we hesitated to begin eating. We paused, and there was a sense of reverence we felt as Sabria was missing from the table. It didn't feel natural or right to eat. I felt my throat tightening as I forced myself to swallow each bite as the table was quiet. I needed to continue to lead the kids, but this was hard. I looked down at my plate and wasn't hungry, but I took another mechanical bite and then looked up and saw Theresa chewing, and as I continued to look around the table, I realized what was happening. We had all looked at each other and down at our plates, and before we knew it, we were eating. This, again, is where our family connected. We knew we needed to move in a direction that was uncomfortable and unfamiliar. We were celebrating a holiday that represented our Independence, yet our Sabria was learning the value and discipline of serving and was unable to come home. We were proud of her, and this day had new meaning to us, and it gave us a new perspective which we didn't see until we sat down for that meal. We all mourned the loss of our old family unit but just needed time to learn to love the new one God created. We trusted he would carry us through. That evening, we watched *G.I. Jane* as this role reminded us of Sabria and then watched the Fourth of July celebration at West Point that was aired on TV. All the kids had their faces right in front of the TV waiting to get one glimpse of their sister. They did! We all cheered and clapped when we saw her in the large crowd of cadets. We felt so close to her, and the kids were saying, "Aww, look at her!" as they gazed at the TV for as long as the program was broadcasted. We were very proud of her. This encouragement prepared us for Labor Day and our second holiday as a new unit. God did provide family for Sabria while she was away, and we learned to recognize these blessings as they came. This is how we learn to roll with the punches, knowing God has a plan and a support for us to make it through.

During our time at home, we wanted to continue to be prosperous. There was a mud issue in our backyard that we had long hoped to correct somehow. This area leading into our house from the driveway was a high-traffic area that we had made worse when we dug the ground up to run a gas line to the detached garage in the back of our house. I was annoyed by this problem and really didn't know what I could do to fix it. It was a large area and would be a big job. I felt discouraged. As my dad was visiting a friend, the friend had told him the neighbor had some rocks in her yard that she no longer had use for and wanted them out of her yard. I love rocks, and when my dad had told me of this, I, of course, asked for the rocks. This, in fact, was no small deal. This happened to be two thousand pounds of large rocks. Most of these rocks were so huge and heavy that I could not lift them or even move them at all. They were beautiful. My brother and dad had graciously moved these rocks to my yard, and this was a hard task. Anyway, these rocks continued to sit in a giant pile in my backyard being ignored as I saw their massiveness and didn't know what to do with them. I admired their beauty but didn't believe I had what it took to best display their beauty and get the full use out of them. As I hated this ugly muddy area leading to my house, and seeing these beautiful rocks, I realized God had set up the perfect opportunity to put something beautiful and strong and of good foundation into an area that was ugly and weak and of poor foundation. Although I now knew I wanted the rocks moved to this area, I wondered how I would scape the ground and design something that would work. My dad came over, and I told him my ideas. He helped me move dirt, cut lines, and move some of the bigger rocks to make a wall to support an upper level for a future brick path to be made from the door to the driveway. As a little got done, I began to get more ideas. It took many months and patience. My kids helped me; and I was able to lay limestone, weed barrier, and make a huge area of beautiful landscape. My dad and I cut bricks to design a beautiful, windy, whimsical walkway which was surrounded on one side by mulch; and the other side was filled with pea gravel, which made a nice spot that was big enough for a sitting area. As the project was unfolding before my eyes, I was able to learn about what it takes to build a firm foundation from one step to the next and how it doesn't just come together but instead is built layer by layer. This was how God taught me the importance of training kids up to have a good foundation in order to be useful and how it takes much patience and diligence to complete this task, and this was why Sabria had to work so hard where she was now at West Point. The larger rocks I could not budge, and being determined to finish this job, I asked God how I would be able to move these rocks on my own. I remembered the technique my kids and I would us in strength training which was to flip tires. I tried one and it worked! I could only move maybe three rocks a day because this was such a hard task. The rocks were big, awkward in shape, and a long distance from where I wanted to place them. It was so taxing. I had a couple bruises and scratches, but over some time eventually, I got all those rocks moved.

One day, while I was at work at the hospital, the kids went out on their own initiative and moved the last load of river rock that we had gotten delivered to our house. The area had already been prepared to receive these rocks, and the kids had paid attention and knew what to do. People would ask how the project got done, knowing those rocks were so huge, and they were amazed to hear I moved them and the kids had helped too. To get this area done, the kids and I used limestone, pea gravel, river rock, brick pavers, and big boulders. We measured the areas we created and went to stores in the area where we could find the right stones to go with those beautiful boulders. I was careful to stick to a tight budget, and over time, we were able to purchase the materials. I was able to share what God showed me with the kids. Stone comes in all shapes and sizes and are resources God gives us and prepares over time to be of good use to us. God also makes a beautiful foundation in our lives that brings joy to others. It will take time, effort, and determination; but if we trust that God grows us during each layer, we will eventually become a beautiful landscape. There is no need to rush the process, instead embrace the journey as it unfolds and understand that every layer has purpose. This was one of the many projects I was able to do at minimal cost as I struggled as a working mom of six with limited resources and while I also struggled to understand my daughter's journey through West Point. All the while, God was carrying me and teaching me about life. I would encourage everyone to spend time outside. God's nature is evidence of him. Spend time in nature, and ask to grow closer to him. My dad helped to facilitate this project and was a part of all of it. He moved the first row of boulders, giving me inspiration as I watched him work with fortitude, showing me that it was, in fact, possible, and leading me to eventually be creative and find my own way to move the rest of the boulders. He is very careful to always encourage my ideas and work because he loves me so much and appreciates the position he has in my life from God, to be a leader, teacher, and parent. He knows if he waters and nourishes my hopes and ideas, they will grow into big projects that are something to be proud of and learn from. Have enough faith to be a resource to your kids but enough trust in God to let him be your guide. God has made them strong and able to do good things. Be careful to know your place in their life so you can be part of their growth.

Now that I've talked of how I kept myself completely busy in life, I'll share of a particularly intense day that I experienced. I had worked day turn at the hospital. I got in the door around 4:00 p.m. and picked up my youngest daughter, Christiana, and then was back on the road. I was en route to my son Dylan's football game. He was a freshman, and as this could be a difficult stage in life for a young boy, I was determined as his mom to show him my commitment to always supporting his growth as a young man. This meant traveling to his game, which was an hour and a half away from home. This would allow me just enough time to watch the whole game and make it home just in time to shower and get back to work at the hospital for night shift. If I thought too much about what was expected of me in the next sixteen hours of my life, I would doubt myself and literally get scared by the intimidating high expectations I set for myself that were God inspired.

So I chose to stay focused on the task at hand and let God lead me little by little. In my weakness, I would ask myself if I would be strong enough to do this or if I would prematurely run out of steam at some point at a time that would be most catastrophic. Will I tank at the end of this fifty-two-hour workweek and end up sick? Would I fall asleep on the road and crash? As I started thinking of these negative thoughts, I chose to block those thoughts and decided, instead, to focus on the positive. As I get older, I am learning that pondering on the positive actually puts a blanket over the negative thoughts, and after a while, those negative thoughts are smothered, and they disappear from my mind. Bobby was working a twelve-hour shift that day and would be home soon to be with the other kids while I went to the game. Christy agreed to go with me to the game, and this sharing of good company was the positive I focused on. As we were beginning on our journey to the game, Christy said, "Mom, I like it here. When I get older, is it going to change? Papa says that it's different here than when he was young, so when I'm older, will it change for me too? I hope I still like it here when I'm older and it changes." As she rambled on, I remembered a prayer that she had said just the other night. She gazed up to heaven with folded hands and said, "Thank you for letting me live my best life." I realized, when she was talking about here, she meant here on earth, the planet, our world. Then as she sat in the backseat looking out the window as we drove, she asked me about heaven. She was wondering where it was and why it was too far to see. She began wondering why she liked it so much here on earth. Why was it so special to her? I explained that when God created the world, he looked at it and said it was good. I wanted her to know that God created the world and that it was meant to be enjoyed, that what she was feeling was her connection to God. She sees and appreciates his beauty in this place, the world.

I appreciate the car conversations I have with the kids. I respect the simplicity of their young lives and thought processes. I love to see the world through their young innocent eyes and learn to view things the way they do. There's so much to be learned from the little ones. This must be why God says to have the mind of a child. God also saw time with children as a pleasure, and I believe he was teaching us all how to act when he told his disciples to "let the little children come to me." He wasn't only enjoying the pleasure of the kid's company but rather was teaching us how to live, in response to kids. As we are figuring out life as people, we should be teaching kids. As we walk along side of children in life, we are to be teaching them to love, honor, and cherish God and his creation; and in the process, we ourselves may, in fact, learn how to love. Instead of having play dates to allow ourselves some alone time with friends or to watch our favorite show or just have some time to ourselves, we should try to take children by the hand into our daily activities, teaching them. Perhaps people are not themselves proud of how they live or don't feel they have anything to offer children, but this should never weigh on their attempts to love a child. God has the power to do all things, and we are expected to raise up children in the way they should go, whether these are our own kids or not. All kids are God's kids. If our country believed this there would be no foster system because everyone would take part. Parents are selfish and constantly fleeing their kids, letting them to stay alone in their rooms or lost in their phones or games and believing this is acceptable. God says otherwise. Don't just be with your kids or in the same house as your kids, but indulge in their existence. Dig into conversation with them. Sometimes I will call on all six of my kids until they all show up to see what I wanted. Then I hand out chore lists. They get upset, and the whole house will fight for a little bit, but soon the fighting dies down, and they start working together. Before long, they are talking to each other, goofing around, and enjoying the good company which leads to making plans for a game or movie night. Sometimes the chores don't get finished, but that's not always what I'm after as their mom. I want my kids to enjoy the company of their siblings and learn teamwork, leadership, and love. I explain to the kids that chores are simply activities of daily living, and we respect ourselves and each other as we get them done. I explain that some people don't have the privilege or physical ability to fold laundry or wash dishes, and by learning to do these simple things, God can trust us with bigger and more important jobs. This is something we revisit often in our "family meetings," *not* only doing chores but having initiative to know when things need done. Through it all, the kids learn they are important to me. I'm always thanking them for their efforts and reminding them how they inspire me to be better. God gives me endurance as a parent, giving the same lecture over and over again and seeming redundant. I know that one day it will click, so I choose to stay on the beaten path and find joy in raising my best friends. The day they spread the rocks outside was a great show of initiative, and this was a day I was most proud. Obedience is one thing, but doing something to show love without being asked is another thing. Both are good, and both are celebrated.

As I sit and smile while listening to Christy's second-grade chatter from the backseat, I am suddenly distracted by a figure I begin to see out of the corner of my eye. A maroon truck pulls ahead in the lane next to me, and out of the driver's side window spills a large burly, dirty man with sun-kissed skin and five-o'clock shadow, which accented his overgrown messy hair. His long arm hung out of the window, protruding from the bright-orange, greased-stained, cut-off T-shirt he was wearing. He forced his middle finger up and waved it at me. His gesturing matched the rhythm of his mouth as I could plainly see him mouthing the words "F you" over and over again as he slowly passed me. His eyes matched mine, and I looked at him, amazed by his boldly malicious actions on the freeway. The ugliness of his actions drowned out the sweet chatter of my little Christy, and I was hoping she didn't see what was happening. It wasn't until he was ahead of me before I realized what happened. My stomach tightened up, and I wondered what I had done wrong. I checked my speed. My speed was good. Did I cut him off? I don't remember changing lanes. What could I have done to trigger such a response from this guy? Then I could hear my husband's voice playing in my mind, "Maybe you shouldn't be driving in the fast lane if you don't want to drive fast." I had a habit of driving in the left lane because it's comfortable for me. I tend to forget that it's the fast lane. I'm just naturally drawn to that lane, but I do drive slowly, and by slowly, I mean I don't like to go more than a few miles over the speed limit. Maybe that was what I did to upset him. Maybe my driving ticked him off. I was really disgusted by this man but refused to let it change my mood. I was smiling before, during, and after this happened. Christy never saw the man do this, and she was still talking. She said she hoped her favorite "Jesus song" would come on the radio before we got to the game. From Christy's point of view, the world was a beautiful place. It was a place she loved. I didn't want to take anything from that by paying any attention to the ugliness. I thought about the man and tried to have compassion for him. Sometimes good people act badly. I know I've had bad days and I take it out on others, and this guy was no different. If we all let things go and focus on the beauty like kids do, the world would be a better place. We finally made it to my son's football game. I had called my husband, Bobby, to tell him what had happened on the road; and my husband, who is one of weak faith, justified the man's response by saying, "Well, were you in the fast lane? That's probably why you ticked him off." I said, "But what about the Army Mom sticker on the back of my car? Doesn't he know I am just a harmless army mom?" Bobby continued on that he believed the sticker meant nothing to this guy and it probably made him feel better to know that he attacked a harmless ball-capped army mom. I realized that evil comes looking for everyone. Babies are not a threat to others, but they are murdered every day. It gives a false sense of power to act in evil against another person. It's laziness to not look for another way to treat someone other than with animallike, uncontrolled, emotion-led action. This reminds me of a conversation that Bobby, Sabria, and I had once. It was during Sabria's senior year in high school at a time when she had broken the all-time scoring record for girls and boys at Fitch High School. It was a huge honor and awesome experience for my daughter, and we were proud of her efforts. At the same time, it was not Sabria's main goal to break records. This was the world's way of measuring Sabria's accomplishments and comparing her talents and efforts to others. Sabria's goal was to be the best version of herself at every level and in all areas of her life to honor God during her time here on earth. Setting records was bound to happen because of her God-given height and talent and passion to work and toil in her life and in this case in the game of basketball. Setting records was the evidence and collateral damage that was left behind as Sabria stormed through Austintown with God on her journey to greatness. She did enjoy the attention it brought, good and bad. She was eighteen, a girl finding her way in this life and trying to figure things out with lots of pressure because of her talent and potential in the game of basketball. She was looked at hard, and much was expected of her on the daily. Once you have set the bar high and made a name for yourself and shown your strength, people will notice when you show signs of weakness, and it will not be accepted. You must be the best and stay the best.

Sabria always had to remind herself that her strength was found in Christ and he was the judge who mattered most. She had to stay focused on that to remain committed to her goals to serve him. So now that she had reached this milestone of putting herself in the history books at Fitch and in the minds of people as being one of the best, if not the best basketball player to ever walk through the doors at Fitch High School, she realized she made history. She did allow herself to enjoy that whole thing for about a week or so, but the celebrating was short-lived. There was a boy who was believed by some to be a good prospect on the boys' basketball team the following year, and he had a sister in Sabria's grade. One day, while at school, the sister had said to Sabria that she hoped her brother would beat her record. Then that week, the school held a sit-down interview with the boy which was broadcasted on TV, and the spotlight was put on him to be the up-and-coming star athlete for Fitch. People were then tracking his stats and trying to predict if he was on track for beating the new record that had only just been set. Sabria found herself in a place she never wanted to be in. People had a hard time accepting the fact that a girl was the one who broke the record and not a boy. There is, in fact, the idea that boys' sports are more influential and important than girls' sports. This weakness is a problem at Fitch, at many colleges, and in families all over the world. This is an idea Sabria was hoping to change in the minds of people. As we encouraged her to remain a role model not for girls or boys and not for records or trophies but for being a witness to all people to have Christ's attitude toward these subjects, she began to see her place of importance in the position that she was in concerning the battle of favoritism and how it is not of God. The only person Sabria ever competed with was herself. Whether in the gym, on the court, at school, or at home, it's always been a point to beat her body and make it her slave so that after she is a witness to others, she doesn't disqualify her own self for the eternal prize in heaven, as it talks in 1 Corinthians 9:27. This is one of our family's favorite verses. In 2 Corinthians 13:5, it talks about examining yourself to see if you are in the faith. This is how Sabria was able to challenge herself and reach levels that had meaning beyond trophies and records. This is what she wanted to see in others. Not that others would compare themselves to her but instead to look into themselves and to see how they differed from God so they could change those things to make themselves better and more like him. If you are a born- again believer, your heart is guarded by God, which then fuels your mind which tells your body what to do. If people don't trust in God, they tend to take a meaningless approach by doing things that feel good or bring some kind of physical or emotional satisfaction. This approach prevents one from reaching their true potential as athletes and in every aspect of life. This cheating approach gets people into trouble because they are putting their faith in the things of this world. This is something that, I believe, forces many kids out of sports, either because they want a feel-good response or because those in authority want a feel-good response, such as winning; so they will force kids out because they lack the faith to invest in a kid they don't see as being worth their efforts at the time.

Sabria felt bad that, instead of feeling positive vibes, she felt like people were instead chasing her success, focusing on beating her records. Bobby explained to her that she had a target on her back. Once you are the best, you are in the lead. No one can be in front of you until they pass you, so, of course, they are chasing you. It's part of the game, and she should be proud of being chased. He had been telling her that for years because she had always been good at the sport and needed encouraged. She was told in seventh grade she would be a Division 1 basketball player, and this was only after playing the sport for a year. She started playing basketball in the sixth grade and was terrible at it. It was hard for Bobby and me to even watch her play on the league team at the YMCA, because it was evident that she had no skill at all. We both loved the game and played it ourselves. We were shocked at how bad our kid was at it. Even running down the court looked unnatural for her, and we didn't think she would ever choose to continue playing after this first experience in the game of basketball. There was a coach there who saw something Bobby and I didn't see. She told Sabria that she would be a great basketball player in the future. Bobby and I were skeptical, but Sabria decided she would continue to believe there may be hope for her to grow in this sport, so she didn't throw in the towel. For some reason, she did not give up; maybe it was her height. She was about five feet nine in sixth grade and thankful to be tall because she was asked by some friends to be on their basketball team that one of the girls' dad coached. Sabria just wanted to have fun and was glad to have friends. This was where it all began. Her passion grew. She wanted to be a good friend on the court, and the game of basketball became a way to love others and have fun. As she started to get better and used her height and new skills to make her team successful, she felt needed. She saw how getting better at this was a way to love her herself, her coach, and her team of friends. It was a way that God could use her, and she realized this was why he made her tall. By seventh grade, a coach from the Cleveland area had heard of her and came to see her play a game in Austintown at the middle school. We didn't know he was there. He appreciated her talent and skill level, and after that game, he introduced himself and told us he wanted her to play for him at SMAC (Score More Athletic Club). He told us that our daughter was different. He asked us if we wanted to stay playing at the level we were at or if we wanted more for our daughter and a chance for her to broaden her horizon. We had no idea what would be involved in this commitment at the time. I knew nothing about travel basketball. I was so uneducated in the subject that I thought when the coach told me she would be traveling all over to different states to play that it meant they went by bus as a team. I had no idea that he meant I would be driving her myself or even flying, in some cases, to these tournaments. I believe God hid some details from me at the time because my weak faith would not have allowed me to believe that I could handle such a commitment. We did wait it out a year before deciding to do it. Sabria decided to play one more year with her local travel team because her friends there were already expecting her to play and this would give her good time to ease into the commitment of SMAC and would also give our family time to plan.

God eased Sabria's mind about leaving the local team after there was some jealousy and selfishness stirring up there, and this was not a place where Sabria could grow. We realized God was pushing us to move on, and we were thankful for the signs. We didn't have a dependable car or enough money in the bank for gas to even get to the practices twice a week that were over an hour away, but we knew God had a plan we couldn't see, so we followed his lead in hope that he would carry us through. Coach Carlos told me I would see a lot of growth in Sabria through his program, and that was what stuck with me. He asked Bobby what growths he wanted to see in his daughter and what her strengths were believed to be. He really wanted to use his expertise and experience to bring the best out of Sabria to build her individually into the athlete and young woman she had the potential of becoming, and he also had the humility of self needed to lead her to the next level. That was when Bobby and I really started spending time talking to Sabria. After every game, it was time to talk. We spent countless hours with her just talking and having conversations about what happens in games and why. Most of it didn't end up being about basketball but about life lessons and how God changes us through our experiences on earth. God had a plan for Sabria, and her experiences in basketball were just part of her journey in life—a very important and special part of the journey. We always brought all of our kids to her games. They didn't play basketball yet. When Sabria first started to play basketball at age twelve, Dylan was eight, Sophia was six, Theresa was four, Quintin was two, and Christy was an infant. We were pretty busy parents, but we knew being a close family was important. After the games, we'd sit in the living room and just talk. All the kids would want to be involved in the conversations we had with Sabria about the games and how they pertained to life around us. We always encouraged the kids to learn even at their young ages that they had a special place on earth and to support their sister and all their other siblings. They listened and chimed in, and we all grew from those talks, as God was the center of those meetings. You never want to get lost in the game or in any other event or situation in life. There is something bigger going on than just what you see in front of you. We reminded Sabria of this in her senior year when talking to her about the chase. We told her to appreciate that she had the target on her back and to know that it was an honor. God allowed her to be in that place up front because she knew how to be a good leader. She needed to accept the gift from God and let him continue to lead her as he's done her whole life. I told her to wear that target on her back proudly and know she was being watched. Her witness is very valuable to God. She should appreciate the honor and respect it as the gift of grace that it was. She should always show God's love to others. He made her a target so that people would see him, not her, so the need to stay humble was crucial.

The topic came up again when she arrived at West Point, and as I wrote about earlier whenever she was out and about, she needed to wear her white-over-grays uniform. She was easily identified as a woman in uniform and stood out as a soldier. Sabria didn't quite understand the rationale behind this practice. I reminded Sabria what she learned in high school about what it meant to be a target and that, as a leader, you're in front. There will be evil always lurking in the shadows to attack those who try to do what's right. Some people will attempt to mock her efforts. Wearing the uniform is a way to stay aware of who you are. It doesn't make you who you are, but it can keep you more alert to your surroundings and to the stand that you take in what you believe and represent. It is just staying in the real all the time. Evil is always ready to break down, destroy, and damage anyone who is willing to work hard to do what's right. Be proud of who you and be willing to display evidence of the side you are on. Just as there are those who will hate and target you because you desire to do the right thing, there will also be those who see you as a target to chase to help motivate them in their own search for greatness, and you will encourage them to do what's right. People need those who are not afraid to be disciplined and not moved from their stand no matter the pressure. These people are real-life heroes. Accept the challenge to wear the uniform which is an opportunity to stay disciplined in your walk and accept it as a gift of grace. Dare to be a target in basketball and in life. Don't throw it in people's face, but you don't need to hide under a bush either. Let your light shine, and be obedient to authority, even God. Some people will appreciate your cause, and some will not. Regardless of the response from those around you, your actions should remain the same as you get your guidance and authority from God.

There was a time in high school when Sabria was in Panera in Austintown with another player from the basketball team, and they sat down to eat lunch. A man from the community walked up to them and told them how impressed he was with the basketball teams' efforts on the court and he enjoyed watching them play. He paid for their lunch and told them to keep up the good work and good luck with the rest of the season. This meant so much to Sabria, and this was confirmation that her hard work and determination did pay off. Another time, Sabria was tutoring a young boy in the library in our town when a man, who recognized who she was, came up to her and dropped an index card on the table she was sitting at and walked away. The card was a letter of encouragement to Sabria about how good she was doing and how he always enjoyed her talent on the court. She was so happy to get such a nice card that she came home and showed me and said she was keeping it forever. She still has it saved with her keepsakes at our house. These are reminders from complete strangers that you can love others through your stand. Sabria met so many nice people over the years because she dared to let God use her to love others through her hard work and determination in life. That day at the library was not Sabria's original plan. The young boy she was tutoring could not meet at the original time at the school, so Sabria agreed to meet him at the library later. God changes your route sometimes to create opportunities to communicate with you. God loves Sabria, and she shows her faith in him by her willingness to be flexible and brave to go down roads he sends her down. She had compassion for the young boy which fueled her decision to tutor him, believing it was an opportunity to help someone even though it really didn't fit well into her schedule; she would not pass it up. She tutored him in math. She had told me one day that she realized the boy really could learn and that he actually learned the same way Sabria did. She found that the boy really only needed the work to be shown to him, but she understood that the teachers did not always like to slow down the pace of class to show work. He could really catch on quickly if he was shown. Sabria had this same struggle, so she had taught him the same way she liked to be taught. He had gotten behind in school when his family split up and was unable to rebound in school after he had missed so many days and lessons. He got put on a list of kids who needed tutored, and Sabria had gotten the opportunity through NHS. She enjoyed the experience. He had struggled with the idea of circumference, so Sabria taught him how to figure it out using a piece of string. This was a learning tool that one of her teachers showed her, and it really clicked, so she used the technique with the boy, and he was able to learn. She was impressed and enjoyed seeing his efforts and interest in learning. One time, we were late to a workout because she had stayed longer at the tutoring session. I yelled at her when she was late coming home, but when she told me that it was because they were really on a roll and she didn't want to leave, I just looked at her amazed at who she was becoming. She had no time in her tight schedule but somehow made time for what was most important, loving others. I was so proud of her for being a positive influence on a young boy who was in a tough position in life and needed her help and support. This should always come before athletics. She was a role model in the area, and people knew her as a good basketball player, so who better to teach the young ones how to focus on what's most important? He needed to see a good athlete taking time out of her day to spend time helping him because this was an example he could follow. She knew what it was like to struggle to learn concepts when the teaching was too fast. Sabria was actually really bright, but having those struggles at times in your life is a blessing because it keeps you aware of the hard times others may be having so you can know how to help them because you've been able to overcome the struggle yourself at one time. She had seen how her brother Quintin had struggled through an experience in school and watched and supported our family as we dealt with it. I'm sure it prepared her to deal with this boy as she did and allowed her to have compassion on him.

Back when my son Quintin was in second grade, he had struggled with reading and comprehension, as many kids do at that age. His teacher had been concerned with his trailing behind and having trouble grasping concepts from stories he read, which caused concern for his progress in her class. I wasn't concerned as all of my kids had struggled in school, and I had always seen a turnaround at some point as we continued to support them, and eventually, all the right things clicked, and they were able to connect with the appropriate level of learning for their age. I appreciate the struggle as I know it is making them better and teaching them to be resilient. The issues I started to be concerned with were the crying episodes he would have at night before bed. I would lay down next to him, and we would talk. One particular night, he became very upset and emotional, which was not normal for him. He seemed very overwhelmed, and I said that I wanted to help him to figure out what was making him so upset about going to school. He opened up to me and said that he didn't want to go to school and see his teacher because she was mean, telling him he would probably be held back from third grade because he didn't do his homework. He said his reading scores were bad and the teacher kept saying he was in the red zone. He asked me if he was really going to be held back and asked me what the red zone was and if he'd be in this zone forever. I assured him that it was still early enough in the year to make a change and nothing was impossible and there was still time to learn and grow before third grade. I told him not to worry, but I was burning inside. Why would a teacher get into a child's head to the point of him having panic attacks before bed! If she had so much concern for my son's position in his progress, why weren't some measures taken to correct the path he was on? Surely, there was an explanation for her behavior, or maybe my son saw things bigger than they really were. I had been contemplating what to do in the situation, and I asked God to guide me and was conflicted until a day that week that I got the phone call from his teacher, and things became clear. My phone rang as I was out with Sabria and Bobby for lunch. We never got to spend much time together, just the three of us, so this was a special occasion. I answered the phone as I saw that it was Quintin's teacher. She started rambling about how Quintin doesn't do his homework, and she was greatly concerned that his grades were in the red zone. I realized this was not a discussion I could have at the table, and I went outside to continue the conversation. She asked me if I was aware that Quintin hadn't been doing his homework and asked in a rude, sarcastic tone if there was a problem at home. She continued rambling in a rough and loud tone that Quintin needed to take the five minutes a night to do his homework in order to do better on his test scores. She sounded very worked up, and I could tell she was irritated about the situation. I said, "So you're saying if Quintin does five minutes of homework a night, he will be out of the red zone?" She scoffed and responded with sarcasm by telling me no and that this was a big problem and that it would take a long time to fix. I said, "Then what's the point in doing the homework if it's not going to help him?" I could see now why my son was so afraid to go to school because I figured this teacher tried to use the same fear tactics to get results from him like she was trying to do on the phone with me, using unsuccessful manipulation tactics. So then I knew my son had a real problem, and it wasn't just with grades or reading comprehension. I said to this teacher, first of all, that she was a teacher and if my son was in the "red zone," then surely there is some tutoring available that he could do instead of extracurriculars and recess and field trips and that the time he spent at school should be spent learning.

I spent much time with my son and knew him well. I knew he was a good boy who grasped concepts well at home and was an asset to our family. She was implying that I did not take an interest in my son's learning and that I did not have a healthy concern for my son's education, because he didn't do the countless hours of home-work. She apparently used this as an excuse for her obvious poor teaching approach, laziness, and lack of good time management in the classroom. I explained that he spent eight precious hours at school, and surely this was enough time to teach him to read and comprehend, and I demanded she do a better job. She could see that I was not on the bashing Quintin bandwagon. I ended the phone call and did some praying, very concerned about how my son must be getting treated at school. I wasn't going to tell my son of the conversation, because I was having a hard time myself filtering my emotions surrounding the situation. I wanted to think and clear my head first before making a move but that very day, Quintin got off the bus and burst through the door, running into the house toward me, yelling, "Did my teacher call you and tell you about me being in the red zone?" His eyes were huge, as wide as they could be. He was in a panic. I was shocked and asked him how he knew about this phone call. He said that he was sitting right there when she called me at 12:00 noon during their specials. He said that he heard her talk about me taking care of him. I came to realize that the reason she was being so loud was so that Quintin and his class could hear her disapproval of him and so she could make a spectacle of him. My niece was in the classroom, too, and she had went home and told her parents how she felt bad for Quintin because, apparently, the teacher would criticize him in front of the whole class all the time about how he didn't do his homework and how he would be behind the other kids. His cousin went home that day and told her parents how she felt bad for Quintin for always getting yelled at by the teacher, and she also let them know that Quintin's mom got called that day about him not getting his work done. Not only was Quintin being shamed by his teacher, a person who should be encouraging him, but he was also encouraged to be bullied by his teacher's attempts to force her agenda, an agenda I did not support. Of course, I sound like that crazy parent, and my son sounds like that noncompliant kid who makes teachers jobs harder. This is the picture the teacher tried to paint of my family. God saw me different, though, and his view of me is what matters most. I would not do what the teacher expected me to do, because her view and mine were not the same. She thought either I would follow along with her and encourage the abuse that was shown to my son in order to maintain the order in her classroom or I would act crazy and give everyone a reason to see me as the person she assumed I was if I didn't comply—an out-of-control, uneducated, unwilling-to-participate parent whose attitude matched her son's. I would, in fact, act on the situation in the only way I could. As my conviction drove me, I was compelled to set up a meeting with her and the principal. I am naturally a nonconfrontational person. I do not look for trouble, because I know I will find it. When trouble finds me, I am ready and willing to be a witness of the love God has shown me my whole life, and this is why I chose to respond to the teacher's display of poor character and leadership. I phoned the principal and said that I needed a meeting ASAP. I was not willing to send Quintin any longer into what became a deleterious environment for him at school. I decided to ask my dad to join me at the meeting for good support. I knew he could bring good insight and perspective. He has a doctorate in theology and has studied the Bible for forty years. He lives his life to love God and serve others. He also worked in schools for many years as a substitute teacher. I wanted the best for my son Quintin but also knew that my vast responsibilities as a working nurse and mother of six did not allow me the time to spend several hours a night doing homework with Quintin, and I also was not willing to sacrifice the little bit of precious time I had with him doing busy paperwork at home. I knew my dad would be a good mediator in the meeting because he could understand both sides, and I did not want to be caught up in a fight which would ultimately destroy my witness of God's love and would, in fact, not help my son in his situation at school.

As we sat down in an office at the school, I was uncomfortable but confident that God would walk me through as I was there to love my son and be obedient to God's call. I began to explain the story of a little boy who had been scared to go to school and now was having trouble sleeping at night because of the recurring negative experiences he had at school with the teacher because it is thought that he doesn't do enough homework at home. The teacher explained that she made a packet for the kids to do at home throughout the year and she worked very hard on that packet. She, focusing more on herself, said that she worked very hard on that special packet to help Quintin. I realized at that moment that my thoughts on the situation were accurate. She was offended by myself and my son that we did not see her packet as important as she did. She was pushing her agenda that the only way Quintin could learn in her class, do well on tests, and move on to third grade was if he did it her way, which was by her teaching from a distance and by him learning at home. God prepared me for this exact response from her. I enlightened the teacher by asking her a few questions. I asked, "Do you know Quintin's favorite hobby?" She responded with a no. I asked, "Do you know his favorite food, what he's good at, or maybe his favorite color?" She replied by saying no. I pulled a folder out of my bag with a packet that was labeled "All About Me." I asked her if she remembered this packet. She replied no. I told her that she sent it home as homework and Quintin and I spent forty-five minutes completing that packet, and she didn't even read it. How could I expect her to teach my son anything if she herself doesn't do what is expected of her? Although my son had been in her class for several months now, she didn't know anything about him or our family, and yet she believed she could give a negative account of what his future would be and what his life is like at home. I pulled out a stack of papers from my bag that she sent home with Quintin after they completed them in class. I told her to look at them. Most of them were coloring pages. Quintin told me they spent a lot of time coloring in class and that he often heard the teacher talking to other teachers about how bad the students were. I explained that most of the papers I received from what was done in class were easy papers or coloring but that the packets she sent home for us to do were very time-consuming, difficult, and things that should be taught by a teacher. I told her that perhaps she should have Quintin do this important packet at school and she could send home the coloring papers for him to do at home. I informed her that he was very good at coloring now, and I was implying that perhaps if she worked on the important learning packets in school, he would be good at reading and comprehension, too, and would do better in his testing. She was sending two hours of homework home a night. I did time this and also spoke with other parents in his class who said it did take about this long to do their child's homework. This homework was not work he could do alone, and my husband and I both worked full-time, I explained. I said we didn't have the time to do the homework she sent home with Quintin and it was my fault he did not turn it in. Our time at home is precious to me. My marriage is precious to me. My five other kids are precious to me. Our evenings were spent at home making dinner and doing chores and extracurricular activities together. We would not be changing that. We had made the mistake of exhausting ourselves in the past with homework, and it always resulted in fights, and our whole house would be chaotic. Excessive homework is an evil thing. I explained that as the kids got older, they began to learn to pace themselves and that they all ended up doing fine; in fact, they did extraordinary in school. My kids all had good grades, and my oldest, Sabria, was being recruited by West Point. I did believe in my system of teaching my kids, and I was not going to let someone with their selfish agenda change my mind.

The principal chimed in and asked if what I was saying was that I didn't want any homework sent home with my son (he was obviously daydreaming while I was talking). I said, "That is not what I'm saying." This was when my dad really took a crucial stand in the meeting. He chimed in to respond to the principal, "I think what Tina is trying to say is that she would like the responsibility of teaching Quintin to be left to the professionals. She already has a profession as a nurse and as Quintin's mother, so she has her own work to do. Let her be Quintin's mother and assist in the teaching process, and let the bulk of the academic-related teaching be left up to the school." I made them aware that my research did teach me that the national PTA guidelines stated that a boy in second grade should have twenty minutes of homework sent home. This is a far cry from two hours. Quintin was a smart boy, so if he was not doing well on test scores, this may be a reflection of the coloring he was doing in class, instead of the work being taught to him. I suggested that instead of him having extra recess and extracurriculars at school and even field trips that more attention would be paid to his abilities to reason, comprehend, and problem solve so that he would have the tools needed to do better on his test scores and get out of the so-called red zone. This is why I sent Quintin to school for eight hours a day. Let me play with my son, take him on field trips, and color. At school, he should be learning, and I knew that school had more to offer Quintin than a complex about how he was a poor student for not doing endless hours of homework after school so his teacher could continue to be negligent and I could be made to look like a bad parent. I also told them I did not support the teacher criticizing Quintin in front of the entire class and bullying him to force him to comply with nonsense. This would stop that very day. This was unacceptable behavior, and bullying at any level should not be tolerated. Teachers are to catch bullying and stop it. Certainly, doing it themselves and encouraging others to join in is wrong. I needed to demand the change in behavior since the teacher openly admitted to encouraging my niece to yell at Quintin to do his homework. She thought nothing was wrong with her technique. They did agree to get Quintin the help he needed to improve his learning. The principal asked if I wanted Quintin to be removed from the class, and I said no. I wanted the teacher to learn to teach and not bully. I wanted her to send less homework home and do more in the precious time she had with the kids. I was raising the standard, and I wanted to see results. This was an opportunity for Quintin to apply himself, pray for God to change the relationship between him and his teacher and his placement in academics. We were not running away from this challenge. God allowed this to occur on our journey in life, and we needed to grow. We ended the meeting, and I walked away with my head held high and confident that God would bless me for my efforts in changing myself and being an example to my son. There was hope after that meeting. I made myself accountable to making Quintin do his twenty minutes of homework, and he really tried hard to be consistent and diligent as best he could in second grade. I was very proud of him. Before long he was on track with his grades. He is in fourth grade now, doing well academically, and has a good heart. I could not leave him to fight that battle alone. Have confidence to stand up on God's word when these situations arise. People are too quick to change classrooms, teachers, and school systems in order to find the perfect place for their kid and escape accountability. There is no perfect school or perfect teacher or perfect parent. Instead gain perspective, and be the change you want to see in others. That's how we can make America great and spread God's love. We must be willing to live at a higher standard so we can have the confidence to expect this out of others and confront them when they choose to fall short.

Some people think you cannot be friends with your kids. I disagree. God says a friend loves at all times, and a true friend will lay his life down for his friend. This is how I treat my kids. I teach, discipline, play, and pray with them. If you teach your kids what a true friend is by being one to them, they will see you as one and could be that to others. I lay my life down for my best friends every single day by putting them first, and this is how I show God's love for them. I was not willing to change my beliefs even under pressure from that teacher, but to treat her with love and respect while disagreeing was something my son can learn from and hopefully do in the future himself. He saw that his Papa and I had his back and were willing to go through fire on his behalf but also expect much out of him as he has much to offer. Family bonds are important. Too many distractions, including homework, can weaken that bond if you let it. This was a lesson in life that even through all the disciple and instruction in our house, I still can be a good friend to my kids, and they love me as a friend too. Sabria used what she learned in this situation with Quintin to help tutor a boy who became somewhat lost in the system in hopes that he would see his worth. She had compassion on him and chose not to look the other way but instead to love him and give him hope to forge ahead in his academics. These experiences I witness with my kids are the reason I can withstand the abuse I get from people around me who choose to treat me badly. The negativity is everywhere, but the good in my life outweighs the bad, and I choose to see it. My dad reminds me all the time that I am experiencing God's precious blessings on the daily and that I am lacking nothing. I'm not missing out on anything. These are the kind of stories I reflected on while I'm driving home from the football game. Realizing that although my life is jam-packed with responsibilities, I have joy in the toil. The rest of that day traveling back and forth with football and working day turn and then going back for night turn in the same day was hard, and the night was even harder than the day, but I made it through, and God sharpened my diligence and perseverance to succeed.

CHAPTER 9

SEEING GOD

Another hour and fifteen-minute drive to my son's football game was underway. This would have been in August-September time 2019, and I was feeling really low and run-down. I needed some encouragement. I was lonely and overwhelmed with life as I tried to continue the constant grind with little support from those around me as God became, in my eyes, the only one with enough power to help me at that point, and yet I still believed I could be a good mom despite the challenges I was facing. Of course, I was edgy about my driving, so I was being careful to be considerate on the road. As I looked up at the sky hoping for answers to my problems and was really feeling down, I noticed the clouds and the bright sun shining behind them. It was a beautiful contrast of light and darkness. It reminded me of a day at the park with the kids. We road our bikes to the school's campus, which was a about a mile and a half from our house. There are several playgrounds there at the schools, and we love to go and rotate around them all until we're tired. Then we drive our bikes back home. It's one of the reasons I chose our house fifteen years ago. It should have been a nice starter house but became a forever home for many reasons. One reason was that it was close to the schools. We can hear the band playing on Friday nights from our backyard, and this has always been reminiscent of many evenings I spent in Austintown as a kid. Now that the kids are older, we can run together to the high school track and run the bleachers. I love feeling close to the kids while they're in school. Going on bike rides is a great way to exercise but also a good way to connect with the kids because they talk a lot during playtime. They relax their minds as they unwind, which leads to unloading their frustrations or concerns with life. Basically, this allows them to get things off their chests that they didn't know was even there.

While at the playground, we were appreciating the sun as it was shining down upon us on a particular summer day. Sophia was twelve at the time, Theresa was eleven, and Christy was seven. We were admiring their shadows that appeared and took shape on the ground as we were talking to each other. One of the girls said, "Hey, Mom, did you know that you only have shadows during the day? Because darkness hides from the sun." The other girls chimed in, "Yeah, that's why a lot of crimes happen at night because the sun goes down and the darkness thinks it is safe from the sun. But the moon comes out at night, and the moon is a witness, so the darkness can never really hide. God can always see us. That's why after you get saved and Jesus comes in your heart, you don't have a real shadow anymore, and there is nowhere for sin to hide." As they explained this to me, I was intrigued at their understanding of the light of Jesus and how we all have the opportunity to walk in the light. This really hit my heart, and I was in awe that I could learn a new perspective as I saw salvation through the eyes of my kids. I was humbled at how God could teach me through these young children, and this is how I longed over the years to spend more and more time with them as God encourages us to do. He is there with them, and he wants to be close to us all.

When you become born again, your faith grows. You will still make mistakes, but you learn and desire to change. As you change and continue to make good choices, God can reveal more of himself to you. This is how your passion grows to want more of him and less of the world. A light shines the brightest in darkness, which is why the most amazing people I've ever met have been through tremendous storms in their life. Experiencing God in a mighty way means you must be willing to go through some dark times knowing he is directing your path. This is where you find him as he is revealed inside of you. On this drive to Dylan's game, admiring the sky and remembering the encouragement my girls gave me on that summer day, I could see out of the corner of my eye that a car was next to me. I could feel someone looking at me from the next lane, and I realized I was driving, once again, in the fast lane! I thought, *How do I keep doing this? Would this be another angry driver that I managed to upset?* I was afraid to look over. I didn't feel anything negative. In fact, I thought I had caught the person smiling. I was thinking, *Why would someone be smiling at me? Do I know this person? Should I wave?* I reluctantly looked over and could see it was a woman. No one I recognized, though, and she didn't seem upset at all. Maybe I was just over thinking again. Then, as her car sped up a little, I looked, and I noticed on the back of her car was a familiar sticker that read "Army Mom." My heart leaped! I smiled and chuckled to myself. She must have seen my Army Mom sticker on the back of my car too! As she slowed again, we were going at the same speed, and she looked over at me, and our eyes met, and we both smiled as we waved at each other realizing the connection and automatic bond we had with each other. We gave each other emphatic thumbs-up as we both drove off. I was so encouraged by this experience, and this moment will forever be in my heart. What a huge contrast from the nasty guy I had met on the roadway just a couple days before this. I thought about how beautiful this sweet lady's face was. Her skin was like porcelain. And her teeth had a perfect white glow. Her lips were rosy pink. She was like an angel. I looked in my rearview mirror to get another glimpse of her, but she was gone—disappeared from the freeway. I thought, *That's weird. I don't remember there being an exit anywhere close by. Could she have been an angel?* I was just filled with such a wonderful feeling that God was with me. He was shining through the darkness and had given me a sign of his beauty. That lady, an army mom, knows what I'm going through. Whether she is an angel of God or just a beautiful army mom, she's amazing to me. My eyes filled with tears as I was overcome with floods of thankfulness for what I had just encountered. Although I have many struggles in life and sometimes relief seems too far off and battles seem too hard to fight, there is hope there to find. Even with the messy house I couldn't find time to clean; the sleep I longed for; the husband who taunted me and couldn't see my worth; a forever-dwindling bank account that tells me its limits outweigh the cost; or all the things the world tells me about how I'm not good enough, I don't have enough, or I won't be enough— God speaks louder, and he finds ways to tell me a different story. He sings a different song. He says I can do all things through him who gives me strength. I made sure to tell my husband about the story and how he had been wrong about the sticker on my car, that it wasn't just a sticker and that it had meaning to me and that God brings power to my efforts to encourage and love others and this is why my efforts are not worthless but will bring forth change even if it's helping one person at a time and even if that person who needs to change is, in fact, me.

The idea that this lady, a perfect stranger, tried to get my attention on the freeway to make sure she could encourage me that day was inspirational. She didn't even know me, and yet she was able to give me exactly what I needed that day at a point when I was feeling so low. She said so many things with that beautiful smile and thumbs-up. She didn't even need to speak, because her actions did the talking. She was able to tell me she understood my humble, emotional, proud, scared, happy, sad, hope-filled, faith-driven, roller coaster ride of a life! I understand that evil is not biased. Evil will come to anyone and attempt to destroy just like the man in the maroon truck. He didn't care about me or have any regard for his actions and the impression he could have had on the little girl in the back seat of my car. So I thanked God for loving me that day the way I needed to be loved and showing me through complete strangers, the battle between good and evil. I saw the importance of living as a witness of God's love and that even if no one validates the hope in my efforts and even if people question my purpose in this life, I can still know my place here has meaning through the signs, letting me know I am living in the light of his promises. It was very encouraging to see another person being bold and positive and willing to spread that power of love to others. The clouds in the sky that day were a perfect contrast of light and darkness, and this contrast is evident in people too. Some are lost in darkness, but people who let their light shine will be bright in comparison. This is how your love grows and your relationship with God deepens. He is there, always.

CHAPTER 10

WEAR THE MASK TO GET ON THE COURT

As Sabria was away for her first three months at the academy, I worked tirelessly to get the house prepared for her return. She would be coming home for a weekend in October to visit, and we were thrilled to have her back in the house. I was inspired by the verse in the Bible about Jesus leaving his disciples as he said he was going to prepare a place for them. I believed that the house should be ready to welcome Sabria so she could enjoy her visit with us and feel the love we had for her. It was hard raising the other five kids while she was away and adjusting to our new way of life. I needed to be many things and shift accordingly to accommodate everyone's needs while making Sabria feel like she was still part of the team, as this was the reality. Encouraging Sabria's dream of going to the academy at West Point was just a continuing of the process of building her up to be the best version of herself, a process that should begin at home when a child is young even still in the womb. She was playing basketball for the one who made her tall. She was serving the country God had born her into. She was playing the game she loved and living life every day for something bigger than herself because it was her call and mission. It's all of our calls to search for our purpose in life and to pursue God's plan with all of our being. People do not always respect the work that goes into this purpose-driven life; but if respect, permission of others, or appreciation from your neighbor for your accomplishments are what you're after, you will surely be disappointed. People had made rude undermining remarks to me all the time during my years in raising Sabria, such as "How did she get so good?" basically making me aware that they believed she didn't have extraspecial parents or a wealthy family or anything else that warranted her success. Others would say that she must have good genes or that it was "in her blood." They would also say things like "I hope my daughter ends up tall so she can get a college basketball scholarship, too, and save me some money." Basically, these people were without success in their attempts to mock my family's faith-driven life and Sabria's discipline to duty, hard work, and fortitude, which were her response to God's calling of her to follow the plan he laid out for her.

These comments lead me to understand that our world is lost. Our world does not believe that God gives us tools to use to succeed. They believe instead in free passes to success, luck, and fantasy. God desires a relationship with us. Salvation is free. Being tall is free. He wants you to take these gifts of grace and use them for good to show his love to others. Our world is not showing this belief to others. People want riches and success in this world to be achieved the easiest way possible, and the truth is that there is no value in that approach. I remind myself often how the Bible tells us that it is easier for a camel to go through the eye of a needle than for a rich man to enter the kingdom of heaven. This passage in scripture has been taken many ways but always with the same idea that being rich makes it harder for you to enter heaven. Why then would anyone desire to be rich? People want to flaunt their fancy cars and big expensive houses that they spent years saving for, and God says these things are worthless. Sabria spent endless nights studying and traveling around the world at the age fifteen, and sometimes it was with people she barely knew, and all the while, her efforts were mocked by some because of her passion to do her best. This was even seen in her coach in ninth grade. This coach was bent on letting the kids know she was the boss. She did not respect Sabria's talent as she encouraged the idea that the older kids earned rank and respect just because of their age. The older kids had more playing time and were given leadership roles even though their performance and character did not support or warrant their advancement. It was a cheap way of running things, but this coach was fueled by her desire to seem important and powerful, which, of course, was a fantasy. Sabria was forced to comply for a time if she wanted to continue to play the game. We believed that God would deliver her eventually out of the hands of the evil she was experiencing. Sabria endured the bullying she encountered in eighth grade by some of her teammates as jealousy fueled their negative and spiteful talks about her good intentions on the court and in the gym. They even held a meeting, which became a Sabria-bashing session. All the girls came together and talked about things that bothered them, and many of them blurted out that they felt that everything was about Sabria. There were some coaches who joined in and encouraged the disrespect toward Sabria as they themselves were poor leaders and could not imagine that they were unable to train or lead such a young girl because she already surpassed their abilities. Instead of humbling themselves to learn from Sabria and from God and maybe some higher-level coaches they should have reached out to and recruited, they instead tried to drag her down to their level so they could feel comfortable in their lowly position as coaches to a girl they couldn't teach. Instead of her teammates learning to get better in order to be able to play better with Sabria at her higher level of talent which would have made them an unstoppable team, they chose instead to try to make Sabria feel bad about their jealousy. Their parents even encouraged and took part in the bashing because they themselves weren't willing to go with their kid to the gym after practice or wake up earlier in the morning to get in a run or spend their hard-earned money on their child to get the best training. If Sabria wasn't so good and I, as her parent, wasn't willing to step up to the plate, the parents, kids, and coaches could remain how they were, and their unwillingness to change and grow would maybe not be noticed. Sabria, in a sense, highlighted their weakness. I wasn't falling for their attempts at manipulation, and I also would not encourage their desire to remain in darkness. Sabria came home from that meeting upset about how everyone felt about her as her main goal was to be a good teammate, friend, and student. I explained to her that she should not believe the lies of weak people and that their actions were petty. We, of course, had a long talk about how she needed to love unconditionally and how this act of love would be her witness of God. She had many gifts, and she needed to use them despite the abuse she would receive for her decision to keep striving. I told her to be an example to those who didn't accept her and to also appreciate the true friendship of those who did love her and to know the difference. So when Sabria was met with conflict in ninth grade, she could see the contrast of good and evil as she recognized it from her trouble in eighth grade.

I had told my kids of my favorite player when I was growing up, Scottie Pippen. He was only six feet one in college, and it held him back. College coaches were apprehensive to recruit him because he was so short, but he had obvious talent to play basketball. He started out as a manager for a team and still played the game he loved and worked to get better despite the height challenge. He impressed the coaches and was still growing in college, and as they liked what they saw in him, they allowed him playing time. He kept growing throughout college and ended up being six feet eight and going on to be more successful in college and then to get picked to play in the NBA, ultimately playing for the Chicago Bulls, noted to be the best team in NBA history! This is an incredible story of how never giving up is so important. God knows what you need, and in time, as you push through the struggle, he will deliver. Who else besides God could have made Scottie Pippen tall? No one. Yet this one thing is what he needed to advance to the next level. He chose not to give up on his dream to play basketball even though he could not change his height. I believe God blessed his efforts by giving him so much height in college. Everyone has a different challenge to overcome. God can move mountains when they get in our way. My dad always tells Sabria to play for the One who made her tall. I find this interesting because in grade school and high school, she was considered tall, but in college she is actually short for a basketball player in her position. If she would have put all her hope in her height and not focused on using that attribute as a tool to polish other skills to get better, she wouldn't have been good enough to play in college. All the abuse she was willing to take mentally and physically in middle school and high school allowed her to play well at the college level at six feet one without a problem. She grew a good hard work ethic and never stopped reaching for the stars. She forged through the bullying she received by some refs who must have believed her talent was a curse and that because she was so big and skillful this meant she was forced to endure torture and illegal blows from her opponents because it was fun for them to watch; and they called the game fair because they believed the other girls were at a so-called disadvantage as her opposition. They would not see that the girls were at a disadvantage, because they refused to change and mold themselves into better basketball players. Instead, it was seen as Sabria was born with more advantage, so she was allowed to be hung on while shooting and allowed to be scratched and bruised up because of her gifts. They must have enjoyed highlighting the unskilled laziness and disrespect of some of the other girls as they attacked Sabria to get a win. If she showed any kind of disagreement with the torture she was receiving on the court, the refs would tell her she was big and needed to learn to take it because if she did try anything, they would call a foul on her. I have pictures of her, even ones that made the newspaper, where girls were literally hanging on her arms and the refs never called a foul.

Sabria learned she would never be enough for everyone else. Some of her teammates, coaches, and refs turned their backs on her. God never did. She learned to have a true love and deep respect for the special teammates, coaches, and friends who did support her and showed her the meaning of a true friend. We told her after each game to thank God she was tall and to fight to be the best, that even though some would be jealous and wish harm on her, God would lift her up in time. Most teams admitted their whole defensive plan against Fitch was to stop Sabria, which she actually appreciated and thought of as confirmation that she was doing her job. She welcomed the challenge and knew they were always after her. It was a compliment. Many games, she was double- or triple-teamed, and if she did get open and get the ball, all focus was on her because she would be the one to deliver somehow. The funny thing was, she never focused just on one area on the court. She loved to be predictably unpredictable. She knew she had to be crafty and creative. She needed to make plays they didn't see coming and think outside the box. This takes skill and intelligence, and she had both. After a specific game in Boardman, the opposing coach who had known Sabria for years and struggled at his attempts to lead his team to defeat her on the court but to no avail had come up to her after the game. He smiled and told her that she kicked their butts yet again and jokingly said that he hoped to never meet her again on the court. He and Sabria laughed, and Sabria walked away that night with many bloody scratches and an achy body, but the feeling of sweet victory she had over that team once again weighed more on her than those simple battle wounds.

She loved that they couldn't beat her team; she would not allow it, and they knew it. Even though their plan every time was to take her down and to extinguish her fire and power on the court, their efforts were never enough. She needed to stay on her God-inspired path, and all would be good. She remained a witness to the coaches, teammates, and opposition that she was a true athlete, loving and bold. She needed to learn to always stay on path so that those who loved her would grow, those who didn't would wonder why they couldn't make her hate them, and those who made it harder for her would see that she rose above the challenge and watched while God still made a way for her to conquer adversity. This was why she eventually chose West Point. It was a tool God gave her to become better. It is not a perfect school. It does not have a perfect screening process. It does not make perfect people. It is, in fact, a place that God can have an opportunity to mold and make her better if she chose to follow him through the process. This was no different from what she experienced growing up in relation to adversity.

In her senior year, she had broken her nose when colliding with a girl from her team at practice. While at the ER, one of her coaches from Fitch met us to give support as he was worried about her after the accident. We tried to encourage her and told her it didn't look that bad. She was embarrassed that her nose appeared crooked, and after the CAT scan confirmed the break, Sabria met with the doctor. He was an ignorant man who told Sabria she should have chosen a different sport like golf. He continued with sarcasm saying that colleges were just throwing those golf scholarships at people and then at least she wouldn't have messed her face up. Sabria was like most teenage girls who felt self-conscious about her face, always finding something about it that wasn't perfect. So hearing the doctor say this to her really hit a soft spot, and I was in shock at his lack of regard for her feelings and poor bedside manner. The doctor tried to turn the knife by telling Sabria her season of basketball, which hadn't even started yet, was over. She would not hear of it. She believed a different story, the one God told her, which was the truth that she could and should play. Bobby ordered her a face mask that very night (after the doctor told us it would be impossible to find one and that only professional basketball players can find those) and although she didn't want to wear it because it was hideous and she didn't like to stand out, she did because it got her on the court. I told her it was just a mask and if it stood between her and basketball and she wanted to play, then she needed to just do the right thing and wear it. People had no mercy on Sabria. Some girls would purposely pull on or move the mask to get to her vulnerable spot. Her face was a target, and she even had to sit out a couple of times in games when she got a bloody nose from girls purposely hitting her in the nose to get her out of the game so they could attempt to pull ahead on the scoreboard while she was on the sideline trying to get the bleeding to stop. The refs never paid attention to this cheating. We're sure her nose broke again at least once more in one of those games as some girls had no honor. I remember her face being swollen, and her nose bruised after most of those games from the tight fitting of the mask on her face and the beating she always took. Still she loved the game. Her plan was to stay the course and hold firm to her anchor and knew in time she would be delivered from the storm and she would be refined after God traveled with her through the fire. I told her she was the most beautiful basketball player I'd ever seen, even in the mask.

Her coaches were so good to her in those last years she played in high school. She really had a solid crew, each having a different personality and each serving a different purpose. Her head coach was inspiring and taught Sabria to have confidence in herself and hold firm to her faith. One assistant was the biggest fan of the girls and always got them fired up as he encouraged and cheered them on. The next assistant was a father figure and, in the fourth quarter of one of the games, told Sabria while she was in foul trouble that she had given enough brut and now they needed her finesse as he believed in her workmanship and ability to transition into what her team needed. The last assistant was funny, even hilarious. Sabria said to me one time that he was the funniest person she'd ever met in her life and he was able to keep the game light with humor and intense with sarcasm. It was the dream team of coaches, and Sabria was blessed by such a great team who she loves to this day. Sometimes Sabria's best was not enough to win games, and after the game, I would tell her that she did great. She would say, "But we lost." I would then ask, "Did you do your job today, Sabria?" That is what matters. Given the game, Sabria's stats would be very different. Sometimes she had less points but lots of steals and rebounds. Other times, it was lots of points but a low number of steals and rebounds. Sabria was trained to be what her team needed at the time. It wasn't about her but about the team, always, even if the girls refused to see it or believe it at the time. If your team needs points, you should score. If your team needs defense, then focus more on steals, rebounds, and blocks.

As I raised Sabria and we hit challenges, I was inspired to teach my kids what I learned as I was brought back to my childhood years in basketball when I watched the Chicago Bulls. Dennis Rodman had gotten twenty-eight rebounds in a game in 1993 when he played for the Spurs. He had zero points that game. This is incredible to me. His team needed his defense, intense energy, and willingness to become a machine; and that was what he brought to the table for the victory. Although his character off the court was questionable, I am only talking now about his extreme work on the court to use this as an example. The Bulls accepted his talent on their team, and he helped them on the journey to become the best team in history. They respected that he could become whatever their team needed at the time to win. This concept was used when I talked to Sabria after games when I could see she played with her whole heart, and her stats would change as she saw what was needed of her depending on the circumstance. I understood how she could break the all-time rebounding record at Fitch, but breaking the all-time scoring record for boys and girls was pretty crazy since she was a forward, and many times, I watched as her teammates kept the ball from Sabria on purpose when she posted up because they were too jealous of her success and wanted more for themselves—a common problem in basketball that coaches need to work to extinguish. It is a problem of character that needs worked on at home first before even stepping on the court. This was evidence that Sabria just did what was needed and didn't worry about records, but the records came, anyway. I told her keep going and don't worry about not getting the ball—go get the ball yourself or do something else that will help the team. Her posting-up skills got really good, and her legs were strong. I told her posting up had its benefits, even if she wasn't getting the ball all the time, because she was learning diligence and working on a skill that she needed to polish in order to get to the next level and no one could ultimately hold her back from getting there. I told her she should always do her job and at the right time, no matter what others are doing or not doing. I had hope that as her teammates were learning from her, she was also learning with them—always staying humble to know that she needed to work on some things, too, and none of them on the team were perfect. I do believe this was a reason that this team was able to win their district championship, which was something that hadn't been done for twenty-five years. I have no doubt that she could have broken the blocking record too. Even though she was known as a defensive beast, she did hold back because the refs liked to call unnecessary fouls on her, and she needed to protect her team from foul trouble, so she backed off, which was an appropriate decision. It was amazing to see. I always enjoyed watching her play as she watched to find her place and purpose on the court.

The goal for Sabria was always to win, of course, but losing had its benefits too. Losing a game makes you look harder at yourself to examine what needs to change. Sometimes she played an entire game, and the only thing that stood out to me was that three seconds when she helped a teammate off the ground or the time that her teammate missed the winning shot and she gave her a pat on the back and words of encouragement after the devastation. There was a particular player whom Sabria knew was good and was a challenge for Sabria's team to compete against. Sabria did not like feeling like there was any competition on the court, but I always told her to appreciate it because this was how she could get a true view of where she was at and what she needed to do to get better. I would warn her before certain games, and a particular game against Howland in 2017 was one of those games. I said, "Remember, the Howland game is coming up, and you know Sara is coming for you. I know she'll be ready to play. Will you?" This, of course, ticked Sabria off, but this was where she needed to stay to get better. Sara had a target on her back too. I would come home from work and say to Sabria, "Did you shoot today? Do you think Sara is taking a day off?" Sabria would pretend not to be listening or tell me to be quiet, but I know it made her work harder. After that game against Howland in 2017, I was impressed at what I saw. Sabria and Sara shook each other's hands and patted each other on the back after a tough battle. They both came ready to play. Fitch beat Howland that day, and in the newspaper, Sara and Sabria both gave the other respect and props for their performance. This is how it should be. I always pushed Sabria to give credit to her team and to respectable and talented opposition because basketball is a team sport and all these girls including Sabria are learning about life and how to treat their neighbor. You should always respect another athlete who challenges you and learn from them, in hopes that you can also teach them something, too, to make them better. How Sabria responded to her team and other great athletes would help mold them into who they would become, and you want good results from your actions. Sara Price told the Vindicator that her team had made stupid mistakes and they let Sabria eat them alive inside. She said they practiced those plays and knew those lobs would be coming. They just couldn't execute that day. She said that Sabria was a good athlete and knew how to execute, she knew how to drive the ball down, she knew how to make super plays, and she knew how to take the game over; and that's what she did that day. Sabria admitted that she brought her A game that day and said that she thought that when she and Sara played against each other that it motivated both of them and brought the best out of them. She said that it was great to play against a player like that because they could both take what they learned and it would make them both better athletes. Sara had finished with twenty-eight points and six rebounds, and Sabria finished with twenty-five points and thirteen rebounds. Sabria was a sophomore that year and had a lot to still learn but was coming along. This was a very difficult time in her life, and to have an athlete to look up to was crucial to her own development in athletics. I appreciated Sara, who was a senior that year; and to this day, Sabria and I respect her for leading Sabria, a younger athlete, by her good work ethic and positive attitude on the court and displaying good character. These were the times I was so very proud of what I saw from Sabria on the court and after the games. Sabria was called a "GOAT" (greatest of all time), a real "load," a "beast," "West Point," and many other names during her career; and this did help to push her as she enjoyed giving people something good to talk about. Sabria met the ugly face of discrimination at a very young age. She understands the concept of forging through the fire of those who want to see you fail while you hold firm to your anchor, which is Christ. These were the stories and memories that got me excited to see Sabria and make her homecoming special. She was my hero, and I wanted to celebrate.

CHAPTER 11

BE A ROCK

This leads me to write about my son Quintin's injury that happened at the very end of September as we were two weeks away from Sabria's visit home for the weekend. It was game day, and as we were getting ready for my nine-year-old son's football game, I was urged by my conscience to call a "family meeting." We only had a few minutes as we were rushing around doing chores and getting ready to head out the door, which was always a task in our house. I wanted to share something with the kids that was on my heart. I had told Quintin and Christy to go outside and get a couple of the rocks we had gotten delivered and bring them into the house. The five kids and I sat down at the table. I held up the rocks and asked them if they knew where they came from. They replied, "The river." I said yes and told them they were called river rocks because they were gathered from the river. I told them to think about what they knew about rivers. So they shared how there is water and a current in a river. I told them to look at the beautiful rocks; and I began to explain that every rock is different in shape, color, and texture. As the current pulls the water over the rocks, exposing them to friction and temperature changes, this actually molds and shapes the rocks, allowing them to take on their own identity. As we experience life on earth, we will be exposed to the different elements that God will use to mold and change us too. As the currents of life flow over us, we will change and take on our own identity. We need to have faith that as God directs us on our journey in life and allows things to happen, he has our best interest at heart. He is always working on his masterpiece in us. We need to embrace the changes God is allowing to take place in us as we become a most beautiful stone useful to shape and sharpen others and to be a firm foundation for growth, insight, wisdom, and understanding. This is how we can love others and teach others about love, ultimately changing the world. All of us will be of different shapes and textures since we all go through different experiences in life. Sometimes life seems too hard, and the elements we are exposed to seem to overwhelm us, and we may not understand how anything good could come from the trial or tragedy. If we stay faithful in trusting God and stay fixed and strong, we will become a beautiful sight to God and others, just as the rocks in our backyard are a beautiful sight to us.

In the world around us, the ideas of mindfulness and self-determination are viewed as the ticket to healing our country. The media and TV push this way of thinking. They tend to leave out the very important point that if your mind and your heart are not fueled by your love for God and your actions are not purposefully reflecting God's plan for our family's lives and our country's future, then we are a hamster running in a wheel and getting nowhere fast. Our actions are worthless and will yield nothing good. We should strive to be everything God intended us to be, and we should encourage this in the lives of those around us. I wanted to share this with the kids in a way they could understand. I do see the importance in taking a stand to raise my kids to believe in something bigger than themselves and not sharing the belief that the answers to life are found only within our human mind and strength. A human who believes this way is weak and will reach the ceiling to his potential at some point and before the problems they face are ever fixed and before the battles in life are ever won. We need leaders in our country who make moves in God's strength since his strength moves mountains, parts seas, and turns water into wine. We ended our family meeting and headed to the game. Quintin had hoped to score a touchdown, and this was my nine-year-old buddy's only goal that day. He loved every bit of football, but that day, all he wanted was to score a touchdown, and he talked intently about it as the end of the season was approaching, as this was something he hadn't done yet that season. He had gotten it in his mind and knew it would be a challenge, so he wanted to get it done. As we sat in the stands during the first quarter, my husband, Bobby, saw the play setting up. He leaned over and said that Quintin would be getting the ball. I got my phone ready and pushed record. As the hand-off was good, Quintin made a swift move and headed downfield, hugging the sideline; and I could see he was giving everything he had to that run. It was the most beautiful run of his young career. I was so proud and said, "Go, son, go!" No one could catch him. I found out later that as we were blissfully watching this run, Quintin had a "bad feeling" come over him. He said he knew something bad was about to happen, and as he saw the end zone approaching, he was no longer happy but instead felt this feeling of doom that he didn't understand, and he was no longer excited to score. Suddenly, a boy came up behind him and missed the tackle but not before leaping toward my son and grabbing at Quintin's foot from behind, pulling, and letting it go like a "slingshot." Quintin could not recover from this, and as his other leg tried to compensate, his whole body was off-balance. At the speed he was traveling, his legs just crumbled, sending him hard to the ground. I was immediately devastated, and even writing this now, I am sick to my stomach. I saw after he landed that his leg shook in an unnatural and uncontrollable fashion that I could see from the stands. It was trembling, which told me that his body went into a type of shock from whatever trauma his knee had just succumbed to. He was banging the ground and screaming in intense pain. My stomach was in knots, and my heart swelled. I knew my son, and I knew this was bad as he could not take himself off the field but was carried by the coaches. As my big strong son they call a beast was carried to the bench, I was broken. My husband did not understand the seriousness of this tragedy and told me to wait and not go to him right then. I'm sure he thought our son would brush this off, but I thought something different. I waited intently on the very edge of the bench until I immediately jumped up as our friend and wife of one of the coaches, Kathy, came and boldly said, "Tina, they need you at the bench." I just zigzagged through the crowds and couldn't get there fast enough, to my son's side. As I didn't want to approach my son looking upset, I held together my signature, everlasting optimism, and just asked my son what happened. Although I saw what happened and even had watched the video on my phone, I could not believe that my son could be hurt. His knee was blown up like a balloon, and the concern in the coach's eyes told me this was not an average injury. Quintin was so tough, but this was something unbearable. I told him it would be okay and that I would help him in any way I could. We gave him some pain medicine right away and iced the knee. He tried to sit on the bench for the rest of the game and support his team, but he very quickly realized this was impossible. He only lasted a few minutes before he realized that his heart was broken, and he was in so much pain that he turned and looked at me, but I could see in his desperate eyes that he was in another world. Tears streamed down his pink, sweaty cheeks as he asked me, "Mom, why did this happen to me?" He said, "Mom, I'm really injured this time. I've never been hurt like this before." His chin quivered, and as I sat next to him and held his helmet on my lap, I was just so upset and wasn't sure where this experience would take us next. After the pain got worse, we decided we had no choice but to leave the game and take him home. They had to carry him from the sideline to the car.

His siblings gathered around him at home, and we all tried to console our buddy. Over the next few days, his leg didn't show much improvement from the ice and elevation, and Quintin had looked outside and said, "I just want to jump again, Mom." Quintin was my most athletic kid. He never stopped moving. Even when he played video games, he stood in front of the TV and jumped nonstop. Everyone got a kick out of Quintin's energy. His leg now began to give out on him without warning. This injury happened about twelve days before Sabria came home for her weekend visit, so by the time she was home, he was able to walk, and the pain was better, but he was still losing balance and would fall down without warning. We figured after she left, we would go through the motions of having this thing diagnosed. He did have an X-ray, which was negative for a fracture, and the hospital was able to issue him some crutches until we could further investigate the problem with an MRI. This helped him get around at school better and prevented the falls. He was forced to use the elevator because the stairs were not deemed safe by the doctor. This was embarrassing to him because he was a shy kid and didn't want to stand out and his weakness made known to everyone, which was then rubbed in and highlighted by the school; and the embarrassment was made worse when the school questioned his use of the elevator and demanded to see proof of the need, which he did have a prescription. They used the excuse for their gruffness by saying that some kids try to fake injuries and use the elevator for fun. I call this stereotyping, and there is no excuse for shaming a kid for doing what he's told. This was one more time I questioned why people who don't work well with kids are put in positions at a school for children.

We decided to go to the last football game of the season to support Quintin's team. He was reluctant to go sit by his team on the bench because he didn't want to look like the "injured guy." I told him, hard or not, it was his duty to support his team and this showed good character because it takes integrity, humility, and honor to go to a football game as the injured guy and cheer on your team from the bench. On our way to the fence leading to the team's bench, his coach met him and told Quintin he would escort him the rest of the way. I was so thankful because I, as a parent, was not allowed beyond that point and I knew Quintin wouldn't have had the strength to walk that route himself. The coach told Quintin that he shouldn't be embarrassed but to think of his injury as a battle wound. Quintin smiled and hobbled off with his coach toward his team. When he reached the team, his teammates high-fived him and patted his back, welcoming him to his spot on the sidelines. Quintin was a very emotional boy who had a lot of passion for life. He was always careful in how he tackled in football because doing the wrong thing could "really hurt somebody." We always talked about playing safe in football and all sports to make sure we were protecting our team-mates and opponents, as well as striving to be the best all while high-lighting the strengths and talents of others. This was how you learn to play with passion. At night before bed, Quintin always poured his heart out to me. He would sing me love songs from a young age and called me "his beautiful angel." So as we lay down before bed a few weeks after the injury, he asked me, "Mom, why'd this have to hap-pen to me? I'm really hurt this time. Am I going to get better? Do you think I'll ever play football again, Mom? I love football, Mom. What if I never get to play football again? Will my knee ever be the same?" The questions just poured out of him. He was in the land of the unknown, and for a nine-year-old, this was an intense place. He believed all things were possible; and so he believed that thing which he couldn't imagine being true but was, in fact, possible—that he may never play football again.

The Bible says all things are permissible but not all things are beneficial. Quintin's conscience was very pure and honest. He just knew all things were possible, but if God found it beneficial to his future to play football again, we did not know. My heart was torn for my son. It just ached at the thought of the reality that this was not a simple injury, as I had first hoped, but an injury that in my heart knew would impact the next year of his life and potentially the entire rest of his life. I thought, *How does a nine-year-old handle such a big situation such as this?* I just focused on Quintin and made it as simple as possible as I responded to his questions. I said, "Do you remember the story I told you about the river rocks at our family meeting right before your game?" He said, "Yea." I told him that God told me to have that meeting that day, and I knew in my heart that the lesson was important for him to hear. I don't always know why God leads me to say and do things, but I try to be faithful and obedient because I know God always has a plan. God wanted Quintin to know that day how much he loved him and that he was molding him. He was using me as a vessel to prepare Quintin's heart to be able to handle what was about to happen to his body that beautiful sunny day on the football field. I told him that he was going to learn new things through this experience and he was going to change. I told him that at that time I knew he didn't want the change but, over time, he would grow thankful for the experience as it would help to form him into the most refined and beautiful rock, useful for good works for God. I told him this experience and journey with God would make him stronger and he would be given a new shape and texture and with more meaning and purpose in life. I told him that we would go on this journey together and that God would never leave our side.

CHAPTER 12

PREPARING FOR OUR HERO

W e wanted to prepare our house for the homecoming of our hero just as God is preparing a place for us in heaven. It had taken the kids and me all summer to spread over ten tons of boulders, gravel, bricks, and stones to make a beautiful sitting area for us to sit with Sabria and relax for the weekend she was home. We wanted an area she could unload her mind and enjoy the family God gave her. My dad helped me to always be inspired by following my heart, and he helped us create this beautiful landscape for Sabria. The kids put together some comfy chairs and a firepit my dad helped me get and that we knew she would love. We labored in love to do some painting and little home repairs as we waited for her to come back. Three days before she was due to come home and about a week and a half after Quintin's injury, my son Dylan had acute appendicitis and needed emergency surgery. This was an incredible experience with Dylan and one I never saw coming. When things happen in life, it is important to ask why. Why did this happen? Sometimes in life, it seems too simple and cheap of a question to ask, but it is brave to ask the question. People often fear asking God or others for help in discovering why things happen in life because getting an answer will not change the outcome or put a blanket over the devastation. What it does is it gives a person the permission to move on from a situation and to realize they still have responsibilities in life and no excuse to stay beat down. This is when knowledge and deep insight are found, which are the purest ways of learning, as they come from God. I have found that learning from experiments is informative and information that you read in books or gain from college or through research is beneficial, but it does not compare to the learning that comes from life experiences.

I woke up one morning into the glim reality of a new day but an old routine. It was 5:45 a.m. and time to get ready for my shift that started at 7:00 a.m. I peeled my tired body out of bed and put my uniform on. Bobby had already left for work. I went into my son Dylan's room to peak at him. He had been in bed the whole day before with a stomachache and slight fever. This morning, there was no change other than his pain was worse. I made the decision to keep him home from school again and headed to work. I got to work and began the shift with a tugging in my heart. I was always busy at work as a nurse, so I really had to focus to keep good time as this was crucial to have a productive day for my patients. I had trouble focusing and getting through report because all I could think about was my son Dylan. *It's just the flu*, I thought. Or was it? After report, something triggered me to pull away for a minute to carefully go over the last twenty-nine hours in my mind. It had all started at 3:00 a.m., when Dylan had come in my room and woke me from a dead sleep and said, "Mom, I don't feel good, and my stomach is killing me. I can't stop shaking." I jumped out of bed and guided him back to his room. He never complained, so this was concerning to me, but his temp was 99.6, so I figured this was some kind of stomach bug or maybe the flu and, once his fever climbed and broke, he would feel better. His fever never climbed, and he never had vomiting or diarrhea. In fact, he asked me if I would give him a laxative to go to the bathroom because he felt like he had to go but it hurt to push. He felt like he was constipated but told me he had gone to the bathroom a day ago, so this didn't make sense to me. Dylan had never asked me for a laxative before this episode, and so I did think the request was out of character. His stomach hurt too bad to shower or brush his teeth, and he was basically too sick to get out of bed. He said he was hungry, but when I brought him food, he couldn't get himself to eat. I thought, *This doesn't seem like a virus I've ever seen before.* I wondered if this could be appendicitis. I looked up the symptoms and called my dad, of course. My dad was very tactical and thought well under pressure. He agreed that Dylan needed to get checked out at the hospital because this did not sound good. I was going to get through the shift and then take him in, but as the morning went on and I continued to call home, I realized my son was deteriorating, and I was working a twelve-hour shift that day. There was no way he could wait till I got off work. He said he had made it to the bathroom but had no relief after. One of the signs of appendicitis is that a person with symptoms could not jump up and down if asked because the pain would be too severe. I asked Dylan over the phone if he could jump up and down, and he tried it. He could not get off his toes, because the pain was so bad. *Bingo*, I thought. I said, "Hang tight. I'm coming home to take you to the hospital." I told my boss I had to leave, and she understood. I hurried home and struggled to get my son from his room to the car. Now that I was convinced this was appendicitis, I was playing beat the clock to get him safely to the hospital before the appendix ruptured, which would make this situation a whole lot worse for my son.

Along the way in the car, I noticed Dylan would cringe at every bump in the road. We made it to the hospital, and they worked him up as usual—IV fluids, pain meds, and an ultrasound.

After being there for a couple of hours, they decided they were confident that he needed surgery and wanted it to be done at Akron Children's Hospital in Akron because it was urgent, and being that my son was fourteen, they wanted it done by a pediatric surgeon. I was fine with that. They began making plans for transport and were deciding if he could handle ground transfer through an ambulance or if airlift by helicopter was a better choice. I went out to my car to collect my thoughts and make plans for my car and kids at home as I would be going to the hospital with Dylan, and this was about forty-five minutes from our house. They decided to go by way of ambulance, and since Dylan wanted me to stay by his side and not leave him, they would allow me to ride in the back with him, which was a blessing.

I called my sister to tell her of what was going on, and she was in shock. "How did you know it was appendicitis!" she said. "You have been so busy with Sabria and arranging her flight home and travel details and all that goes into her being at West Point along with working and raising six kids and fixing the house up! You have so many distractions, and even after Quintin's injury, I just can't believe you were able to pick up on this! You never take your kids to the ER, and the one time you do, it's for a thing that every parent is afraid of missing when their kid has stomach pain! How did you know to take him in?" I told her it was a feeling in my heart that I couldn't ignore. I just knew that God was telling me that something was wrong with my son. This was an experience where I learned that with all my distractions in life, God is the one who keeps me focused. I always pray that he will direct me as I raise my kids and that he won't allow my shortcomings to interfere with their health, safety, or success. God will never let me fail as long as I trust in him and have faith to act when he tells me. This was a moment that I saw grace in my life and thanked God for the opportunity he gave me to help my son. My sister is always a big defender of mine. She always knows what to say to give me a jolt of confidence. She reminds me of Micky from the *Rocky* movies. She's always in my corner telling me that I'm a machine and I can't be broken. She tells me to always keep fighting and that I'm doing a great job. She has the gift of encouragement.

Dylan and I made it to the hospital, and the doctor ordered antibiotics to be given overnight to calm the infection and for the surgery scheduled for the morning. My alarm went off at 6:00 a.m., and I rolled off the couch in the same scrubs I had on from the day before. The nurse was by his side and promptly getting him ready for surgery. I followed them to the presurgery area and sat with my son not knowing what the outcome of this would be, but I hoped he would pull through and this would be over soon. They took him away, and I went out to wait. I then realized I was snatched out of work, ending up at this hospital in a big city with nothing but the clothes on my back, which were my hospital scrubs that I'd now had on for thirty hours straight. I had no family around, no car. Once again, just me and God on a journey together. For everyone else, the world was going on, but for me, time stood still. Even though I had six kids, Dylan was on the forefront of my mind right then. I just dropped everything to be his aid and to help him as best I could. All my kids were special, and I didn't see them as numbers. They were all different, all special. I was on pins and needles while he was in surgery, praying that God would protect him. Finally, the doctor came and gave me an update. Everything went well, and they were able to get his appendix out before it ruptured. I was so relieved and thankful that this had worked out the way it did. I was taken aback to see him, and I was honored to be the one Dylan saw when he woke up from anesthesia. He said, "Hi, Mom!" I was so relieved to see him, smiling. All he wanted now was for his dad to come see him and to bring Chick-fil-A with him. I believe, in his postanesthesia stupor, he asked for six Chick-fil-A sandwiches. He would have to stay at the hospital for a couple of days, and his dad did come that day and honored his request for

Chick-fil-A. He didn't bring six sandwiches, as he knew this was not actually what Dylan would want, but he did bring a feast for him. It had been several days now since he ate well, and he was starving. His dad and I dropped everything to be there for Dylan, and this whole situation gave my son perspective on life. When his food trays would come, he would not eat unless his dad and I had something to eat too. He kept offering us the food on his tray and refused to eat if we didn't also have food. He is a sweet and valuable young man, very loving. I was finally able to get a break from the hospital and change my scrubs after being in them for thirty-six hours straight. Bobby stayed the night with Dylan, and I went home to take care of the other kids and clean the house and get the yard ready as Sabria was flying home the next day. I was back at the hospital early the next morning to relieve Bobby to go to work and to help Dylan shower and walk in the halls in hopes that he would be allowed to be discharged.

There were two other kids who had been injured on his football team earlier in the season, and Dylan and the rest of the team had visited them at their homes to encourage them. I had let the coach know of Dylan's situation, and Dylan expected a visit from his football friends, but no one ever came. He didn't talk much about it, but I know it bothered him. He would not be able to finish out the end of the football season, and as I would find out later, he was losing interest in playing football at Fitch, anyway. Dylan was learning the value of family and love, teamwork, and support. This was being learned at home. This is where the learning should take place before any athlete tries to walk onto a court or field. Many athletes and coaches, for that matter, never learn of these attributes, and I have watched and witnessed this firsthand. Finally, after spending two nights in that hospital, I was given permission to take my sweet boy home to recover. We celebrated after the doctor left the room, telling us we could go home. I took Dylan home, and he rested. I quickly transitioned into get-Sabria-home mode. I made a double batch of lasagna and the kids, and I hopped in the car and headed in the opposite direction from where I drove to get Dylan in Akron, Ohio, that morning. Now I was driving to Pittsburgh to meet my girl at the airport. Dylan couldn't make the trip, because riding in the car was painful, so he stayed behind to rest. I figured I could give him the job of turning the oven off when the timer rang for the lasagna we made that was still baking in the oven. When I had called home to remind Dylan to shut the oven off, he didn't answer. I was in a panic after calling several times with no response. My brother Dominic ended up going to my house (he lived very close to us) to find Dylan in a nice deep sleep. He was on strong pain medicine and welcomed the sleep during his recovery, even as the lasagna was in the oven! Thankfully, the house didn't burn down, and Dylan was, in fact, okay. I felt like I was managing a three-ring circus every single day at every moment, and it was intense as I was constantly shifting and going into all sorts of directions and yet remained focused, always ready to troubleshoot or pull up a plan B.

We continued on to the airport. Sabria had learned of both of her brothers' incidences and had felt bad that she couldn't be with them during their struggle. As their big sister, she felt responsible to tend to their needs of support. This made her homecoming that much richer because these events had just happened and she could be there for the boys. It helped her to know that our whole family was striving to overcome our own adversities and this knowledge she could use to persevere through her own battles. Our family was growing as we were always meeting up together again as a unit forging under fire. When we arrived at the airport to get Sabria, we waited, hoping she would find her way out of the airport and to our car. She was worried about flying alone; but I told her if she could be dropped off in the middle of the woods with a map and a compass and could find her way out to the destination, surely, she could find her way through an airport. We watched intently on that warm fall evening, trying to get our first glimpse of her. The air was crisp, and the lights were bright as the excitement built. The kids hadn't seen Sabria since we dropped her off on July 1, so it had been over three months since the siblings had seen each other. They made a welcome-home sign and were waiting in anticipation. It was Sophia and Christy's birthday, October 11, that day (they were born on the same day, six years apart) and felt special, and it was like a special birthday gift that their sister could make it home. I watched as the kids yelled, "There she is!" They looked back and said, "Could we go get her?" I yelled, "Go get her!" They ran up to her as soon as our soldier girl came in to view. The shining of her black buffed shoes glistened under the airport lights, and when they saw that polyester uniform and black-rimmed hat in the distance as she walked with perfect posture toward us, they screamed and ran toward her. Her siblings gathered around her and squeezed their best friend as happy tears streamed down their cheeks. I was shocked at all the emotion that came with the reunion. When it was my turn, I grabbed her and couldn't let go—crying as we embraced in the airport parking lot, not caring who was around to see our emotion. As my body sobbed uncontrollably, I thanked God in my heart for the experience and relief of seeing my girl finally home and safe in my arms. All of what my family had been through in just a few short months all came together in that moment. I was so proud, and she looked as beautiful as ever. Her bunned-up hair, perfect posture, and clean-cut uniform made me see her in a different light. She grew up and had a sense of independence about her. She had made the trip by herself, flying for the first time alone.

We took her home and surprised her by unveiling our backyard masterpiece. Our family—including her aunts, uncles, cousins, Papa, and even my mom—were waiting at home for her and had the firepit lit and an open spot to sit and relax for our girl. We all ate what she longed for a home-cooked meal of lasagna and sat outside for hours, just talking. She couldn't believe all the work we had done, and she said it all looked so good. We told her we labored in love and she was our inspiration. Dylan enjoyed the company and sympathy from his big sister, and I'm sure this was good medicine for his soul. As we sat outside, relaxing together, she just talked forever of all she had experienced. I just looked at her in awe of how we had reached this point in her journey and how we were all together to share in the fellowship of each other. She was doing what we all believed she could do, and she was telling us about it. She felt the love we had for her; and she realized while she was away from home and working so hard that her family was at home working so hard for her, preparing, and eagerly waiting for the time she would come home again. We were keeping our family bond strong. This was how we would remain close and connected through love. All of my kids are important to me, and I really connect with the Bible story about the shepherd and his sheep. It talks about how the shepherd will leave all ninety-nine of his sheep to go out to find the one lost sheep that got away in order to bring him back. This is how I felt about Sabria leaving, Dylan's surgery, and Quintin's injury. Although I was proud of Sabria for leaving and understood the process, we all were still a unit, and she was always on our minds and in our hearts, and it only felt right to have all my sheep together. Having her home even for just two days was a reason to celebrate, and that's exactly what we did. Taking her back to the airport was tough after our good time together. I looked over at her to see her wipe away tears. She was emotional for the entire hour-long trip to the airport. I knew God had blessed me with this time with my daughter, and I prayed that we would be strong until we met together again. The time spent with her was like a tall glass of water—very refreshing at a time when our souls needed it. Now it was time to work again, and I knew that it was time to get back to it. God had proved to be faithful, and I knew he would stay that way. This is how we were willing to move onward and continue the grind.

CHAPTER 13

REVEALING OF TRUTH

We had our appointment with the sports medicine doctor the day Sabria had flown back to New York, and she was actually FaceTime-ing us from the airport after landing. This would have put us right at about October 14. She was sad to go back and was already getting homesick. She waited for other planes to land so she could travel back to West Point with her friends from the airport who were also returning after time with their families. She was missing us already, but being in this appointment with Quintin and seeing the reality of his challenges that were coming really put things in perspective for her. As the doctor started to examine Quintin, he said that he was 75 percent sure that this was an ACL tear and he would set him up for an MRI. I was in shock and could not believe what my ears were hearing. Even though I had suspected this was the case, I had hope still that it wasn't true. I asked how this injury could be possible since Quintin was only nine. The doctor said this type of injury was, indeed, uncommon for such a young boy, and given his age and the special precaution that must be taken to protect the growth plate in the knee, there were only two surgeons in the entire area who could be trusted to do this surgery. I knew in my heart that God would be Quintin's surgeon and that he would work through the one given the task of performing the surgery. The honest concern shown from this sport's medicine doctor was overwhelming but encouraging as I did understand the seriousness of the situation. Sabria had many friends who had experienced this particular injury, and it was devastating to any athlete at any level. For a nine-year-old, it was just completely unbelievable to me, and I was sure this would be a life-changing experience for my whole family. Sabria was familiar with the impact the injury made on the person who sustained it and knew the pressure that would be felt for the entire family in general. We chose to remain optimistic as we found hope in our favorite verse, Jeremiah 29:11. We named it our family verse as Sophia always brought it up in our family meetings, and it encourages us to see the silver lining in any situation. It states, "For I know the plans I have for you declares the Lord, plans to prosper you and not to harm you. Plans to give you hope and a future." When Sabria got to West Point, she applied a sticker of this verse to her laptop to remind her of the hope we have in every aspect of life. This verse gave me much comfort a few weeks later on the day I got the results of Quintin's MRI. They had told us we would need to wait for twenty-four to forty-eight hours to get results after the test was done, so Quintin and I decided to run around and do some errands after leaving the hospital before going home. While we were in one of the stores right after leaving the hospital, my phone rang. It was the doctor. He said he looked at the MRI after we had left and told me that, unfortunately, it was the worst-case scenario. Quintin had a complete tear of his ACL and possible tear in his meniscus. Not expecting the results after only an hour, I was in shock once again. This was the reality. God already knew what Quintin's injury was, and I was only now finding out. I closed my eyes and just couldn't breathe or speak or move. I was unsure what to say, and really my ears didn't want to hear anymore, so I felt them turning off as the doctor continued to talk. I finally gained a hold of my thoughts and asked what the next step would be. I was at a point where I could only take one step at a time. He said the next step was to call the pediatric surgeon he recommended and set up and appointment. As I collected my thoughts and shifted to this new reality, I took comfort in the fact that Quintin had a complete tear of this ligament, which was a good thing to me because it took some of the guesswork out. God knew I appreciated the clean-cut facts that this would only be repaired with surgery, so there was no question as what to choose to repair this. No amount of therapy was going to be enough to repair this and get him functional enough to play sports again, so surgery was the only option for Quintin. The doctor agreed. I told Quintin the news, and as soon as I got to my car, I called my dad. He could tell I was upset, and I told him what we had just found out. He said, "Wow." He then continued, "Well…you can cry about it if you want, but it's not gonna change anything. This was already written for Quintin. All you gotta do is go through it with him. Quintin is tough. This is nothing for him. God's gonna continue his plan for Quintin no matter what, and if he's meant to play sports again, then that's what's gonna happen. God's plan for Quintin is going to be carried out, and an ACL tear isn't going to stop that." He asked me, "Can you change this?" I replied, "No." He said, "Then do what you can do, and be there for Quintin." I felt like I was being put through a meat grinder. I felt like I was in a hurricane, drowning, and when I finally got one opportunity to catch a breath of air, it comes in the form of my dad, encouraging me to keep going and battling through.

I thought of all the details. Work was slow, and I kept getting canceled on my shifts, so we were living on our last dollars. We planned to go to see Sabria for Thanksgiving because she was devastated that she wouldn't be allowed to come home because of their basketball schedule. Would we have enough money, and now, then the question, could Quintin even travel? This was about three weeks before we were planning to leave. How would I take off work to care for my son during this very tough surgical recovery? So many questions I had, but I knew God had already worked out the details. I was reminded of something that Sabria taught me. On R Day, as we sat in the auditorium and Sabria was told she had sixty seconds to say goodbye to us, her parents, I wondered why she seemed so strong. She hugged us and walked away through the crowds of cadets and parents as everyone said their goodbyes, and she never looked back. That room was overwhelmed with the heated emotion of goodbye, but she didn't seem to be bothered by it and instead stayed focused. I found out later that she had told my dad that she would know when she walked through the doors at West Point, it was where she was meant to be, and she would know it for sure that moment she stepped foot through those doors because God would never let her leave her mom and walk through those doors if it wasn't meant to be. This allowed me to see that he allowed me and Quintin to be in this situation and he would see me through till the end. I knew it was meant to happen, and this gave me the courage and confidence to forge through the fire. I didn't have all the answers, but I didn't need them. I only needed faith to continue.

The end of October 2019 was rough as the days leading into my birthday were filled with mixed emotions. Sabria's birthday was the day before mine, and we always celebrated together. I always told the kids of how God knit them together in my womb and how they were fearfully and wonderfully made. The day of their birth was an unveiling of God's masterpiece that he made for his pleasure and in his own image. To not be with Sabria for our birthdays was excruciating. The weekend of our birthdays fell on family weekend at West Point, and we originally planned to go and visit, but our financial situation shifted our plans. We decided instead to visit her on Thanksgiving since she wouldn't get a leave to come home, and we didn't want her to be alone on the holiday. It did make sense, but her time alone in her dorm while the other kids were out spending time with their families that weekend was difficult. Thinking about her alone there without her family was too much for me. I tried everything to keep busy but was unsuccessful. I tried cleaning but finished too quickly. I tried working, but there were no shifts available. I began to feel sorry for myself. This is a mood I hate. I felt like I needed advice from my grandma, but she had recently passed away. My mom was battling liver failure still in the Cleveland Clinic, and my dad was there helping her at the time. I didn't want to burden them with my misery. The kids were at school, and Bobby was at work. I found myself alone with my thoughts and unable to escape my chains of despair. This was to be a day of celebrating, but I couldn't figure out what to do. I decided to get a Jillian Michaels DVD out of the box. I put it in the Xbox and pushed play. I had been so busy and off-kilter that I hadn't gotten a workout in for several weeks. I felt sloppy and undisciplined, and this was very out of character for me. I had let the anxieties of my life collapse on me, and I was feeling the weight of the crumbled debris that remained after the storm. I began doing the moves I saw on the screen through my cried-out swollen eyes, hoping I could blow off some steam. As I attempted to make a sloppy effort at a workout seem valuable, I caught a glimpse of the fall leaves on the trees outside the window. I told myself something I tell my kids to do: "Be like the trees." I watched as the wind was blowing. The branches and the leaves moved gracefully with the wind, but the base stayed firm. I reminded myself that as the winds of life blow through my life, I need to remember to move with grace but hold firm to my anchor and not let my base be moved but let it remain steadfast, solid, and strong. I remembered sending Sabria a letter during basic training telling her this and how I saw that she was steadfast and solid like a tree and, as the winds of life blew through her, she would feel the breeze but her base would remain firm and solid. I just broke down and started crying that day in my house doing that workout—all my emotions flooding out of my body. I was still exercising through this because I didn't want my emotions to control my body. I wanted my heart to be in control of my mind and my mind in control of my body. This is when there is unity of the body, soul, and spirit; and God is the head of this unit. I knew I was getting broken down to be built back up. I told myself to breathe, stand up straight, hold firm, and breathe. I cried through the whole workout because I realized my life was changing. My old life was gone, and I needed to breathe and let my heart heal and beat again. Battles in my life were coming from every angle, and I didn't have the people in my life whom I once had to help me through. I needed to be stronger than ever but felt like I couldn't ask anyone for help. Everyone had their own problems and agendas. My dad was always a strong tower in my life. Even when he couldn't be around to help me or give advice, I had what he taught me from the time I was a small child. The good news was that God never leaves me. These were the times in my life that I grew closer to God. He let me know that he would be my strength. He loved me, and this was only the beginning of my journey. I had meaning. I had purpose, and through all the struggles, I'd be okay I couldn't be there for Sabria like I wanted to be. I couldn't make enough money even though I worked all the time. Our bathroom had been under construction for over a year, because we only had enough money to do the remodeling ourselves. My son Quintin had this ACL injury, and my other son was recovering from acute appendicitis and emergency surgery. It wouldn't be long before the medical bills were pouring in while we were already penny-pinching to get by. Amazingly, I felt good during this workout. I was releasing all of the self-doubt and letting God give me the confidence boost I needed to continue. People watched how I lived, and some would call me an over-achiever because I always tried so hard. Some people called me a goddess, supermom, superwoman, or energizer bunny. People would say I just had a motor in me because I never seemed to stop. My kids would even ask me if I ever got tired. This day in this workout, I realized that all this meant was that God was continuously doing miracles in my life to get me to my next step. He was my energy. He was my strength, my fuel, and my confidence in continuing the work he put in my path. My life was hard, but I took pleasure in my work because it was a testimony of his love for me. My perseverance always came from the one who made me, so I never really found myself without support.

God is always there, so you don't need to feel alone. I always revert to Romans 1:20: "For since the creation of the world God's invisible qualities—His divine eternal power and divine nature—have been clearly seen, being understood from what has been made, so that people are without excuse." This is why I always look to nature to remind me of God and his presence in my life. No one and nothing can take this from me. No threat of violence, sickness, disease, distance, or turmoil can ever remove the hope I have in God and his presence in my life. This revealing of God through nature is there in all times of need. I teach the kids about this whenever I get the opportunity because these lessons are eternal and make impressions on the heart. I realized that day that I could celebrate my birthday and I should, even if it was just in my heart. Couple of things I was reminded of that day: do whatever you need to do to reconnect with God, and do it often. Exercise is good for your soul, as well as your body. Don't wait too long to get back to a healthy routine if you get offtrack. Let God reveal the answers to your questions and fill your voids.

CHAPTER 14

HELPING CHILDREN SEE HOPE IN THE FUTURE

M any of us don't understand why we were put in the situations we find ourselves in. I look at my husband, Bobby, and me. I know we don't deserve to be the parents of six amazing kids. We both grew up in two very different types of homes, which will take us back to the '80s and '90s. I grew up on the west side of Youngstown, Ohio. This is a town that was once rich in Italian culture and tradition, but as the years went on, some of it soon became known as the "ghetto." There are still some very nice neighborhoods, though, and I appreciate the authenticity of people who are raised in this city, especially the streets of Elberen and Imperial. We were a low- to middle-class family who believed in God and were taught to work hard. My mom stayed home to raise us, and my dad was a man who worked as many as three jobs at a time to make ends meet, who never seemed tired, and who spared no expense when it came time to play with my three siblings and me. He always made time to build giant snow igloos and ice slides in our backyard and take us on adventurous bike rides that always ended with a trip to get ice cream. He always included the neighborhood kids when we had snowball fights and would fill up our minivan with kids in the summer to take us to Rocky Ridge and all over Mill Creek Park to climb the big rocks and play kickball and Indian ball. After a long fun day, he would always make time to tuck me in bed and say bedtime prayers every night. If I woke up with an infamous stomachache or nightmare, he was always there and made the problem or fear disappear. He made sure to keep our rich Italian traditions important along with my mom's Polish and Slovak background. He was very respectful to our Greek orthodox neighbor whom we came to realize was offended when we cut the grass on Sunday because it was against what he believed was right. So we didn't cut the grass on Sunday out of love and respect for our dear friend and neighbor. I began to realize that some things are just not that big of a deal and to love your neighbor can be a something that you can achieve if you learn to be flexible.

When I was around eight, my dad wanted to introduce our family to a good friend of his and made plans to take us over to his house so we could have dinner and all enjoy each other's company. This family was of very rich Pakistani culture. They had a big family as we did, and there were lots of kids running around when we got together. Although their dad read the Quran and was a Muslim and my dad read the Bible and was a Christian, we were all good friends. My dad enjoyed the friendship he had with this family and always showed God's love to them. The kids I played with were very nice, and their mother dressed very differently from my mother, always wearing a long beautiful dress of many colors with a matching head covering; and I always marveled, as a young girl, of her beauty. They ate very different food from us, and when we went to their house, we enjoyed a delicious meal that their mom worked so hard to prepare. All the work that was put in was evident, and I appreciated this energy expended for me. What I enjoyed about that meal was the love that was shown to me, and even as a young girl, I was humbled by it. My parents taught us to always be thankful for food that was prepared for us. My dad taught us that the Bible teaches that we come from all walks of life and are all different but that God teaches in Galatians 3:28 that there is neither Jew nor Gentile, neither slave nor free, nor male and female; for you are all one in Christ. He taught us that God teaches that there is only one race and this leaves no room for the sin of prejudice or racism, which was never a thing in my house and still isn't to this day because God says we were all made in his image. I believe what God was teaching was that, sure, there are different races and genders but this should not be something we focus on in life, because it is so small compared to the big things God planned in advance for us to do and these are the things we should be focused on. Gender and race are just small details of the big picture, and yet, somehow, we waste so much time being distracted by them. I was taught to respect other people's beliefs even if they weren't our own and to love others as God loves us. We should never allow color, race, or religion to become a barrier between people or an excuse to sin or show favoritism or hate of any kind. My dad was my hero from the beginning and will always be for teaching me truth. My mom was always tending to the house and making home-cooked meals that we all looked forward to, and our neighborhood friends of all different backgrounds always wanted to eat over at our house. I knew my family was different from the beginning, and kids from the neighborhood were just drawn to the love that was evident at our house. We never had much money, but it never mattered. My parents still live in that old house, and although the neighborhood changed, the memories remain.

My husband had a much different upbringing. He was born in South Carolina and then moved and lived in Maryland for much of his childhood. He moved to Ohio when he was twelve years old and never felt like Ohio was his home. He remembers the bushels of fresh crab they would get from the Chesapeake Bay, which were much cheaper back then but were a priceless meal. He dreams of going back there one day to have crab cakes, which he swears is the only place that makes them taste the right way. He says you haven't had real crab until you've had crab fresh out of the Chesapeake Bay. He moved around a lot, and his parents divorced when he was young. His father was not in his life for long. His grandparents were in and out of his life, as was much of his family, and no one really seemed to stick around. His mom became a single mom and did what she had to make ends meet. Bobby will remember things about his childhood that will pop up every now and then that seem to have been hidden in his mind somewhere as he learned to cope with the dysfunction.

I met Bobby when we were both thirteen. We met at the roller-skating rink. Our eyes matched up, and I never looked at anyone the same after that. We were hand in hand since eighth grade, and yet there are things that I am still learning about him to this day that I never knew—Some good, some bad; but when you are committed to love someone, you take the good, bad, and everything in between. Perhaps one day, I'll write a book about marriage if a challenge of that caliber is in God's plan for me. Marriage is not for the faint of heart. We are not a wise people for thinking that marriage should be something to jump into without being prepared and doing it the right way. Bobby and I are very different, and we look at situations very differently, so being married and having kids together is a complicated and sort of twisted thing. We don't always agree, and with God, I am able to somehow gain perspective, and God can allow Bobby and me to somehow work together despite our differences. God works miracles in our house daily as we live together but are so different. For instance, whenever our kids had struggled in school, we didn't worry too much, because we had found that they eventually grasp concepts and would learn. We did agree on this particular subject partly because of how my eyes were opened in the story of my husband's childhood in school. My Quintin had trouble in reading, and as I shared that story earlier, there was thought he may need held back but ended up doing well. Sophia was delayed in talking and also needed to be in a remedial reading program for extra help in school. Now only a few years later, she has straight As and is advanced in the gifted program. These are just examples of how much could change in a child's path. Encouragement for growth and enriching kids at home emotionally, intellectually, and spiritually along with getting the right help at school can impact their development and future. A few years into my marriage, I learned that Bobby didn't learn to read until the tenth grade. He told me this, and at first, I didn't believe him and thought he was joking until I started to think back and put two and two together. So many times, at our youth group meetings at church, he was asked to read as we went around the room and he would ask to be skipped. It appeared that he didn't want to participate and was being defiant or socially awkward, but really, he just couldn't read and was too embarrassed to admit it. Some thought he was shy; others thought he was disobedient. The truth was that Bobby was facing giants that others didn't see or care to know about. I knew of his tough life but didn't understand why the church didn't better invest in his safekeeping. Why were they able to overlook opportunities to help him to have more stability? Why did they not see his worth as I did? I don't really know what attracted me to him, and others questioned what I saw in him as well, because we were raised so differently and were polar opposites. I was just drawn to Bobby. My dad told me several years into my marriage, as I often questioned my place and purpose in it, that he believed Bobby saw me as his angel; and that is what I cling to as I push myself to still love him after all of these years and all the struggles we've encountered. I watched as most people disserted him, and he did not have the opportunities I did, which were simple but impactful.

I do struggle to this day finding purpose in church as in many cases hypocrisy is most widespread at church. I choose to make church inside myself and in my home, making outreach my main mission in my daily life and not my side job. I don't want to make it appear that I am involved in "church" but neglect to make my actions match my appearance. When Bobby was in high school, he never cared about his grades. He was always moving to a different area in town and was often the minority. He ended up in fights with the neighborhood kids who protected their turf from the kids who were different and didn't fit in. I'm sure most of these kids had no discipline or attention at home and were also abandoned by their dads, as Bobby was. They weren't raised to see others who appeared different as special. They saw them as a threat. Bobby was taught this, too, through the fights and harsh treatment he received from the ill-mannered kids he encountered. He couldn't go home and have his parents explain that the problem was sin, but instead his mom glorified the sin by calling it prejudice or racism and accepted it as just the way things were, instead of taking a stand to change it. She would tell Bobby to fight back and show them who he was made of, never correcting the problem but instead allowing the hatred to grow. All the kids in these neighborhoods suffered from a lack of self-confidence, lack of purpose, and poor self-esteem. They should have been taught how much God loved them, which should have been displayed by their parents and churches, but this was not the case.

Bobby shared with me a flashback that plays over in his head. It was Christmastime. He was about seven years old, and he was walking home from school with his brother, who was about five at the time. They went into their apartment expecting to see their mom but were met by unfamiliar people who he later found out were social workers from Child Protective Services. They told the boys they needed to go with them and that their mom had been taken away. Bobby was scared and confused and wanted his mom.

He looked over at the Christmas tree and knew that the wrapped package under the tree was a BB gun. He dashed for the gun in order to protect himself and his little brother against the intruders. The social workers, of course, overpowered the boys, and they were placed in foster care. His foster parents were very loving to the boys, and Bobby called them aunt and uncle. The boys were with this family for maybe eighteen months or so. The family took the boys on vacation and spent quality time with them, treating them as their own. Bobby holds a special place in his heart for this family who showed him the meaning of unconditional love. They gave him a glimpse of what family should look like and that what he experienced at home was not how things were everywhere. Bobby remembers reuniting with his mom about eighteen months later, but there were mixed emotions. He had missed her so much during their time of separation, but when they were finally brought back together, she was pregnant and expecting another son. Bobby's excitement quickly turned to a feeling of betrayal. He had waited so long to see his mom again and maybe thought, while they were apart, she was preparing a place for him to come home to, but here she was ready to give her love to another child. Bobby loves both of his brothers and to this day is still thankful for them and their friendship. He did help his mom care for the new baby, even feeding him bottles and changing his diapers. He moved around from town to town with his mom and brothers and was never able to get rooted in a particular area.

Bobby and I fight to this day because I search for joy in all situations and am always reaching for the stars; and he, however, is content with simple pleasures and has trouble being motivated to better himself and those around him, stemming from his battle within to love himself as God loves him and to see his worth and purpose. I believe this is because most of his life was spent just surviving and getting to the next day, always hoping for unconditional love but instead found love that came to him at a cost.

He remembers drinking powered milk and eating saltines crackers and ramen noodles for much of his young years while they waited for their welfare check and food stamps to come. Sometimes he went to bed hungry, sleeping on a dirty floor coated with dog hair because they couldn't afford a bed for him to sleep on. He never knew when his mom would decide to pick up and leave town at the drop of a hat. He just remembers helping her pick up their belongings, whatever fit in their car, and moving to the next house or apartment. When he finally moved to Ohio, he went to live with his grandma for a while and then his aunt and uncle who lived in the area and who bought him new clothes and taught him how to clean and have responsibilities that yield the learning of discipline and accountability. It is hard to appreciate the value of this learning at the age of twelve. These should be taught from a young age and should be witnessed in the parents every day as a young one grows and develops. Bobby continued to bounce around from house to house. As issues came up, he would be turned over to the next house. He never had stability, and it wasn't until tenth grade when his aunt made a bet with Bobby that he couldn't get all As and Bs on his report card. He was intrigued by the challenge and started to try in school. This is when he finally learned how to read and taught himself. He finally started doing well academically. He tells me how all the words had appeared jumbled on the page and the letters were backward or in the wrong order. I assume he may have had dyslexia and maybe some other learning barriers, but he just wanted to win the bet, so he figured it out. All those years the schools had just moved him ahead while he did a lot of guesswork to just squeeze by on tests. Now that someone gave him a challenge, he had given a lot of effort, was willing to try, and was rewarded with encouragement. He ended up moving back in with his mom in his senior year but didn't want to change schools. The school system in Youngstown that he was in had deteriorated, but the alternative school was worse. (Bobby and I never went to the same school. I went to Youngstown Christian School. It housed preschool through twelfth grade. The tuition rates there were a reason my dad worked so hard and had several jobs.) Bobby desired to just stay at the school he was at (Chaney High School). He did not want to move schools once again, but the bus wouldn't come that far to pick him up, and his mom didn't have a car. He decided to walk the five miles to and from school every day. He walked through the ghetto and through Mill Creek Park, the same place that brought me joy as a kid as our family fun days were spent there. Bobby appreciated the landscape as a scenic route on his long journey to school and from school every day.

We both appreciated the park, but it represented something different for us both. Collectively, it was a place of peace that separated the troubles of life from the freedom of a clear mind. I spent many family outings there playing games and learning to have good fellowship with my siblings. Bobby was alone much of his life and walked through the park with much time to think about all that was on his mind. He didn't play organized sports, but I can't imagine having the energy to do that when you spend so much time being hungry and struggling just to get back and forth to school and then going to bed at night on a hard, dirty floor or maybe, if you're lucky, an old couch. While I was excited to enjoy the trip after a nice bike ride to get taken to Dairy Queen to get ice cream, hesitating to choose my favorite (a peanut buster parfait) because it was the most expensive treat on the menu, my dad insisted I get what I wanted. Bobby, on the other hand, was excited for the times his mom gave him a food stamp so he could walk to the corner gas station by himself or with one of his brothers to get himself a bag of chips and a Big Gulp, the biggest soda pop he could get. He played football for a bit in high school but quickly realized he couldn't manage that kind of commitment, having even to wash his own clothes, sometimes by hand, and not having a ride to practice or the right food to eat. He got really good at basketball because he dribbled all the way to the basketball courts as he walked the couple of miles from his house. He loved to play pickup games at the park, the spot everyone called the Cages. It was called this because of the fence that surrounded the courts. As he got better and better at the sport, Bobby earned the respect of the street ballers who would always pick him first to be on their team. This was a far cry from getting beat up for not fitting in. Basketball was therapy for him, and Michael Jordan was his idol. To a young boy with nothing, dreams were everything. He shares the passion of basketball with Sabria, and I'm sure when he watches her play, he does what she does and just escapes into passionate freedom to be the best. He and Sabria differ from each other in a big way. Bobby wanted to be the best and crush everyone else on the court. During those games at the Cages, Bobby could (in his mind) get back at everyone who ever let him down in life and turned their back on him…which was a lot of people. He didn't learn the value of team and humility to build others up. He had nothing to lose when he hit the courts, and basketball was seemingly the only thing in his life that he had control over. He could choose how good he would get, and he was great. He would go to a hoop by himself at a park in our neighborhood called Borts Pool. He would attach weights to his ankles and just run and jump under the hoop over and over again. Finally, after much practice, he could dunk at five feet eleven. His three-point shot was always on point, and he was really quick on his feet.

I know he celebrates with our kids as they succeed and reach milestones because it feels like his efforts of getting good at something when he was young was not wasted time. That heart and determination, he shares with them. Even though he never got the chance to excel at his talents and get to a level that reflected his talents, passion, and drive, he can love his kids enough to give them opportunities he never had and even a nice bed to lay down in at night to recharge for the next day. This is what he gives to our kids.

Bobby still struggles with letting God fuel his passion. He reverts back to his young mind that tells him that he must battle on his own. Our own strength is never enough to withstand the wars that are waged on us daily. People will let us down, and as parents, we must do a better job at raising our kids to not live according to the agenda of the world around us but to live under God. God was with Bobby as a young boy walking through the park, playing basketball, and buying his own treats. God never left his side, but sometimes it is hard to imagine such love and friendship of a God who never leaves you when it is not displayed by those around you whose very purpose is to love you and show you God's love. As parents, we need to teach our kids better. They are not underprivileged kids. They are not White kids. They are not Black kids. They are not rich kids. They are not bad kids. They are God's kids. If we see them this way, we would learn to discipline them better, love them better, and teach them better. We stereotype our own kids by not trusting them to God. We let them believe they are vulnerable because they are Black, privileged because they are rich, justified because they go to church, entitled because they are poor, prejudice because they are White... The list can go on forever. It's all garbage. We are who God says we are. He is our one and only judge. As parents, we will be accountable and judged by God for false ideas we put in our kids' heads. Be careful to make the most out of every opportunity given to make the most out of every situation in order to teach truth to your kids.

After having many different jobs and dabbling in different careers over the years, it was clear to me that Bobby was searching for purpose. He was always good at fixing and building things. I've heard stories of how even as a young child he would take things apart, like the vacuum cleaner, just so he could try to put it back together again. He wanted to see how things worked. This was his built-in gift or talent. Bobby searched over the years to do different jobs but always was brought back to the thing he was good at. I believe God was always leading Bobby, but he wanted to try things on his own because he was raised to believe he was alone in life, which was a lie but one that he believed. He let his pride build after any accomplishment or good work that he did, instead of humbly giving credit to God. This caused much trouble in our marriage as he began to believe he was excused on days he wanted to relax and not indulge in the responsibilities of our household or to even be involved in get-togethers or special events with the kids. He would drive separate to family get-togethers so he could leave early whenever he felt like it, leaving me alone with all the kids. Sometimes he stayed away from the events all together because he just didn't feel like parenting or socializing and would decide to be alone. One time that comes to mind is the day we went to a lake with my sister's family. It was summer 2011. I was seven months pregnant with our sixth child, Christiana. Bobby drove separate to the lake, so I had anxiety the whole time wondering when he would decide to leave. Finally, he walked up to me while I was in the water playing with the little ones and said, "Okay, bye, I'm leaving now." I asked where he was going, and the knot formed in my stomach, knowing I'd be stuck there pregnant and alone with five kids. Sabria was only ten at the time, so all the kids were still young, and this was a hard time for Bobby and me as this is the time as parents that you don't see what your kids will become and you only have hope that your efforts will eventually yield something good in them. I always had to believe that simple acts of love that seem mundane, like changing diapers, cleaning up toys, and wearing puke on my shirt till I had time to change would all be worth it someday. Bobby said he was going to play basketball with his friends. He did this all the time, so it wasn't shocking to me, but my sister's family was astonished. I always made excuses for Bobby's absences and poor decisions toward me and the kids. Today there was nothing to say, and I didn't try to make it look a certain way. He left me there with my car, which was, of course, the family car because I was the one who was the one responsible for everyone, the family. Bobby left me there to watch all five kids who were all under the age of ten. I was largely pregnant and feeling the effects of the summer on my pregnant body, but this was nothing unfamiliar to me. I looked around at the heavy cooler, messy picnic table, diaper bags, and water toys lying everywhere and then, of course, had the questions from those around me: "Your husband, where is he going? Is he leaving? Wait a minute. Is he really leaving you here with all the kids?" I didn't lie, because I wanted to be true to myself. God was my husband, my companion, my friend. Bobby was fighting the same battles he'd always fought, and I was not enough to change him. He did not always value me or his position as father and husband, but it did not mean that I could not remain valuable. His bad choices did not define me. God defined me, and God said I was valuable. I told them that he had made plans with his friends and didn't elaborate.

This experience, along with many others over the course of our marriage, is what I blame my anxiety disorder on but only in my weakness. My anxieties and panic attacks are only a sign of weakness in my faith. I learn to cast my cares on God, and he always delivers me from my worries. I encourage others to do the same. If you have been hurt by someone you trusted or by someone you don't even know and it is causing you to have trouble trusting, loving, and coping with certain situations in life, learn to pray to be delivered. This, I have tried myself, and it has allowed me to separate myself enough from the negativity surrounding Bobby's actions to still love him and include him as an asset and tool in the kid's lives and mine. This, as I'm sure you can imagine, is no easy task; but that's why God, in his power, is the one who rescues me from the situations and helps me to cling to him. Be delivered today from your worries. There is no reason to wait. Bobby struggled to find reason to suffer along with his family but instead removed himself at times from challenges at home and could not seem to enjoy the simple pleasures of raising a family. He seemed to think that because his childhood was so hard, he had paid his dues in life and now he should be able to rest easy. He believed he was doing us all a favor by sticking around and was already better than his own father, so he deserved our respect and appreciation. He would tell the kids, "Do as I say, not as I do." By saying this, he let us all know he expected us to always go at 100 percent but that he was not measured by the same stick and was not willing to perform at the level he expected us to perform at. What was actually going on was that he relied on his own pride and strength which he knew in his heart was not enough but refused to believe that, with God, he was already good enough. This is the very popular "woe is me" attitude, that allows one to feel like a victim and encourages them to remain unproductive in life. When I would remind Bobby that I, too, was clocking in and out of a job and that if he was home first he could start dinner or maybe help to get my work clothes washed as I washed his, he would say that he worked harder than me at his job and so he couldn't be expected to help with any chores at home or with the duties of raising the kids so the brunt of the work was on me and he needed his rest and his time to wind down in the evening. He was hiding behind his feelings of inequality by puffing his chest out at us and demanded to be the king of the house. I forced my beliefs on Bobby that we are all held to a high standard and that is God's standard so none of us could boast about the good work we do or feed into our weaknesses, which in God are made strong (Ephesians 2:9). Bobby began to resent me; and I came to realize, after many years of marriage counseling and really through God ultimately opening my eyes to see, that I could not fix Bobby and I shouldn't try to. He was not my project but God's, and he wanted that privilege of building his masterpiece in Bobby. My job was to stay steadfast on the path God led me down to be a good wife to Bobby and a good mother to my kids and to walk in faith every day so that Bobby could see God in me and then also find God himself. This was an unnatural stand to take. The only thing I had then was faith. God met me where I was and knew I was willing to be led. He guided me, and with his help and power, I would have what it took to live the purpose-driven life he called me to live.

My nature wanted to divorce Bobby as he chose to separate from us, his family, daily on so many levels but physically was still in the house. My duty and commitment to him and God was clear to me, though, and loving Bobby meant I needed to live my own life and be responsible for myself and the kids in hope that one day our parallel lives could intersect and we could all become one as God intended. I dreamed of the day Bobby would see himself as God did, because this was the only way he could truly love his family the right way and it really was the answer to life in general. As I thought about how Bobby loved taking things apart and putting them together again as a small child and now worked as an impressive industrial maintenance technician, I began then to wonder how many times he had to do this very act to himself as a child—pick up the broken pieces of himself and put them back together. I never saw Bobby as he was. Even when we were young, I saw him as God saw him. All his weakness and flaws were made perfect through God, and this was the only way I could see him even through such grim situations and experiences I went through with Bobby. As long as God asked me to, I would stay in this marriage, and at Bobby's side not moving on, giving up, or changing course until I was given the direction and instruction from God to do so. This was a passionate and purpose-driven life I was living, and it is not for the faint of heart. God also was teaching me that in order to accomplish the things he had for me to do in life, I needed to stop depending on Bobby the way I had been and to make a move before getting stagnant as I waited to see him change. I needed to realize that God was my provider and friend and that he had things for him and me to do together and I needed to start growing in faith and otherwise to be able to be a useful tool to him. I was not perfect either, and God wanted me to know that there was hope for me, even though I questioned my decision I made so many years ago in marrying Bobby and maybe we weren't meant to be. God told me otherwise. He told me that my journey was beautiful and that he was leading me down a beautiful path that I could never mess up. He told me he would allow me to enjoy life and to see its beauty in all its splendor. He told me to trust him and not to be afraid to go on the walk of faith with him. I gave my marriage to him. As I began to take more and more responsibility for the family and to shy away from my own insecurities but to indulge in the call to become a leader for my household, Bobby made sure to take credit for the success in situations and would say, "See, aren't you glad I am always so hard on you? Look what you have been able to do and how tough you're becoming." He could only mock me in his mind. God was the reason that I could accomplish anything good in this life, and he was molding me despite Bobby's constant ignorance of reality. This was a short circuit in Bobby's world. He chose the fantasy he believed in and allowed it to bear fruit in his own mind. It was a twisted way of thinking that he had developed, that he could excuse people in his past (instead of forgiving them) and ultimately what he was doing was giving the credit to all the dysfunction in his life if he did anything good and honorable. It is what so many people do in life, and this is how pride builds in a person because they want to rationalize all the trauma they went through in life and give it meaning. It's meaningless. Read the book of Ecclesiastes in the Bible. It really can help us to understand life and is very refreshing but only if you desire a deeper walk with God. I'm not saying that any trauma one experiences in their life should be ignored; but there is a reason one endures tragedy, bliss, happiness, and trials of all kinds. It is a shameful waste of time to go through life allowing oneself to be identified by their own accomplishments or tragedies they experienced in life but instead to grow from these experiences and travel through them with the one who created their very existence on this planet, getting the most out it and moving forward to fulfill the ultimate purpose of our existence in this life.

CHAPTER 15

BIG BLACK

I'm led to write about a portion of my life that helps me believe that God is bigger than any obstacle. This was a portion of my life from August 2015 to February 20016. Going into August, Bobby and I had finished our first year with Sabria in travel basketball for SMAC. Sabria was in eighth grade at the time, and we had taken a year to prepare for this commitment as we were confident that this was the right path for Sabria. After she was beginning her dealings with jealousy and prejudice from those around her, we saw her potential and hunger for greatness and wanted to feed it. Our eyes were opened to the commitment that was necessary to continue on this journey as the first travel basketball season that went from March 2015 to July 2015 came to a close. Much financial expense, travel, and planning were in our future. I could see early on that this was going to be out of our league, and this was why we did wait that extra year before committing, but even so we struggled. So I began to put our family on an even tighter budget, opened a separate bank account, and set as much money aside as possible. The second-to-last tournament in that first season was in Maryland, and we rode home on fumes. Even after all the planning, we still struggled. We took the whole family on that trip as we tried to make the most of it so as not to stir up jealousy but instead to encourage unity among the siblings. Some would say this was a financial mistake, and even my husband at times disagreed with my style, but I always look for opportunities try to keep my kids together as much as possible so they can learn from each other and develop good friendships. Our family car was on its last leg; and we couldn't afford to complete the very last trip of the travel basketball season, which was a combination back-to-back tournament to Kentucky for a few days and then on to Tennessee for four more days. It was an impossible task to make it to both tournaments, which would have been a whole week of traveling. I borrowed my brother's car to take Sabria to the tournament in Kentucky, and on this trip, I took only Sophia with us. Sometimes, as I couldn't afford to take all the kids, I would take one or two and spend quality time with them; and this was also an opportunity for them to see other states and be adventurous. My brother had a small car that was good on gas and was reliable, and he graciously let me borrow it. When the tournament in Kentucky was finished, it was the dreaded moment of saying goodbye to Sabria and sending her off with another family who would take her on to the next tournament in Tennessee. This was such a humbling experience for me and one I will remember for the rest of my life. It changed my life, to be honest. So many feelings came over me during this time. I was thankful for the family who offered the time, money, space, and responsibility of taking Sabria under their wing for those few days—for making sure she ate good, felt welcomed, and had a clean uniform. Coach Carlos also looked after her and made sure she had everything she needed.

I had the luxury of knowing she was in good hands, but I did not take this lightly. There would be other trips in the future. As Sabria became a reliable asset, the coaches would use her at times on the older team to help ease the rigor of long weeks of play and promote longevity of the other players by having a sub. This was a good opportunity for her, and as long as Sabria was up to it physically, she would do it. Most of the time, these were opportunities I could be a part of, but I do remember once leaving her in Georgia the following year to go to another tournament with the older team, which was an unexpected opportunity. I was scheduled to work and couldn't stay, so I headed back to Ohio, and Sabria stayed in Georgia after our team played in Atlanta, and then after that, the older team was moving on to Augusta for one more tournament before returning home. This time in Kentucky the year before was different. It was a time of vulnerability. I knew I was leaving her there to go on without me because of my own faults. It was not a last-minute change or an opportunity that sprung up out of nowhere. This was a time in my life that I felt vulnerable, weak, and dependent. I was bound by my work schedule. I was dependent on my husband. I was held back by the chains of my self-doubt to be everything my kid needed me to be. I hugged Sabria. She was fourteen at the time and I watched as she got into the back of her teammate's car. Sophia and I headed north, back home to Ohio, and Sabria headed south toward Tennessee. My mind was a wreck driving home, beating myself up for leaving my daughter behind and not being with her. She and I talked about the plan, and she was comfortable going on this trip without me. It wasn't the ideal situation, but she understood that I couldn't go, and she was thankful for the opportunity to play and get better at the sport and to be useful to her coach. I was proud of her for going on the trip and on my way home vowed that I would never be stuck in that situation again.

I didn't know why I needed to go through this experience, but a few years later, I was blessed with being responsible for another girl in our area with talent who was recruited to SMAC and needed a way to get to these tournaments. I didn't know it at the time, as I drove home from Kentucky, that God needed me to do a mission in the future and needed to prepare me then for that future task. He knew that this trial with Sabria would fuel my ambitions to be a better mother for my own kids and to other kids who needed help. This brings me to tell of a most difficult journey I embarked on. After Sabria came home, she told me all about her trip and that she had done well and had a good time. I had talked to Bobby about how we needed a new dependable car and needed to have money to continue on this journey in travel basketball. He had no clue how much effort and money it had already taken to get us through up to this point, and his nonchalant attitude was annoying to me but caused me to understand that him and I were different and that I had my own callings from God. I knew at that point that I needed to appreciate Bobby's efforts but that it was time to find that inner beast in myself because without it, we would not be successful in being a help for our kids. It was time to not just talk about the change but to be the change we needed to continue on the journey. There was no one else who could do it, because God had put the responsibility on me. I prayed hard and did some math. We had about seven months. That's it. Seven months to save up enough money to buy a car and save up enough to make all the trips. I started looking online for cars that would fit my family of eight comfortably. I found a Nissan NV 3500. I'm not surprised if you've never heard of it. I had never heard of it until this moment that I was online looking at it. It was perfect. It was a twelve-passenger commercial van that was built on a truck frame. It had leather seats which were all removable with a durable interior that was all easy to clean and was made to hold up for long trips. I never saw myself driving a van, anyway, so I figured, why not go all out? It was definitely different, but so were we. I never saw one driving around or knew anyone who even had heard of this vehicle, but I knew it was the one. I told Bobby we would need to save about $2,000 a month in order to make the seven-month deadline and be able to have a down payment. This was the only way to buy this car and to make our monthly payments affordable before next travel season. He laughed at me. We were in debt as it was, so this figure was a true fantasy and a laughable expectation. I told him it was the only way. He didn't believe it was possible. One thing that is true about me is that when someone tells me I can't do something or that my idea is impossible, it makes me want to do it all the more. I called my brother Mike, whom I talked to daily in those days and whom I considered one of my best friends. He encouraged me and was similar to my dad in telling me that anything was possible. I had a family meeting and told the kids the situation. I explained that we needed a family car that we could all fit in, would have room our friends and luggage, and would get us to the tournaments to see Sabria. I told them I would have to spend a lot of time at work and they needed to understand that this was only for a time and not forever. I did not want to leave my kids to go to work and in my heart wanted to blame my husband for this.

God told me to be brave and reminded me to be humble and to do what needed done. He had put this mission in my lap and would be the one to carry the burden. I didn't even know if the amount of work would even be available, but I had to try. I was faithful and started signing up for shifts. I worked whatever was available, seldom saying no when asked to work extra hours. I had direct deposit; and after every single payday, I walked into the bank and transferred as much as I could into a separate account, keeping my goal in mind. I always asked for a printout of my balances. I could have manually transferred this money through the computer, but this way had a bigger meaning. My little one Christy was only four years old at the time. She was still small enough for me to carry. As I walked away from the bank teller with my slip in one hand and my other hand cupping Christy's leg and I looked down at the number on the slip and being proud of my earnings, I would squeeze Christy's little thigh that poked through her little shorts. I held her body close to mine and would look at her as she held the lollipop she got from the bank, and I needed that dose of reality to keep my mind aware. This was how I poured salt into my own open wound to make sure I felt the damage. I always dreamed of being a stay-at-home mom, and this dream never came true. This was not where God took me. However, he had a plan, and as I walked to my car, I learned to hate money. I hated those numbers on that slip that kept me from my kids, but I kept on pace as God directed. I signed up for more shifts and made more money. I began to feel like work was my home. Many days I ate breakfast, lunch, and dinner at work. I spent the night at work. After every single pay day, I walked into that bank with my kids and transferred that money, in person, squeezing my baby and believing this would all work out and eventually be over. Some pay days were better than others, but I never faltered or lost faith. None of my paychecks were small. Sometimes I wouldn't be able to keep all the money in there as I could remember we needed to buy one of the kids an instrument for band and then had a problem with our toilet and septic that was an unplanned expense, but I listened as God told me not to be discouraged and to keep going and not to give up.

My schedule for work looked like a road map. I could remember working three back-to-back sixteen-hour shifts and then a couple of twelves that week too. My boss at the time came up to me and asked me if I knew how many hours I had worked that week, and I said I didn't know. I honestly didn't know. I just kept going because that's what God said to do. She looked at me and said, "Seventy-two. You worked seventy-two hours this week! You're are a crazy lady." I just smiled as I looked at her and thought, *Wow, that is kind of a lot.* During those months, though, it was just what I did. She didn't even know that many nights after those sixteens I had to stop at the grocery store at midnight before I could go home to bed. Many times, I went straight home to clean the house and make a late dinner after my twelve-hour shift and then got to bed late, and I would get back up and head out for another sixteen. It was intense. My boss at the time appreciated my efforts and looked out for me, but she was also sweet and admired my perseverance. The hospital really needed my help at the time, so it was a perfect scenario, and those opportunities to work now were not available, and I know that God set up the time and place for me to be able to have all these things match up for his ultimate plan. It really wasn't even about making money. It was about trusting in him, building faith, and growing perseverance.

I never seemed to miss a beat with the kids, indulging in every opportunity to take them places and play and to also take care of the house for them. This was inspired by the life I watched my dad live when I was a child and how he would strive to spend time with us even with grueling work hours, giving me no excuse myself to cheat my kids out of quality time with their mom. They were my inspiration through this time, and I always told them that. I prayed that God would watch over them while I was on this intense journey. I didn't want to lose time with them or to overlook problems or concerns they might have been having. God kept us connected. He allowed me to still have energy to be a good mom and to love my kids. After several months of this grinding, a friend of mine at work helped me get in touch with a credit union in my area who was able to assist me in the process of getting a loan and to get a low interest rate. This friend was always giving me good life advice and helping me navigate through the mechanics of life that I wasn't good at and couldn't depend on my husband for. I am so thankful that she sensed when I needed help and was ready to give me advice from all that she had learned in life. I continued to call my brother Mike. I would literally tell him what my paychecks were to somehow keep myself accountable and mentally on target. He would encourage me and keep me grounded.

I ended up eating, sleeping, and breathing work for those months and saved $12,000. This was awfully close to my goal of $14,000, and I contributed the difference to some unforeseen events along the way that I mentioned earlier. I always realistically overestimated. I found that Nissan van I had hoped to get in Medina, Ohio. This was a little over an hour from where I lived. I made an appointment to go and see it and brought my dad along. The dealer took me to the vehicle, and as I walked up to it, I questioned whether or not I could even drive it. It was a lot bigger than I imagined, and even being five feet nine, I had to use the handle to pull myself up into the seat. I was petrified. The van's roof is seven feet high, so sitting in this vehicle seats you above most other cars and trucks on the road. The confidence I had gained over these last few months allowed me to give it a chance, and as I started on the test drive, I did not allow my nervousness to be seen by the car dealer. I never liked driving. I especially hated driving long distances. Now I would be driving all over the country in this beasty truck van. I thought, *What in the world is happening to me?* I was giving up everything for my kids and for the sake of living a purpose-driven, God-inspired, passionate life and letting nothing stand in my way. The dealer had told me that there was a few hundred miles on the van, so it was on sale. There was a basketball team that needed a large vehicle and used the van to travel to a tournament. This was yet another sign from God. I bought that van, and it became known to everyone as Big Black. Everyone knew it was me when they saw my van because no one else in the area had one. You couldn't miss it on the road, and most people had never saw one ever. It really fit my personality because this life I was living was not like anything I'd heard of. It was unique. I really had a good laugh one day when I was out with my dad and all the kids when I was parked and a man stared at my car for a while and then looked at me with a serious face and said, "That is a badass van!." My dad and I just laughed and nodded in agreement and said, "Thanks." I feel this van sort of displays how I feel as a mom. I'm not tired, vulnerable, overworked, or weak. I'm willing to take this job of motherhood on and be a beast at it. It doesn't define who I am. God defines who I am, and he tells me I should go all out. My confidence was built during the purchasing process as the credit union made it very easy for me. As the car dealer tried to get me a "good deal for payments" and "a good interest rate," I said, no, thanks, smiled, and said, "I already worked out the finances." It was a good feeling that I did something so big on my own but with the help of my beautiful supporters and the love of my life and strong tower, Jesus. I had some leftover money after we bought the van (imagine that), so I put up a giant playground in the background with a play yard surrounding it. I designed the area with the help of my dad and siblings. My kids picked it out, and I told them it was their reward for being so willing to go through the storm with me as we saved for Big Black. They helped put it together and even saw that their hard work of supporting me through the months had paid off. I want to encourage everyone through this story to be aware of the time you spend earning money. It is very costly to be away from your kids, and you must measure the worth of what you are doing and where you are spending money. Teach your kids the value of money and that it's important to keep it as a simple thing in life. Don't live to work. Rather toil in passion as you work to live. This was a valuable lesson I learned, and I still can picture myself and remember the soft touch of Christy's thigh as I held her close to me as we walked out of that bank so many times. I'm willing to continue to move with the rough currents of the waters of life to be molded by the one who made me, and I will always look for the lessons to love through the storm.

CHAPTER 16

BE TOUGH ON TRANSITION

After learning of Quintin's diagnosis of a complete ACL tear with meniscus involvement, I held a family meeting to tell the kids the situation so we could discuss any worries that they may have. This was about three years after buying Big Black, several years of travel basketball under our belt, suffering from financial strain, my mom's chronic illness, sending Sabria to West Point in July, Quintin's injury in September, and then Dylan's appendectomy in early October. We were realizing the next year of our lives would be garnished with Quintin having a major surgery and hospital stay, followed by several months of intense rehab and more months of physical therapy in order to return to sports and live a normal life. I started out the meeting by asking the kids if they thought that Quintin's injury was meant to happen. To my surprise, they all said, "Yes," and Quintin yelled out, "Yes!" I laughed and thought, *Wow, what am I gonna teach these kids?* They had learned to really roll with the punches and to trust in God's plan. So we read together in 1 Corinthians. It talks about how we don't receive the spirit of the world but the spirit of God so that we may understand what God has freely given to us. This was important in understanding that we had the right to believe that Quintin's injury was a gift and that Quintin was still in God's hands. This way of thinking allows us to continue on the path and to know that God has a plan for the future. It gives us freedom to be tough and freedom to weather the storm in hope for a bright and good outcome. This gives us the opportunity to respond to any trial with confidence instead of questioning the reason and asking why. It is important to ask why but only as a way to better indulge in the mission. It is important to move on even before understanding the why in order to stay in the moment and reap all the blessings from God. If the goal is to grow your faith, you may not have an answer to the why for a long time. I explained to the kids that this would mold Quintin into what God was going to build him to be. Quintin had already taken a new look at the situation. He was so upset when this first happened but now saw hope. He had to be tough on the transition, which athletes are always asked to do on the field or on the court. This time, Quintin was doing it in life. He didn't have the choice to run outside and grab the football and play the game he loved. His new Lebron James tennis shoes he intended to wear to basketball would instead be worn to go to therapy sessions at the children's hospital. We had hope God would renew his strength in time and soon he would have that chance again to do the things he loves to do with his friends. There was also a possibility that Quintin would never be the same, and this was something we had to understand. He couldn't change what happened, but he did have control over how he responded to the situation and control over his attitude as he took the next step. I wanted the kids to all know this journey would be long and seem to never end, but just as our battle in the process of working and saving to buy Big Black ended, so would this. Months were going to go by, and Quintin would feel like giving up, but together we could all help to push through and come out victorious in the end. I encouraged the kids to see the hope in the future, or should I say the kids showed me the hope for the future? We help each other through tough times and communicate the doubts we may have so that, no matter the situation, we can remain hopeful to fuel the passion to be great and to forge ahead even in times of distress. We are always careful to look back at our lives at all the times God had carried us through and use those times as encouragement to continue. I understand that, although the process of saving for Big Black was tough, it helped build my family's hope, faith, perseverance, diligence, discipline, and trust. God was using life experiences to build us to be able to deal with things that were to come. More experiences to shape us as his beautiful stones. It was a process, and we were willing to go through the storms with him.

CHAPTER 17

WORKING OUT
THE KINKS

As we waited to hear when surgery would be scheduled for Quintin, life around us was still going on. It was November now and time for Sabria's first basketball game with West Point. Bobby and I were beyond excited. It was a home game to be held at Christl Arena. We desperately wanted to make the trip, but after looking at our schedules, it was looking grim. I looked at him and said, "So you're telling me that you're going to stay awake for forty hours straight and we're gonna drive six and a half hours straight to the game, watch the game, and then drive the six and a half hours back home and then you will go straight back to work?" He thought for a second and then said, "Yep, sounds like a plan." I knew this was too crazy not to be our plan, so I didn't argue. This was how our life was. Nothing ever came easy, ever. Sabria didn't know all the details of our crazy plan but knew we'd be at the game, all seven of us. The only thing she asked for was a pair of new white Vans. Why anyone in the army would want a pair of white shoes during wintertime in the snowbelt is funny to me, but it's what she wanted. Even though I was on afternoon shift and crunched for time with prepping for the trip, I was used to last-minute requests from the kids that seemed to make no sense to me. I threw my scrubs on and jumped in the car and stopped before work with minutes to spare to get those shoes, even spraying them so they'd be ready to wear. Within an hour of her request, they were bought, sprayed, and in the trunk. I sent her a pic of the shoes, and she was in shock. I love being able to do those little big things for my kids. She felt loved and said she loved me so much. It wasn't about the shoes. It was the effort to love that she noticed, and this helped fuel her ambitions. Be accountable to show up for your kids whenever it's humanly possible, and when it isn't humanly possible, have faith and ask God for some help, and then watch as he guides you through the miracle. I expect Sabria to be accountable to her squad leaders, coaches, teammates, and teachers; therefore, I need to show her accountability as a parent to try hard and love her the best I can without excuse. I choose to be bound by my desire to love my kids and hope that they extend that love to others.

The next day, we made it to West Point. We made good time of six and a half hours, which was impressive, especially with five kids in the car who always wanted to make stops. We were so excited to make it there that even my little one Christy said the drive was worth it and she couldn't wait to squeeze Sabria. We walked into Christl Arena during warm-ups, and Sabria spotted us. Her face lit up, and she was smiling from ear to ear. This was a far cry from when she was younger and would say, "Do you have to bring everyone to the game?" Her big family had a big meaning now, and she was no longer afraid of what people thought, because having a lot of people show up to your basketball game when you're in the army is a valuable asset. Not only that, but as Sabria grew up and realized who was always there for her, she understood what a true team was made of. We were her squad, her army, her backbone. We were there to represent, and she felt the love. This was what my hope was when the kids were young. I believed that through my efforts to keep them together and supporting one another even through times that seemed to have no meaning, they were learning the action, routine, and discipline of love. All those times the school administrator, teacher, or PTA mom charged me that ridiculous ticket price for my whole family to get into the game, they thought they were justified because it was "fundraising" work for the school, or they thought maybe I just had a good job and could afford to come to the games. Really what was going on was I was working extra shifts just to be able to pay for my whole family to get into all the sporting events so my kids could support their siblings. In my opinion, parents and siblings should get into extracurricular events free. In fact, I believe kids should get extra credit for the show of good character by going to the sporting events for their friends and siblings. The reason this is not encouraged at the school is they care about making money, not building kids of good character. I refuse to hear and believe any garbage talk about how the school needs the money and how they lowered ticket price. It is an act of poor leadership and is a systemic problem that extends all the way up the ladder throughout politics. This act of charging spectators astronomical amounts just so parents can support and teach their kids to support and love their family is wrong. They make it hard, but God makes it possible. We gave effort, and he made our paycheck go further. Bobby and I were spending hundreds $200 to $300 a month, sometimes more, sometimes less, to make it to all the kids' games, band concerts, during basketball season, etc. So many times, we forced our kids to stay home because we literally ran out of money to support our kids by the siblings being present. The school systems are hypocrites in this way. Support the teams they say. They don't care about support. They care about money. Money will never be the thing to raise a young man or woman of good character. If the school wanted the kids to support each other, they would let them in for free and give the kid a reward for their good support. They want compliance. They want support of an idea and agenda that has nothing to even do with the child. Kids are smart. If they know their worth, they won't hesitate to skip an event when those in charge are pushing a selfish agenda. I found myself getting burned out as I pushed against the grain, getting splinters the whole year round, in order to push in the right direction to help build good character in my kids and to promote positive supporting and loving team players in my kids while trying to push against the hypocrisy at the school. The schools and communities need to do better to promote support of what's right instead of wasting time supporting entitlement and the acts of self-indulgence.

I was proud of Sabria's smile as we walked through those doors, and my kids were confident that they were where they were meant to be, which was on the sideline for their sister. She warned us on the way there that she wasn't asked to warm up with the girls who played a lot, so she wasn't expecting to see much court time. I think she prepared us so we wouldn't expect too much and so she wouldn't be inviting the possibility of disappointment or maybe preparing herself as she was not accustomed to sitting on the bench but expected this would be the case. I could never be disappointed, because just seeing her at all was worth the trip, but I wanted the best for her, and I knew how hard she worked, so I was hoping for that hard work to be rewarded with playing time. As I sat down and could relax for a minute, finally, I started to have an eerie feeling about what she told me, and I began to wonder why she would not be getting playing time, as this, I was sure, would not be the case. Bobby knew her potential and how her skill level ranked on this team, so we knew reality was that she would be given a big part as a leader on the court. We were wrong. As I got my camera ready and they called out the starting five…Sabria remained on the bench. I stopped filming and remained calm and irritated, thinking, *Oh, Lord, what did we get ourselves into her? More politics?*

Is this ninth grade again? I knew the obvious that Sabria deserved to be on that court, and I knew she did not have a place on that bench, but humility is a virtue, so I watched and waited. The kids were shocked and were all doing what kids do. They were asking, "Mom, why is Sabria on the bench! She's not starting!" I told them it was okay, and we all watched intently waiting for our hero to get a chance to shine. Bobby and I had both texted her before the game. I had told her to let off serious steam and was led to tell her to rock the boat and make the team aware that they needed her out there. To make an impact. To be the help they wanted and needed. I told her to do one thing, her job. That's it. That's all that she should do—what God expected of her, which was a lot (to whom much is given, much is expected) if she stayed on target, then doing her job would prove to be enough. I told her to serve and not to be served, because that is where all the power is. I told her that grace allowed her on the court and that was where she was meant to be so she should own it and to let no one take her pride or her place out there. This was her team, her coach, her ball; but at the end of the day, she should give glory to the one who made them all and give credit back to the team. This was how to be a savage and beast of a player but remain loving and humble toward others. This was to play and act in honor. I told her to have a good attitude and to know the Lord was proud of her witness of him. Bobby had sent her the verse from Joshua 1:9, knowing she was nervous about the game and what she would be facing. This verse reads, "Have I not commanded you? Be strong and courageous. Do not be afraid; do not be discouraged, for the Lord your God will be with you wherever you go." This was my prayer as she sat on the bench, that God was preparing her to get out there. I hoped that Bobby and I did enough to help her and her mind would be clear and her heart ready to take care of her team. I knew she had a conflict going on inside of her. The battle between God telling her she was good enough and the coaches not making her a starter.

This was a confidence issue for sure, but I knew God would win that war. It was okay that she was on the bench because if nothing is expected of you, then you have nothing to prove. She was taught to respect authority, and God would handle the rest. Sabria and I had talked about this in the past. These are opportunities to get out there and just unleash, let loose, and have some serious fun! So this was what I was thinking when we all saw her stand up and go toward the sideline and wait at the table to go in. I thought, *Oh yea, baby, time to unleash!* My kids all cheered, "Sabria's going in. Look! There she is!" We all were in our glory, watching our girl. She was playing so tight and seemed uncharacteristically scared and unsure of herself. I just kept praying that God would fill her up with confidence and let her come alive out there. As I watched her from the stands, I knew that she was taking this whole experience in and she was happy, smiling with contentment. She was aware of her place and time and knew her purpose. She had a way of watching the other team and how the game was unfolding, and by doing this, she could figure out how to interject herself to be the best asset to her team, fitting in where she could best use her talents and strengths to support the whole team. She was a good analyst in this way. This is the most important aspect of any sport in my opinion. Sometimes coaches do not teach it or look for it in their players, because they either don't know how to look for it or don't know its worth and maybe don't have it themselves so they can't recognize it in others; but it's how to play with courage and honor, and without it, nothing else matters. That's what she was doing in the first few minutes. She was getting loose and analyzing so she could play the game with courage and honor by finding her proper place in that game on that day.

This is a tool people should use in their everyday life because every day is different and God's plans for us and our role and purpose in life may change, given the day. Learn your place and purpose in every situation by assessing first. This is one thing I love about nursing. Assess is always first. If you skip this step, your whole mission is kinked. The best way I can explain this is to compare the kinking to a water hose. We all know what happens when you get a kink in your water hose; no water comes out. A water hose that is bent at some point along the way will eventually wrap at the weak point and pinch off the water supply, preventing good use of the hose to supply the potentially good resource of water for whatever is was needed for. For what good is potential if it stays bottled up and is never put to good use? Likewise, the potential of water can never put out a fire, only the good use of water's potential. This is how I look at a basketball team or a team at work or school. If anyone veers offtrack, then the weakest one on that team will eventually cause a kink or break in the whole team, preventing success. These weaknesses come in all different forms, but if not noticed or taken care of, the team cannot function well or even function at all—which unfortunately is a very common problem I see in our world today. Sometimes the coach is the kink. Sometimes it's the boss. Sometimes it's a player or an offense being run that doesn't work. Sometimes it's a weak conditioning program. Whatever the case, kinks should be removed or straightened out to promote growth and success. We enjoyed watching Sabria strategize as she was assessing the situation and working out the kinks, and by the second half, her hose was ready to spray at full capacity. She was ready to put her potential to good use by finding her proper place in the game for the sake of her team. She ended the game with fifteen points in only twenty-one minutes of play and was the second leading scorer of the game even though she was only given half the playing time of the starters. She also had seven rebounds and some impressive and 1's. Whatever the coaches didn't see in her before the game, did they see it now? Maybe this was the part where only God saw her potential, but that would have been fine. It's all for him, anyway, and we were so proud of our girl for doing her job. We always teach the kids to humble themselves and let God raise them up because trying to raise yourself up will cause you to fall. Coming off the bench and being the second leading scorer was really Sabria's style, anyway. Be nothing, but show the world everything. The coach had told me that Sabria was her own worst enemy because she tried too hard. I don't believe this is a weakness. I believe that people don't have faith enough to encourage players to play the game with heart first, and this is a real disappointment to me. Sabria didn't have trouble with discipline or confidence. What she had a problem with was listening too hard to authority. She respected people and would listen and be obedient, but that was what held her back. The best thing someone could do for her and the team was to let her truly know that they had faith in her decisions on the court and to let her be a leader and ball out. They could have done this by showing her their support through facilitating good communication concerning her strength and conditioning training and in nutrition counseling and sleep support and by encouraging, even demanding, her to speak up and tell them how she felt she could do better. This would have shown that they had an interest in her ideas and had faith in her self-evaluations. She needed to have permission to play her game, do things that worked for her. Otherwise, she would continue to be held back from her true potential, and this would be unfortunate. In any case, as long as Sabria was faithful, God would raise her up as he did her whole life. I do believe that good coaches and good teachers, if they truly want to train others, will eventually be surpassed by their own students. Those coaches, teachers, and others in authority who can't handle their pride getting knocked will not be able to take a step back and allow good players to get to their highest level. Some people make it to the top but lack the vision to see that they stand in their own way of real success and in the way of others. As God can move mountains, he can also move roadblocks, so this is no big thing to worry about if it happens but instead something to pray about. I hoped those in authority over Sabria had vision, and if not that, Sabria could teach them and show them how she learned to see. After the game, Sabria told us that us being there meant everything to her and it gave her a boost to continue. I found out that she only had twenty hours of sleep that entire week. She had a history paper to write after that game, many big tests that week, and SAMI (room inspection) before heading to Arizona for her next game. This knowledge of her week kept me balanced as I had been overworked as well. She and I connected on this level. Sabria was getting pressed at every angle and was holding herself to the highest standard. As her friends who were playing basketball as college freshmen in regular schools were taking twelve credits and living a sedentary lifestyle, she was taking twenty credits and living a military lifestyle, believing it was an opportunity to choose to forge under fire. She was anxious to get to her studies after the game, so we all hugged and kissed her over and over again and then said goodbye. We headed home, tired, and our energy level and moral was reflected in the fact that it took us eight hours to make the drive home, stopping several times to change drivers. We made it home by 5:00 a.m., and Bobby had catnapped on the way home, and the kids slept. This way, Bobby was able to head straight to work, and I was able to get the kids off to school. It was crazy for all of us, but we don't really remember the trip so much as the time spent with Sabria. We drove for fourteen and a half hours that day but mostly remember the hour and a half spent with our girl, and that weight lifted from her to see her family from home and to feel the love of that mission were fuel for her, and we recognized the importance of that.

CHAPTER 18

FLUSHING CERTAIN THINGS DOWN THE TOILET

The next game was in Arizona, and we felt like we gave Sabria enough boost of encouragement to make this game without us. There would be no way for us to make it that far, so we planned to watch the game on TV. Bobby, the kids, and I gathered around and just could not wait to see our girl on the court. It was so exciting as the anticipation was building. Once again, she was on the bench to start. I was thinking, *What is the problem here?* Did I miss something? Why would she be sitting on the bench when she was obviously a much-needed asset to the team and proved that in the last game? I had a flashback from Sabria's freshman year in high school. I made it to my first parent meeting at the high school. I was sitting in the bleachers, staying alert and watching everything going on around me since this was my first experience with a child in high school and I didn't want to miss anything and really wasn't sure what would be expected of me. I was excited about what this basketball season would have in

store for Sabria. Up to this point, Sabria had already been playing for her elite basketball team, SMAC, in Cleveland and had
traveled all around to Kentucky, Tennessee, and Maryland playing
against some of the best talent in the country and was even playing
on an older team and still being an asset. She was predicted to play
at the Division 1 level, so we hoped her talent and discipline would
be respected there at the school. We were sure her expertise and
experience would be taken seriously, and we were ready to see her
placed in a leadership position on the team and were ready to hold
her accountable as she led her team.

As I sat in the stands, an upperclassman walked past the
stands and, with a sarcastic tone, yelled out as she bobbled her head,
"Freshman…balls!" She then trotted off to get a drink of water and
relax after the practice while the freshman started gathering the
balls. I looked on in amazement and raised eyebrows at the gull
of this bratty child and thought and looked around like, *Is someone
gonna get their child? Where is this girl's mother?* Then I watched as
Sabria listened and ran around and cleaned up, and I was about
to lose my mind, but I remained calm. *Who exactly was going to
talk to my kid like that?* I thought. This was clearly going to be an
interesting year of basketball. I talked to Sabria after the meeting,
and she told me that the freshmen were responsible for cleaning
up the equipment and water bottles after practice. I told her that I
expected her to always help clean up after practice no matter how
old she was and that I never wanted her to speak to younger people the way that older girl spoke to her. She said, "I know, Mom.
I wouldn't do that." I explained that cleaning up is everyone's job,
and I asked what her coach said about that girl's behavior. She said,
"It's the coach's rule, Mom. She wants it that way." I was shocked
and then told her I didn't agree at all and didn't want her taking
part in this abuse of others. I asked her if I sat around and ordered
all my kids to clean while I relaxed? She said, "No." I said, "Do you
order your little siblings around and then sit like King Tut while

they do all the work?" She replied, "No." I said, "Being older does not mean you have less responsibility. If anything, the older you are, the more you should have. Those younger than you watch your actions and learn from how you act." We all act as a team at home with chores and responsibilities, and this is how it should be on the court and in the locker room. Leadership roles should be given to those who earn that role and who show evidence of good character. It should not just be thrown at kids who are older because their age says they are ready to lead, and being a leader does not mean being a slave driver and mistreating those who are under you. Sabria did understand what I was saying. I knew I was going to have to watch this coach as she obviously had different views and beliefs from my family's. Sure enough, as the year went on, Sabria was suppressed by this coach who wanted to make it a point to be in charge and to teach Sabria something. Everyone knew Sabria should be in the games, but her coach left her on the bench for half of the game and only let her play one to two quarters a game and thought of herself as generous. Her Cleveland coach was baffled, and people in the community who knew of Sabria's talent and reputation would ask me why this coach had the best player sitting on the bench. I knew that the coach just wanted credit for the future greatness of her team, so she was sitting on things until it could look like she built the team up, but reality was that she was too proud to admit she could not teach Sabria, since she had already surpassed the coach's expertise and was at too high of a level now for her to manage.

I was tired of waiting for this coach to do what was right and admit she needed help, but instead, she kept Sabria on the bench and out of her hair because she could not deal with a player of that caliber. I began to look for other schools for Sabria to escape the abuse she was receiving even being punished for making good decisions on the court whenever those decisions questioned the coach's authority, authority that was misplaced and distorted in the first place. I looked into Ursuline High School and Gilmore Academy, but neither seemed a right fit. Sabria began to question herself, and her love for the game was disappearing. Her stats weren't what they should have been because she wasn't given time on the court. Her team was losing games, and everyone expected her to do great things for this team, but because of the coach's power trip, she was stuck and not able to use her potential to bring any success to herself or her team. She came to me one day and said, "Mom, I am beginning to hate basketball. I don't even want to play anymore." She began crying and didn't understand how the thing she loved most in life was something she now dreaded. Basketball was part of her identity. It was understandable that she didn't know herself anymore because she didn't know the game anymore like she did before. She wasn't allowed to enjoy it. It always felt so right and natural to play; but now, because of all the drama and negativity surrounding basketball, she could no longer find enjoyment in it and just wanted it to be over. I was distraught and really disgusted with the situation. Two other girls, both seniors and good players, had already quit the team because they, too, lost interest and would not tolerate the coach's behavior. I watched from the stands when Sabria was shoved or yanked by her jersey when the coach got upset. She was reprimanded when she shot a three-pointer because the coach said she wasn't allowed to do that. There was a time when the coach got so angry that she kicked over the whole Gatorade water stand during a game as all the players looked on in dismay. We watched as Sabria deteriorated before our eyes, and as parents, we felt helpless.

I prayed for her, talked with her, and tried to support her through this; but she began to suffer socially, academically, and spiritually. I don't like confrontation, but once again, trouble found me. I remember being at home and getting the call from Sabria's coach. By now I was picking up the pieces of my daughter and dealing with personal issues with her that stemmed from her feelings of self-doubt. I was ready and willing to talk to the coach. I answered the phone and spoke on a very personal basis, which I had never done before with her. She began by saying that she heard a rumor that Sabria was leaving the school and possibly going to Ursuline. I corrected her by saying that it, in fact, was not a rumor and not a secret at all. I also enlightened her by saying that Ursuline was only one of the many schools we looked into already for Sabria. If she knew Sabria at all and cared about her as an athlete, she would have seen the deterioration in her and would have worked to help her. I told her that I was looking for a way to best help Sabria to thrive as an athlete and young lady and that I wasn't willing to subject her to the abuse she was receiving from her, even being taunted because of her desire to leave the school that was holding her back from reaching her potential. I told her she had held my daughter back long enough and that she was gracefully given the privilege to coach one of the best basketball players in Ohio and she had not taken that gift seriously. I explained that, not just I, the entire community was questioning her motives and qualifications in her position as Sabria's coach and I was tired of trying to answer the question as to why Sabria was not on the court, a privilege she most certainly earned and was most qualified to have. She had pushed Sabria to the point of not even wanting to play the game, and I would not sit idly by and watch her dreams get flushed down the toilet. I told her that she basically destroyed Sabria's season, because her stats did not represent the player she was. She had the right to prove herself on the court, and that right was taken away from her. I also mentioned the other girls that quit, and she said that since those girls had quit, this gave the coach the opportunity to put Sabria on the court. I told her it was too late and that the season was already ruined and almost over. She tried to correct me by saying there was still half of the season left. I said, "No, there is a quarter of the season left, and you've wasted three-fourths of it." Not to mention the fact that I was disgusted with her talk of those other girls as if them being forced out of the sport was a justified act and implied that it was good because it now opened a spot for Sabria on the court, as if Sabria needed an opening in the first place. She said, "I will put Sabria on the court." I told her that was a good move and that was the least she could do. I told her hopefully Sabria was still willing to play the game. Up till now, she thought of only playing travel ball where the game is played fair—a place where your discipline and hard work is rewarded with time on the court and respect. There is no drama there; there's no freshman or senior. If you perform and listen, you play.

There was a girl who was very impressive in fifth grade (Shyanne Sellers) whom Sabria played with at SMAC. She was three years younger than Sabria but often played with the girls who were four years older than her and at the elite level. This was because her talent and skill allowed for this, and she wanted to be challenged and was a good asset to any team she played with. Several years later and just recently in 2020, she would be recruited to the University of Maryland. For Sabria's coach to tell me a spot needed opened for her to play just magnified her lack of vision in the world of basketball. I just wanted her to put Sabria on the court and get out of the way—that's it. What's in a reputation if there are no actions to back it up, and how can there be actions when you are chained up on the sideline? This allowed me to look at stats a different way. I don't completely believe in them, because politics poisons their reliability. We are not always able to see the full potential of a player by looking exclusively at their stats. They are not a complete reflection of a player. In a perfect world with coaches who know how to coach and players who know how to pass and play the game with honor and dignity, yes, stats would be completely accurate; but we don't live in a perfect world. I had watched a show on TV where a very respected women's basketball coach had implied that there was a spot on his team for a young girl in middle school. Come to find out her dad was a famous basketball player. This was a college that mostly chose All-Americans, and the best of the best basketball players went there. How then could it be known that a girl in middle school would become good enough to go there? It's called politics, and it's an ugly thing. I have lost much respect for many so-called coaches over the years because they displayed the character of hypocrites. The truth is not in them. Yes, hard work and determination will get you far unless a famous person's kid wants that spot. I flushed everything that coach ever said down the toilet after watching that and vowed that I would never encourage any of my girls to ever go to that school. I was proud of the phone conversation that day that I had with Sabria's coach in her ninth-grade year—putting gossip, deception, and egos in their place. The challenge was far from over. This is why Sabria has never indulged in remotely breaking records or having amazing stats. She doesn't get too worked up about it, because she learned even when you are doing your best and striving, your lack of success may be caused from something you have no control over. Her fundamentals, knowledge of the sport, talents, and good work ethic were no match for a coach with an ego and agenda and a team that wished to sit on the new girl and teach her a lesson.

Sabria learned to strive to do her best even without the title or recognition, and if you can do that, you're a true athlete, and perhaps the reward will come in the end, but even if it doesn't, you were true to yourself, and God will be proud of your efforts. Not giving in to failure and pressing on even when things seem glim is how you grow and reach success. This is what we said to Sabria to try and encourage her, but she was a shattered girl. That season in basketball forced her compass into a tailspin. She picked the wrong friends, trusted boys who said they cared about her but treated her badly, and lost vision of who she was. I was looking at the shadow of a girl I once knew and had no idea how we had gotten so offtrack. I was despondent over Sabria's crushed spirit and didn't know how to help her. She finished the season clinging to the little bit of joy she could find in the game. We weren't sure what to expect in the future concerning basketball. Her grades were dropping, and she didn't seem to care or have the energy to bring them up. She began getting herself into some trouble and couldn't see that she needed to make a change. Her self-esteem was low, and she was depressed. All she had to offer the world, and she couldn't see it. Her dad and I were constantly having to redirect, which was grueling. I had called my dad on the phone and said I didn't know how much more I could handle with this kid. He encouraged me, and I told Sabria that she had five siblings watching her and she needed to change her ways and realize the value and importance in herself and her position. I looked at the shell of my once strong and beautiful daughter and watched her admit the truth as she said, "I know, Mom! I can't help myself! I don't know what to do!" I knew I was losing my daughter, and that, I was not willing to do. I looked right at her and said, "Well, I can help you, and I will! From now on, this is going my way. If someone comes to this house and shows their face, one of those who are aiding in your hopelessness, I will make them leave. None of your so-called friends who are acting out will come to my house and disrespect my daughter. That's it. I'm done." I was separating Sabria from everyone and everything so she could cleanse her soul. She wanted a fresh start, and I knew it. She wanted to be rescued from this misery, and I would not rest until my daughter was safe, God's way. I said, "You can tell that boy (her boyfriend at the time) he is not welcome here. He has treated you like crap and disgraced you and me and our entire family for the last time. He better never show his face on my property again." I knew in my heart if Sabria was going to survive this, I would have to go hard on her. My position as her mother was more important right then than my friendship with her. In fact, I realized I was going to show her what a true friend was. No more being nice to her boyfriend and buying him Christmas presents and giving him rides here and there. He was using us and using her. Her fake friends were using her. No more. We started to monitor her phone 24/7, and she was locked down. Her dad was on board, and we took her phone and rummaged through it consistently, letting her know we would not be made fools out of and her little friends would prove to be no match for her parents who loved her more than she could imagine and we were ready to go through the fire with her. She didn't really mind the siege, though. She gave me attitude, but Sabria was very bullheaded, a true leader, and I knew if she really wanted to fight me, she would have won. This was how I knew she trusted me and trusted God. She knew she needed the help, and she was willing to give everything up for a fresh start.

As soon as I saw that Sabria was giving me some leverage to help her change, I jumped on it. Was she in it for the long hall? I didn't know, but I was, and my endurance and perseverance would be enough to be her asset through this storm, like she had been to so many others when they needed help. God would be my strength. I would not give up, and I knew God was stronger than all her little fake friends and little boyfriend. I will tell you that for months it was painstakingly hard. I would take one step ahead and take two steps back. She didn't believe that she was worth the fight, but I prayed for her constantly and told her she was in God's hands. We did have to fight off the demons, so to speak. At our family meetings, we talked about our problems and hopes for the future, so this is how we stayed focused even through times of despair and doubt. She was supersensitive and vulnerable through this time of healing, so even the slightest letdown from one of her real friends was hurtful to her. The ex-boyfriend tried to make amends, and we had to battle through that, too, as Sabria still wanted to trust him and believed good could come from a relationship with him even though negativity was the only result every time. He would no way be given another chance. I held firm to my anchor, and as I suspected, he was not strong enough to continue fighting. This struggle went on for months, and it was kind of like a game of tug-of-war. But I would not let go. Bobby and I did not waver in the battle for our daughter; and we were both fighters till the end in our hopes to rescue Sabria and restore her hope in herself, God, and her dreams. We gave up everything, time, money, freedom. Everything revolved around Sabria and our family unit. Sabria and I had little arguments, but we started really talking about everything, even things we didn't want to talk about. We brought out the ugly and dealt with it. We prayed that Sabria would be renewed by God's cleansing power and that she would be restored to be able to find her way in the world.

That summer in travel basketball, she came alive again. We were so thankful for her smile. Coach Carlos and Coach Andre never doubted in Sabria's abilities, but Sabria had to believe in herself. They were always encouraging to her and expecting the very most she could offer, and Sabria needed this pressure in order to keep her focus and to redirect her compass. There is controversy in travel sports. Is it necessary? I say follow your heart. I can say that, because we had such amazing coaches and met some really great athletes, it helped my daughter to align herself athletically, socially, physically, and spiritually, as it really helped her to see that God had a plan for her. It also helped push her to her limits and beyond and gave her self-confidence and self-worth. During her time of finding herself, she was met by her coach once in the middle of the court at a game, and he got in her face and asked her when she was going to start acting like an f——king woman. We all laugh about it to this day; and this, Sabria will tell you, is what she needed, and she never forgot this experience. He turned the switch on. Everyone has a switch. You can leave it off or turn it on. That day on the court, Coach Carlos gave Sabria the *permission* to be the woman she wanted to be—permission to unlock the chains that held her down, and this was something she used to get her through this downtime in her life. Knowing that people do believe in you and see your worth is powerful, and it can change your course if you let it. Being back at the elite level of basketball where everything seems clearer to an athlete was what she needed, and she remembered what Coach Carlos asked her that last season on the court. She finally realized that she could be whatever she wanted to be, and she held that power. Her coaches in Cleveland would tell her that she was not there without reason and she needed to woman up to the challenge. These coaches were vital to restoring Sabria's self-image. They expected her to bring her best to the court, and only her best was enough. Whenever I talked to Coach Carlos, I would thank him for working with Sabria. He would respond by saying that he was blessed. He would then thank me for the opportunity of working with my daughter. He always referred to us as family. I told him that he helped us raise Sabria, and he told me that it takes an army. Sabria's coaches at SMAC are the epitome of what a great coach is. They always gave good advice to her and words of encouragement during regular season and off-season. They never stopped coaching. They lived it. They would even come to watch her play at her high school when they had the chance and were proud of her efforts. They taught her the meaning of a true friend, family, and team. When she asked Carlos for advice about whether or not to leave Fitch, he responded with a question: which would be harder, to leave or stay? She said to stay would be harder. "Well, there you go. That's what you should do," he said. Sabria agreed, and she and Carlos thought the same. He helped her see the value in herself and to believe she had what it took to stay. Staying and hitting the challenge head-on would be more beneficial for Sabria, her teammates, and the program at Fitch. This way she could be an inspiration to her siblings and the other kids in the school system; and this was what it was all about, anyway—not stats but inspiring, teaching, loving others through the sport.

After the travel season, we heard of the high school coach leaving and a new coach taking her spot. We were hopeful and on a mission. Sabria was excited to start the year off and continued on the road of recovery. She and this new coach bucked heads a little at first, but this was the start of a beautiful relationship. I knew this program needed a coach like this to train the girls. Sabria still had some residual attitude left over from the year before, but I knew what she'd been through and how far my girl had come; and now she was not only my daughter and my friend but was something even more amazing, my better half, even a prodigy. I would have her back to the very end, and nothing could ever break that bond we had. That season went as good as it could with a new coaching staff and some resentment, harsh feelings, and negativity left over from the year before. The coach called me one day to tell me he was upset with something Sabria said after the last game as the season ended. As she was walking off the court, she had made the comment that she was glad the season was over. He said that she had poor body language and that was something she needed to be careful about because college coaches want to see good body language and this was an attribute of good character. I told him I appreciated the phone call and I respected him as a coach. I told him I had no problem with what Sabria said after the game and that her body language could use a little work but that it would come. I do believe he was shocked at my response. I explained that Sabria was just being honest and he needed to realize that being on that team wasn't exactly a great experience for Sabria in the recent past and, quite frankly, I shared in this same feeling of being glad the season was over. I basically felt like we were cleaning up and rebuilding from a hurricane and this rebuilding would take time. Sabria had come a long way. There was too much drama associated with high school basketball at that school, and we were glad to get a break from it. She was glad to start travel basketball again because her experiences there are inviting, drama-free, and fun. It's all about the game of basketball and polishing your skills and learning about teamwork, leadership, and the value of pushing yourself to your limits and beyond. There, she could play real basketball, which meant no drama and no politics.

There it was just girls coming together to play the game. Some girls traveled several hours just to get to practice twice a week to play the game. Sabria and the girls on her travel team learned a real respect for themselves, their parents, and the game of basketball. I told him to reduce the drama associated with the sport at the school and make it more of a privilege to play the game. Sabria appreciated the respect the girls at SMAC had to give up their time and their summers to go to other states to play their best. It's an honor to walk onto the court, and this attitude is shared with the girls who travel. I believed that Sabria's body language would change when the girls started to respect the court and the game of basketball, instead of always thinking about themselves. Even if they didn't, Sabria would continue to learn to lead, and I knew this would be displayed by her attitude and body language. It would come. I saw so much growth in Sabria over that last year that worrying about anything at this point, after all she'd been through and conquered, seemed petty. Her heart was right. I told him that I believed he was a God-send to us and to the team. Sabria needed coach Schnurrenburger, and so did the Fitch program. I told him of some things that Sabria had dealt with in the last year and that she was on the road to healing and learning self-worth. I told him she respected him and saw new hope in him for basketball at Fitch and this was just the beginning. I knew she would give him her best, and he needed to challenge her, and they would make a good team. I trusted Dan and knew I could be honest with him, and he would take what I said the right way. He knew I wanted the best for the team and Sabria. Sabria saw how I stood up for her and yet showed respect to her new coach who she wanted to impress, and this deepened our relationship and her trust in me. She did listen to me about body language and understood the importance of it and agreed to work on it. She trusted and respected Dan as her coach and wanted to be accountable and was learning how to be what she saw she could be. She could see that I was a good friend to her and had her back but stayed honest about her shortcomings. She appreciated that I made the coach aware of Sabria's position, and she believed it let him see her heart better and her passion that ran deep. He could now connect with her on a high level because she wanted the challenge, and I could help her with her attitude by explaining to her that the coach is represented by Sabria's actions. So she needed to be careful about how she represented her coach. I told her that being a good teammate meant having a good attitude on and off the court and that it did matter. What she was doing while she wasn't playing the game did matter. After this, she finally put a complete end to the relationship with that certain boy. Whatever was left of communication, which wasn't much, was gone. I believe she saw that she could trust me by her side and she didn't need him. She saw the contrast between a good man, like her coach, who wanted the best for her and wanted her to respect herself and others and the boyfriend who always used her and ended up hurting her every time in the end. Her Papa, both travel coaches, HS coaches, her brothers, and many more were all good men in her life who gave her examples of what a good man is; and they were enough for her. She found that she didn't need a boyfriend. I learned through this that kids have a hard-enough time learning who they are and parents who encourage their kids to have boyfriends or girlfriends are stunting their kids' growth. It is a bad idea. Encourage your child to indulge in their relationship with their family and God, and leave those fantasy love connections alone. It is not reality and will distract your child from reaching important milestones. It will appear to be a good idea or harmless, but it will suck your child in. Kids need to learn to take good care of themselves and learn to be a good leader before getting trapped into a relationship that yields no benefits but requires much energy and attention. This is my advice. Sabria and I continued to work out together, and she started going to Bible studies on Thursdays at my dad's house where she made good friendships and gained confidence in her purpose. She began to deepen her faith and understand the world around her and why people act the way they do. It helped her to start to see God's plan for her life. As she saw the path God had her on, she began to grow fond of her scars. She did not feel guilty of her past but knew that her battle wounds were part of her journey and God was still molding her even through her downfalls. He never left her and always loved her. She started to pay close attention to how she looked to others and knew she was on a mission to display God's love to the world. It became more about how to serve others and how to use the game of basketball as her mission field.

Jump stretch helped keep Sabria aligned and focused during her high school years. Jump stretch is an athletic circuit training program using rubber bands that create resistance to promote gains in strength, flexibility, agility, and speed and also to prevent injury. We were introduced to this class at the perfect time. I was just getting to the YMCA one day when Coach Carl came up to me and told me about the program that was offered there. It was an old program that was started several decades earlier by Coach Dick Hartzell in Youngstown but new to the Y at that time. I knew this program would help Sabria to get to the next level and would be a good tool for her. She and I signed up for the class together. We were intrigued. It was very challenging, and we were able to see a difference early on in her lateral movement on the court and in her overall conditioning, flexibility, and an increase in her vertical jump. We went twice a week together, and some days we wanted to skip it because it was so grueling and intense, but we stayed committed because we knew the hard work would pay off and she'd be a step ahead on the court. After the classes, we would walk out to the car and say, "That was the hardest class ever!" We'd say this after almost every class. Every class seemed harder than the last, and they never got old. We were always learning new things and taking our bodies to the next level. This was a healthy lifestyle for us, and while I was pushing Sabria, I was staying healthy too. We continued to go to the classes, and before long, we were taking the other kids too. She was learning to be a leader, and she began to complain less and pushed her siblings to get better. She began to indulge in taking care of her family, and our bond began to grow. The kids liked the attention they got from their sister, and we enjoyed our family time together getting healthy and more athletic. The classes were built for kids ages ten and up. Every month, I paid the ten bucks per kid (which was a discount because we had a Y membership). I signed up myself, Sabria, Dylan, Sophia, and Theresa. This was an extra fifty dollars a month to budget, but this is the kind of thing I spent money on. We weren't a family who went to the movies much or went shopping. We always tried to do something athletic together because this was a healthy way to spend time together—laughing, learning, loving. It also kept me, their parent, at their side and available to talk or help them through struggles they were having. They knew they could trust me, and this was important. We grew more bonded through jump stretch. Coach Carl would always find ways to enlighten the class. He explained things and gave advice in class to the kids and talked in ways they could understand and made them feel that he believed in them but also let them know they needed to believe in themselves in order to succeed. He would say that your biggest competitor should be yourself. No one in the class really compared themselves to the one next to them. If you were running next to them, you were definitely racing, but it was only to measure yourself and to help you get to your next level. It had nothing to do with beating your neighbor. This way of thinking was so that no one could boast. He would say, if the workout was easy, you're not working hard enough; if the workout was too hard, you're out of shape. This was how an athlete could continuously grow and never put a cap on their potential, which is key to having hope in an athlete's future. It was never okay to slack off. It was important to always bring 100 percent of yourself to a workout because how hard you work in training will be reflected on your play in the game or in the competition. These workouts were crucial to Sabria's development as a young woman. She wanted to be challenged. She wanted to be accountable for showing results to someone who believed in her and invested their time and energy to train her and lead her by giving her benchmarks. We always said thank-you to Carl after class for kicking our butts. Carl was someone sent to our family from God and at the perfect time. God knew I needed help raising these kids, and when he calls you to do something, he sends resources and doesn't let you go it alone. Carl is a great resource and friend to our family. Sabria had a few really bad ankle sprains over the years. He taught her how to prevent them but also how to treat one if it did happen to have the least amount of downtime. He showed her how to use bands to aid the ankle in healing. The technique is to tightly wrap the ankle with a compression band, which restricts the blood flow, and then use resistance bands attached to the wrapped ankle, and rotate the ankle back and forth and side to side for about a minute or two. This will help remove old blood from the area and release tension, swelling, and joint stiffness, even as it's done immediately following an ankle sprain. Once you release the wrap, new fresh blood rushes to the area to battle the trauma.

As the Bible tells us, there is healing in the blood. This is true about our bodies, as well as our spirits. God gives us ways of understanding his love for us, and even through an injury, he wants to help us. God shed his blood for us on the cross; and this was to make us pure, cover our sins, and heal us, giving us redemption (Ephesians 1:7). When our bodies get injured, it is a reminder that God provided a way to recover from injuries. He had a plan before the injury even happened. Everyone wants to jump to ice after an ankle sprain, but I saw Sabria's downtime was significantly diminished using heat, compression, and resistance bands. It hurts like hell to move that foot around, but doing this a couple of times a day is worth the effort if you want to play. One specific tournament we went to, she rolled her ankle the first night. We were devastated over the idea that the entire weekend may be ruined and Sabria held back by this ankle injury. She remembered what Carl taught her, and she was determined to fix this and play. We went to a local store in that area and purchased bands and Epsom salts. We went back to the hotel and worked the heck out of that ankle, and her team was shocked to see her walking on that ankle the next day and asked if she was okay. She played every game that weekend, soaking it in warm water and Epsom salts and doing the exercises with compression, and had no downtime from that bad sprain. Once we got home, she rested it. She was amazing to me that weekend, and I respect her dedication and toughness. Sabria treated her body like it was God's temple. God was teaching her to respect and protect it and use it to serve him. That comes with much responsibility and the more she was willing to learn, the more God would show her. I knew it hurt. It was badly bruised, and she grumbled through the pain. But she wouldn't let it keep her off the court. Her friends would call her after that if they had an ankle sprain and were in a pinch and wanted to play. Not all athletes will do this technique, because it requires determination and a strong desire to succeed. I appreciate that I was able to witness this in my daughter. Sabria learned to trust Carl, and he and she developed a good friendship and bond over the years as she was able to extend the same love to others that Carl extended to her. She was learning and indulging in all that God was putting in her path; and these experiences of hardship followed by opportunities to grow and people to guide you in the right direction were the perfect recipe for Sabria to get out of the rut from ninth through tenth grade. After that, she was unstoppable, and that was the hope that kept me strong for that year and a half. The diligence had paid off, and as I always saw Sabria as beautiful and with great purpose, she now saw it for herself, and this was a true miracle to witness. This was the new creature that was born, and this is the girl I have been talking about in this book. She was moving on and doing what she had hoped to do and learning to love her body as God's temple and becoming a living sacrifice for him for the sake of others. He was her hero as she was becoming one herself to others. This is how the love of God can spread to the world. I tell this part of the story so that people can see that God uses the broken. No one is without a past or without failure. No one is perfect, and as we get broken down, God can build in us a most beautiful masterpiece.

CHAPTER 19

LIVING IN GRACE AND ENJOYING THE JOURNEY

All the times I stood by Sabria's side and helped her see the silver lining were experiences she could share with others. I saw the fruit of my labor the day I met with the pediatric orthopedic surgeon who would repair my son Quintin's knee. It was the beginning of November 2019 when we were in the office. I sat across from my nine-year-old son as he was wearing the oversized paper shorts he was issued, and I was wishing we weren't in this place. His face told the story of a little boy loving life but struggling to play and live life with a leg that just didn't work the same anymore. For the past five weeks, he had stopped playing sports, used the elevator at school, and never knew when that leg would decide not to hold his body up anymore and send him without warning crumbling to the ground. He sat very quietly as we waited for the doctor to come in and discuss this thing that had taunted us for the last month. The doctor came in and sat down. He looked at me and Quintin and, with concern in his voice and with compassion, carefully explained to us about Quintin's injury. He used the sculpture sitting on the counter to show us what Quintin's knee was like before, what it was like now, and the process to fix it. He gave us options and then looked at me and said that, basically, Quintin is never going to have the knee he was born with. That knee is gone and can never return. He said they could do their best to give Quintin the best knee possible but wanted me to understand that it will never be the knee it was before. He said that this was such a serious injury for such a young boy. He said that there may be things in life that he just cannot do. I had to bite my lip and hold back my tears, and as the doctor handed me a tissue, I had tried to be strong as I did not want my son to think this was a time to be sad but instead to have faith and be tough. I was so very sad to hear that my boy was in this situation, and I just had a hard time hearing what this doctor was telling me, although I so appreciated his honesty. The doctor did not want to give me any false hope because he could not promise me that this would go as we hoped, but he did tell me that he could promise he would do his very best to give Quintin a restored knee that hopefully would do everything Quintin desired it to do for him. I knew in my heart that this man would go with Quintin into the operation but that God would be the surgeon and would work through this wonderful man to restore and repair my son's knee and it would not be the same knee he was born with, it would be a better one. We decided to go forward with the surgery as Quintin's knee was going out on him all the time, and there was no question that this needed done. The doctor set him up for surgery and gave him a brace, and out we went.

I took Quintin to Chick-fil-A afterward at his request, and we sat down to eat. Sabria happened to call me right then. I was so relieved to talk to her, and I could not hold back my emotions this time and didn't care who was around. I just started balling my eyes out in the middle of the restaurant. Quintin just stayed quiet as I explained what the doctor had told us. She was quiet for a second, and I'm sure she was wiping her own tears at the thought of what our little buddy was going through and how he was injured so badly. Sabria said, "We know that the doctor can't promise a full recovery, but God can. He's the one doing the surgery, anyway. If Quintin's book says his knee will be perfect, then it will be perfect again. Trust him." She started talking to Quintin and encouraging him, and he started smiling. This all made perfect sense to me. Sometimes we put too much pressure on ourselves and think that our actions are going to change our existence, but our stories are already written, and God is the author. We just need to go through the story day by day being confident in God's strength and wisdom. He knows what we need even before we know we need it. He's already prepared a way through the struggles.

Sabria's faith in the situation with Quintin gave me hope that she was confident in her position on the basketball team. When I was on the phone with her, she was telling me how she had been having such a busy week with much on her plate and getting ready to leave for games in Arizona and Colorado. She was still so focused, and the fact that she could transition herself to a family event and talk to her mom with such grace and wisdom told my heart she was okay. She wasn't a starter yet; but I know that she knew that if God wanted her to be a starter, she would be and if it was in her story to be a starter, then that's what would happen. She trusted the author of her book and was living day by day faithful to stay the course of her journey. Everything she had been through in her past had proven to her that God had her back. I was so thankful he was my endurance to persevere back when she was in high school and was trying hard to find herself and her great purpose and position in life. Years later, I was so thankful that I stuck by her side and was strong enough and willing to be used by God to help my daughter and not give up on her. What a humbling experience to see what a beautiful life she is graciously living and that she appreciates the journey. God does give us the desires of our heart if we truly pursue to be found in him. James 4:3 reads, "When you ask, you do not receive, because you ask with wrong motives, that you may spend what you get on your pleasures." Sabria understood that when you learn to serve God, he will give you the desires of your heart, so having selfish motives is never necessary. You will never lack in anything, and you will find real peace and contentment when you choose to put God's plan above yours. If you are struggling in life with a certain thing and you can't seem to figure out why you don't seem to be getting what you want from God, search your heart. God is waiting to lead you.

The third game that season would be against Air Force in Colorado. Sabria had a few things against her. She said when she was running it felt like her lungs were bleeding. Colorado is at a different elevation than New York; so this can cause things such as dehydration, headaches, shortness of breath, etc. It's important to stay hydrated. There was a two-hour time difference and a forty-five-degree change in temperature. We don't always take things into account when we're watching sports on TV, and up until now Sabria never had to play basketball under such circumstances, so this was interesting. Sabria said they were taking precautions and drinking lots of water. I told her to be careful and to listen to her body. I'm sure she was rolling her eyes as she said, "I know, Mom." The game came on, and the Hunter family gathered around the TV. I had sent her a text before the game that read, "Remember, today has already been written. Go through the day in confidence that God knows what you need before you even need it." The game started, and Air Force was slowly gaining the lead. Before too long, they had a good lead as Sabria came off the bench and started to play basketball. She always plays better when she has a reason to try, and she enjoys a challenge. She was making a presence on the court and working to help close the gap. She was fouled right before halftime and landed on the ground, but the refs didn't call the foul. I watched her as she smacked the ground with both hands, furious, and that's when I knew, she was coming alive! The kids and I were cheering and saying, "Oh, man! Here comes Bri. She's pissed! She's gonna come out hard in the second half ready to slay!" We knew our girl, and we were right. She came out and scored the first six points of the second half! I jumped off the couch with both arms in the air; and our whole house was cheering, screaming, and jumping all over the living room for our hero! It was a 10-0 run for Army in the third quarter. They kept plugging away and closing the gap. They ended up winning that game by two points after being down by twenty-one points! *How did they come back from that?* I thought. Grit and passion played a huge role. The Air Force coach admitted that it looked like her girls ate sushi and West Point ate steak and potatoes. She believed her team had better players and talent but that West Point had more brute. I believe it takes more than what you eat or how much power you have to win games. Sure, eat right, get tough, but if you don't have attributes of heart, you can't win games. To come back from a twenty-one-point deficit is crazy! The kind of determination and perseverance it takes to do this is special. Sabria had her first career double-double in that game, thirteen points and ten rebounds. Sabria led her team and once again did it after coming off the bench. Nothing could hold her back. She was named Patriot League Rookie of the Week on November 18, 2019. She was proving she was sold out on her mission to stay focused and give everything she's got for her team and coaches—not for herself but for them. She was ready to be a useful tool, dependable and able.

Don't wait for people to believe in you. Give people a reason to believe in you. Make a move, even if it's just one, because that one move can lead to another and before long, you're moving along the path you hoped to be on. Sometimes you won't get to your goal right away, but that's not a reason to lose heart or give up, because as you keep trying, you're building perseverance, which is a wonderful tool to use. Imagine all the tools you'll pick up on your journey if you don't give up. Sabria sent out a family text that read, "I'm starting!" She was now a starting five! I was so proud, and I told her to lead by example. I told her to be contagious and encourage the other girls to lead too. Her team is going to be something great with leaders all around. They are all growing, and all have so much to offer. I hope those girls find that inner beast and work on their own to be better for the whole. This is the best way to form chemistry of a great team, in my opinion. Many times, on my journey of raising my kids, I am reminded of the story in the Bible of Peter walking on the water. Walking out of the boat to Jesus when he called, took faith but as his fear distracted him, he began to sink. Jesus was right there to catch Peter. We all get distracted at times and are afraid to take on projects that seem too scary. Even sometimes we will walk in faith and then get distracted as Peter did, and we fall offtrack. Jesus never leaves us and wants us to succeed. He will always catch us when we fall, so we should never be afraid to take that leap of faith. This brings me much hope on my journey. If people ever ask how you do the things you do in this life, you can just say, "Jesus keeps me afloat."

The next game was in Brooklyn, New York. Sabria had gotten her first double-double and was now going to be starting for the first time in college. Bobby and I didn't want to miss it. We made the drive with literally a few minutes to spare. I was driving through Brooklyn like I had done it a million times but had no idea what I was doing. We were doing another drive-by game. So Bobby and I, between our shifts at work, were just driving the 650 miles to Brooklyn, a ten-hour drive one way from our house; watching the game; then turning around; and driving back home. No money or time to spend the night in a hotel, but we didn't need to. We just needed to see our girl. As game time was approaching and I was mesmerized by all the smoke in the streets, steel staircases in the alley ways, and lots of trash bags lining the streets, I decided to choose a spot on the side of the street and park my car. I had no idea if I was even in a parking spot, but Bobby and I looked at each other and said, "Yep, looks good." We got out of the car and quickly went into the building to surprise Sabria since she didn't know we were coming. We walked into the arena and saw one of her friends down on the court as they warmed up, and she recognized us and whispered in Sabria's ear, and she looked up and saw us in the stands. I blew her kisses, and she smiled in disbelief. I brought her some things I knew she'd been hoping for (we always had a running list): popcorn, ramen, face cream, and pictures of her siblings—you know, the essentials. She didn't expect to get that package that night or to see us, but we hoped it brought her comfort. This was a good night. Making that drive was crazy, but to be honest, I don't remember much of it, only the experience and seeing Sabria.

I enjoyed seeing Brooklyn as it seemed familiar to me. An old rustic, noisy city. Reminded me of my childhood in Youngstown, where I lived, on the West Side up the hill from the old mill. The Coke Express train ran through the bottom of my street, so we had lots of noise in my neighborhood. My dad always took me down there to the "tracks," and we walked those tracks and under the big bridges for hours, just investigating. We always found really awesome rocks that I'd like for whatever reason and would take home with me to add to my self-admired collection. My kids now bring rocks home from there still today when my dad takes them there, to the tracks, to investigate. The bridges in Brooklyn took me back to my childhood. To this day, I find trains as a source of comfort because they remind me of good times with my dad. Sometimes if I have trouble sleeping, I put train sounds on my phone, and it just plays as I fall asleep. It takes me back to my bed at night in that house in Youngstown when I'd have the window cracked, just enough to hear the sweet noises of the night and feel the soft breeze of summer. I would wait with patient anticipation to hear my dad's footsteps as he came up the stairs to tuck me in bed at night and got down on his knees next to my bed to listen as I said my prayers and talked out my concerns or worries from the day. He would hug me and tell me good night. I was then left to fall asleep but not before waiting for the comfortably consistent and predictable appointment the train made with me as I heard it coming—the screeching of those steel wheels of the cars against the tracks and the bumping and moving of that locomotive, which was very rhythmic and satisfying to me and was just what I needed to help finish off those childhood presleep anxieties. The train ran through our town, it seemed like, several times a day; and I always loved to hear it. Sometimes we kids in that neighborhood would yell, "Train!" when we heard it coming, and we'd all run down the steep hill of our street to watch it close-up, letting the wind, from its force, blow through our hair and easing in the calm after our heightened adrenaline rush. I felt at home in Brooklyn and appreciated this trip God made possible for me to take, reminding me of my childhood.

This was a good game, and I was proud of Sabria. I had realized Sabria's form looked a little sloppy, and she really looked tired. A man from one of the papers in that city came up to Bobby and me and started talking, and we shared why we were there. He said he couldn't help but wonder why Army's bench was so long. He asked Bobby and me why they recruited so many girls, and it struck me with wonder as well. I said that with the rigor of the program, maybe they expected to see a lot of injuries since these were soldier girls whose bodies go under much stress in the program. He seemed unsettled by my comment, and I became unsettled then, too, after I thought about it. *I hope my daughter will be safe*, I thought. Why would I assume that just because a program was rigorous, injury would be a possibility or threat? This should not be a common assumption, and I didn't know why I even thought that way. Was this why the bench was deep? So that the team had enough players to still have games after all the injured girls were out recovering? It was something I couldn't get out of my mind, but I did focus that night on Sabria and the task at hand, to give her encouragement and support.

The next couple of games were good, and the girls were really getting into it. After a game against TCU, a little girl came up to Sabria and asked for her autograph. Sabria's first autograph signing, how cool! This was Tuesday, November 26. This is what it was all about, to make an impact and be a positive influence. This is how you use the game of basketball to make the world a better place. Encourage and teach the little ones to have a good attitude and lead by example. It's not about stacking your *stats*. It's about loving your teammates and those watching. Sabria would rather make a good pass to assist the shot rather than make the points if passing would have a better effect. She didn't want to be selfish with her play, because this was not good to teach the little ones who watched or her teammates who wanted to know she saw their worth. Sometimes you'd see her under the hoop with her arms spread like an eagle to ward off opponents so her teammate could get a rebound. She would make a wall with her body, not letting anyone in, after the shot went off. I would tell Sabria to do what she could to love her team. Do your job, use your resources, get creative, and think outside the box, I would tell her. Do what makes sense. If you don't have position to get a rebound, don't just box out; be a wall. She became like an eagle. Isaiah 40:30 says, "They that wait upon the Lord shall renew their strength, they shall mount up with wings as eagles, they shall run and not be weary, and they shall walk and not faint." This verse reminds me of Sabria on the court. This is the only way I think the game should be played. Anything less is not worth anyone's time. She would go through the last quarter and the last minutes giving everything she had till the end. This was what she trained for. Coach Carl would always say that games are won in the fourth quarter. That's when the truest athletes compete because only the toughest have what it takes to play well through to the end. That's when all the blood, sweat, and tears become worth it. He would also say that if you don't sweat in class, you'll bleed in the game and you don't need to be scared to sweat, because no one ever drowned in their own sweat.

The day before Thanksgiving, Sabria's team lost their privilege to use the locker room. They use the locker room to eat, take naps, and shower. By the time Sabria had gotten to the locker room to see that it was locked, it was too late to make other arrangements to eat. Since they are not allowed to leave the base; the mess hall was a thirty-minute round trip of walking, a journey that would have required two changes of clothes; and plebes are required to wear their uniform whenever walking from one destination to the next, Sabria figured she would have to skip lunch. She had all of her travel belongings with her because her barracks closed up for the holiday, and she was moved to a transient barracks for the time being and had not moved yet to that barracks. She ended up sitting in the gym with no lunch, nowhere to lie down, and nowhere to put her bags. She doesn't usually vent to me about her dealings at West Point, because she doesn't want to worry me, and she also realizes that most times it's easier to not talk about it. Today was different. The chronic lack of sleep was catching up. She didn't get much sleep at night, so her naps during the day were crucial. She was going into practice tired and hungry and being punished for reasons that were unclear and seemingly unjust. She was overwhelmed and irritated. She had called me, feeling desperate, and I could hear in her voice she was discouraged and worn out. Using the locker room may sound simple, but to a cadet under these circumstances, it is like coming home after a long day of work and being locked out of your house. I couldn't even imagine this, and I was annoyed at the decision that was made to do this as it was not a constructive form of punishment, in my mind. I understood my daughter was a soldier and needed to be tough, but I couldn't see a connection between the punishment and an opportunity for growth. Even so, I tried to encourage her and be supportive from my position. Understanding that the game of basketball for Sabria was always an outlet for her frustrations and a way to see her issues in life a little clearer. I felt helpless as I could tell this was becoming a stressful area of her life, too, leaving her nothing to help her see clearly and nowhere to dump her frustrations; but I told her it would be fine and to focus on what she did have control over, not on things she couldn't change. God wants us to be in the now and look for direction in our time of trouble, not wallow in the discomfort that our trials bring. I told her to focus and to make sure to make it to the mess hall in time to get dinner because I wanted to make sure she ate a good meal that day as she needed the nutrition. I told her every day was special and to not let this ruin her attitude or her day. No one is promised tomorrow, so let God take care of you today. This was a team punishment, and she had no reason to feel guilty, since she wasn't involved in the actual act that was being punished. She just needed to go through it, not be part of it. She loved her team, so this needed to be no big deal for her. She just had to know it was only a moment in time. I told her siblings about her day, and they sent her Bible verses to encourage her.

Sabria did survive this day, as expected, and we were on our way the following day to pick her and her friend Kam up for Thanksgiving. They weren't given pass to leave West Point, because the basketball season didn't allow them enough time to make it home and back. This is why we made the plans to bring Thanksgiving to her. Sabria was so relieved to see us and was refreshed to get away from the base. We had planned two nights in a hotel and dinner out at a restaurant that served Thanksgiving dinner with all the fixings. It wasn't the same as home, but we were all together, and I don't think we could've asked for more. We went shopping together at the mall just for something to do, and when I looked around amazed at how good God was to me for bringing my whole family together, I looked down at my shoes; they were Quintin's. I told Bobby, "Hey, I wore Quintin's shoes today." They were nice shoes, my size, and looked good with my outfit; so I wore them. He had other shoes he preferred to wear, anyway. Bobby looked down at his feet and said, "These are Bri's." Sabria had a collection of nice shoes, and she wore Bobby's size. I then noticed that I had Theresa's shirt on, Sabria's pants, and Quintin's shoes. This was a moment that I stopped for a second and smelled the roses, like my grandma taught me to do.

Bobby and I gave everything we had to the kids. I rarely bought stuff for myself, and with six kids, there were always hand-me-downs that I made work for myself. My girls always share each other's clothes, and never do we have much money to buy new things at the store. One day, we did go into a fun store, and the kids did have some money to spend, and they bought each other friendship bracelets. I was really intrigued that even when given the opportunity to buy for themselves, they instead chose to buy for their sibling, who was, in fact, their friend. Kids do learn love, and we as parents need to hold firm to these teachings, too, so that we can continue to teach our kids what is really important in life. We as a family have never really shopped much, but we always have what we need. I've always taught my kids to focus more on what they do in life than on what they have in life. My sister would sometimes have a hard time buying Christmas presents for my kids because they could never think of anything to ask for. They would tell her simple things like a pair of fuzzy socks or a new pair of gloves. She would say, "Tina, your kids are so hard to buy for because they never know what to ask for other than simple things." I would laugh as my sister loved my kids and wanted to spoil them at Christmastime; but the truth was, they were so very content, learning that they could have fun and joy even when they weren't always buying new things. When they did get something new, they were very appreciative because they knew it came at a high cost for our family. They weren't kids that went without—always had a nice trampoline in the backyard, sports equipment, bikes, and, of course, necessary electronics. The rest, we didn't worry about. We don't go to the doctor unless we need to, because our health insurance is expensive and, in my opinion, a real rip-off. We end up paying out of pocket a lot, so we are careful and mindful of running to the doctor or ER. We learn to use sense and go to the doctor when it's necessary. We don't go on vacation but teach the kids to make fun wherever they are. We travel around enough with basketball and would rather take little day trips when the opportunity comes up to do so. This is how I believe one can learn to have passion in life and to be grateful and have a cheerful heart. This reminds me of a situation that proved to me that my kids were learning something more valuable than just fitting into a social class.

A few years back, Theresa was in fourth grade. I was invited to her school for an awards ceremony. I worked a lot, so to actually be off this day was special, and I was thankful for the opportunity. I don't believe that a kid should do anything just for the sake of winning an award, but sometimes it is encouraging to have the positive feedback as a young person. I figured I would go and show my support for all the kids at the school whether my daughter was getting an award or not. I made it to the cafeteria and joined the other parents who were there to support the kids and applaud them on their accomplishments. I sat down and tried to ignore the voice in my head telling me I didn't look as cute as the other moms. I don't have a lot of time to coordinate outfits, so most of my clothes are roughly thrown together, and I'm sure I often look disheveled, but I do try to look presentable for my kids. I sat down at a random table alone with tired eyes and waited to see my girl and hoping she would be happy to see me in the crowd as a proud supporter. I thought maybe she might get an award for a job well done in spelling or math and thought of little ways I could tell or show her I was proud. As they began calling up kids and passing awards out for the jobs well done, the kids' faces were bright, and their smiles were big. I was really happy to be a part of helping to boost their self-confidence. One of the teachers got up and spoke about being a good friend, what it means to be a leader, and a good example to others by our actions. She was giving a special award out that was called the FLIP award, which was given to someone who showed good character in the form of leadership and who displayed good behavior in the act of being a good friend and a good example to others. The teacher called up a young girl from the crowd. The little girl pulled out a letter she had written. As she read her letter out loud, she explained that she had diabetes. She talked about her routine at school which involved daily trips to see the nurse where she would get her blood sugar checked and receive her shot of insulin. She talked of a girl whom she considered her best friend because she went with her on her trips to see the nurse, and this gave her the support she needed to deal with this disease because she didn't have to be alone. As I listened to this story, it brought tears to my eyes to imagine the silver lining that was in the situation. The value of a friend was revealed to a young girl dealing with such a thing as diabetes and, as she struggled through the learning process, realized that it was possible to find balance and to live a good life even while dealing with a difficult disease. Through this process, she had found a good friend, and this made her life a little easier. *What a touching story*, I thought. She said that after going through this, she decided she wanted to be a nurse when she grew up. She then revealed that this special friend she spoke of was Theresa Hunter. My heart skipped a beat. My eyes welled up, and I gasped. Everyone clapped and cheered as Theresa walked up to receive this award. I was never so humbled. This was the fruit of my labor. This was relief for my tired body and eyes. As we stood up to applaud the kids and take pictures, my heart was full. I did not know that Theresa did this every day for this little girl, her friend. She was so genuine and did not think she was anything out of the ordinary. She was just being herself and following her heart. Being a nurse myself and always pushing my kids to serve others, I was just so overwhelmed and very proud of my sweet daughter for her actions. Sometimes as parents we hope our kids hear us and take the advice and teachings that we give, but we don't always get to see the effects, because we are so distracted and busy. We don't always know at the end of the day if what we do and say actually penetrates. This day, I was honored to be given the opportunity to slow down and see effects. Even though I worked long hours and I sometimes felt like I wasn't strong enough to be a good parent, God showed me that he was good enough and he had my kids in his hands. He would not let me fail at my biggest and most important job of teaching my kids to love one another as they are loved by God. I was not worthy of raising Theresa, and I knew that, but this day, God said to rest in his presence and find relief and to enjoy the gift of grace I was given from him to be her mom. This humility that I was taught by God through my kids was what pushed me to believe I could bring Thanksgiving to those two girls at West Point. It wasn't all planned in advance, and so I only had booked one hotel room. They were fine with this, and we played board games and talked until late at night, just enjoying the company of each other. It was two nights and three days for our whole family and Kam (nine of us) to relax in the now and take some pressure off the constant grind that came from the amazing program at the academy. It was another refreshing tall glass of water that we appreciated before getting back to work and preparing for our next big adventure of Quintin's ACL surgery.

CHAPTER 20

QUINTIN'S SURGERY

We made it to December 2, and it came time to take Quintin to have his surgery. We prayed for a miracle, and as I found myself once again sitting in the waiting room at Akron Children's main hospital, I was a little more comfortable being alone in an unfamiliar city and in the uncomfortable position of waiting for my son to come out of surgery. It had only been about six weeks since I was there with Dylan having his appendectomy, back on October 10. This time, I was in the waiting room trying to convince myself that I would have a way to somehow be off work when my son needed me and would have all the needed supplies to care for him at home. I was a nurse, but I knew that caring for a nine-year-old boy following ACL surgery would be no easy task. Our bathroom was on the second level, and as I knew that if there was probable meniscus involvement, he would not be allowed to bear weight for approximately six weeks. This meant he would have a straight leg brace from the top of the thigh to his ankle and must use crutches for the first six weeks following surgery. Using the toilet would be hard, and having the toilet on the second floor made it even harder. How could I keep him home with no help when I had scheduled shifts to work?

There was no one to watch him. There were so many things to think about, and I just paced around the waiting room hoping my son would be okay. I prayed for God to do a miracle in my life and to pull me through this experience as I was relying on his strength and direction and my family was depending on me to be a leader.

A few hours later, the doctor came out and told me that everything went beautifully. He said that, as expected, Quintin's meniscus was torn, as well as the ACL. He was able to repair both tears and was able to successfully use the IT band from that same leg to do the repair. He said he believed and was confident that Quintin would have a very good knee to use after it healed. I was very relieved as he smiled at me, and I could tell he was proud of his diligence as I could still see the indentations the gloves made on his hands from the long surgery. I so appreciated those hands that I knew God worked through to heal my son and give him another chance at an active life. I went back to the PACU to see my boy, and as I walked toward him, he smiled, and his voice cracked as he said, "Hi, Mom." He smiled and then closed his eyes. I watched as his bottom lip puckered out, and his chin quivered as tears streamed down his pink cheeks. He was in so much pain already. The nurse told him it was okay and that even big strong football players have pain and that he was doing a good job. She softly swiped her hand across the top of his head; and as her fingers moved through his hair, she encouraged him, teaching me how to love my son from the bedside, from a position she knew no mother wanted to be in. I looked at him in his pediatric gown that was covered with little Tiggers and his leg in that very recognizable black ACL brace that encased his brand-new knee, wondering how in the world we had ever gotten to this place. The next two nights in the hospital were intense. I would lie down for maybe thirty minutes before getting right back up to move his leg even an inch just to give him some kind of relief or hand him the urinal. I would answer questions like, "Mom, why does this hurt so bad?" or to calm him as he squeezed the bedsheets in that hospital bed and grumbled, "Mom, I hate this so bad. Please help me." The reality of this situation could only be seen now for my son, and he was really overwhelmed. We tried to watch movies to stay distracted from the obvious. I handed him my phone to show him an inspirational video of a young boy who also sustained an ACL injury and who told of his successful journey back. This did help to encourage my son even though he only had enough strength to deal with the now. That was okay. I myself only had enough in me to deal with the now, and together, we understood this battle. "Today" was the only day God had given us, and we would be hard-pressed and focused to not just survive each day but to strive and to fly as eagles through each day, giving it everything we had.

Before leaving the hospital, a physical therapist came to teach him how to use the crutches with one leg straight and without putting weight on it. She taught him how to use the stairs, which was terrifying to watch, and I decided right then that we would only do the stairs to get into and out the house, and that was it. I found my way back to my car and pulled it to the door to pick up my son after we were discharged. Even with the passenger front seat all the way back, it was excruciating to try to get that leg into the car, keeping it straight out in the brace. I was helping to hold the leg, and we squeezed it in and then propped it on several blankets because he was in too much pain to put his foot on the floor of the car. Even the man who brought him to the car felt compassion for my son, and I appreciated his kindness. This was an ordeal for sure. I just headed home because this was what I needed to do next. I was going one step at a time because taking one step was all I could do. He was on Percocet and Motrin around the clock, and I never left his side. Just like when he was a newborn, I parked myself on the recliner couch right next to him, knowing I'd be getting up constantly to tend to his needs, and this was what I was willing and ready to do. After a few days, he didn't need pain medicine and didn't like to take it. He really did impress me. I borrowed a portable toilet from family, and thank God, I had this to use for Quintin. He would not have made it without this. The only bathroom we had was on the second level and getting to it was impossible for him. The first time he had to use the toilet was a nightmare. He broke out in a sweat getting from the couch to the toilet, and he was yelling at me as he tried to get positioned. My poor son was in agony. His nine-year-old anatomy did not allow for him to use the bathroom the traditional way because the brace had to remain on and straight at all times, in order to not bend his knee and jeopardize the repair, and was in the way of everything functioning the way it needed to. I was stuck to my son's side, helping as I held his leg up and held the urinal as he had both hands on the handrails of the toilet. Sometimes as you try to go to the bathroom one way, the other way wants to work too, and this was the only way to manage both so that he didn't pee all over himself. Even if it was just a dribble, he could not stand to feel like he had no control over himself. He would cry in pain as this all was such a struggle. This was a moment I would cringe at what we were going through. He would yell at me and sometimes swear and apologize later, telling me he didn't mean it but that this situation was so hard. I held back tears as I looked at my once athletic, tough, cheerful, innocent son who was now a pile of misery and embarrassed to have me take care of him in this way and as he would have to breathe through the pain and give himself a pep talk just to get from the recliner to the toilet. He would say, "Mom, I hate this so bad. I'd rather be at school than do this!" I told him I understood and realized that would be our life for a while, later finding it would go on that way for the following five weeks. As I said before, God only gives us enough information to get us to take that step, in faith. Getting too much information up front is not necessary and could even induce fear. I am glad Quintin and I just took one day at a time, not knowing it would last so long.

That Friday had come quickly for Quintin and me. I had strongly advocated to get a therapy session scheduled on this day as recommended by the surgeon to prevent more downtime and stiffness from building up in his knee, and waiting through the weekend would have wasted precious time. We were only about four days postsurgery when we were headed to this appointment for physical therapy. He was unstable on those crutches, partly from not walking much over the last few days, partly because he was so uncomfortable, and partly because he was still on pain meds. Of course, it was wintertime in Ohio. We had to be careful as we walked on ice and through snow and slush to get back and forth to the car and using the stairs. I was trying to stay close to him; but if he slipped and I, too, slipped on ice, it would have been a disaster. Coming out of our house and walking down the stairs were terrifying. I just kept praying for God to help us. He vomited in the parking lot on the way into the office and then again on the way back out to the car, but thank God, he didn't fall on the ice or pass out. We met Dan that day for the first time. This would be Quintin's physical therapist for the next nine months. He was very encouraging and helpful. This appointment of us getting established in the PT office was important to me as I wanted to keep a clear line of communication open so that if questions or concerns came up, Quintin and I could address them efficiently. I was also given some teaching and advice on his dressing and incision care as questions had come up after we went home from the hospital. We made it home in time for me to get ready for my afternoon shift at work. I was able to leave Quintin for short periods when I knew the kids would be home from school soon or Bobby would be getting home from work, and usually these periods of time were under an hour. I was still working my shifts but remained available for Quintin and his needs. It was a miracle how God was able to manage my time for me. When times were rough, I told him it would be okay, but I really didn't see the light at the end of the tunnel. I relied on hope and persevered in faith. I had talked to the school to set up a time to go back. But after two weeks had passed, he still couldn't use the bathroom on his own, and it was such an issue. I would not chance him being embarrassed, so we decided to homeschool for the rest of the month. He ended up recovering at home for about six weeks. I actually never knew what day it was. I was so tired when I got up that I just knew that it was today. Every day became today. I continued to sleep in the living room with him in case he needed anything because I didn't want him to try to get up alone and have the chance of falling when he was tired and the room was dark, as he was off-balance at times. I knew he may try to do things on his own as he got better, and I wanted to be sure he was ready and had the help if he needed it. I was still working my shifts at the hospital, taking the other kids to their school and sporting events, cleaning the house, grocery, shopping, supporting Sabria, paying bills, and getting Quintin to therapy several times a week. The living room became his prison and the recliner, his bed. This room was the place where he would recover, go to the bathroom, and take sponge baths from his mom. I tried to preserve his self-worth, modesty, and privacy as we developed a bond that we didn't really want but did appreciate the strength and versatility it built in both of us. The Bible teaches not to worry about tomorrow for today has enough worries of its own, and this is where God kept me and Quintin, in today. I no longer even knew what tomorrow meant.

As I was at home very busy with Quintin, I still worried about Sabria and prayed for her often. When we had visited her for Thanksgiving a few weeks earlier, she had told me that she felt out of shape, and this continued to weigh on my mind as I took care of my son. Sabria's friend Kam had also vented this concern to me as well. We had all three talked, and I had told Sabria that she looked like her knees were bowing in again, and I had noticed it recently at the Brooklyn game. This specifically was concerning to me as this was something we worked to correct at home before she left for West Point. Coach Carl, in jump stretch, had noticed that her groin muscles and inner muscles of her legs were stronger than her outside muscles. This imbalance can be corrected by strengthening the weaker muscles, which she did. Now at West Point, the problem was back. She said that she had gained weight and felt unstable on the court. Since she hadn't been doing exercises that supported both inner and outer muscle strength in her conditioning there, she knew she wasn't conditioned well enough to keep her in good shape and lost some muscle mass, especially in her core. She was tired all the time, and this left her potentially vulnerable to injury. She was afraid she would end up getting hurt. Kam agreed that she, too, did not feel athletic. They said that as a team, they all felt uneasy and concerned as they were unable to maintain the athleticism they once had. She was doing well and still able to deliver on the court, but I felt this was only because her heart was in it. Her body was failing her, and I could see this and knew it would lead to no good as she lacked power and energy. I felt that my attempts at being her mom and friend were not good enough from a distance, but I didn't know what else I could do to help. I was not at peace with this situation and told her she needed to get in the gym any time she could to work on some things, especially her core and balancing those muscles in her legs to prevent injury, and this was crucial. I did not think she would be able to do this, though, because their time was managed so tightly in their plebe year and she was always lacking in sleep. My opinion was that the time spent in practice and conditioning should be more geared toward results and not sticking to a plan just because it was the plan but doing something that worked better for the athletes. I just prayed that God would be with my daughter where I couldn't be. I just encouraged the girls to be more vocal and to try to better voice their concerns and to also, in the meantime, try their best to get small workouts in when they could that would help them stay healthy, and surely there would be a turnaround. Any good news I got from Sabria was enough to keep me going and taking care of business at home.

CHAPTER 2 1

HERE COME THE BRICKS

I had made it to work that afternoon after Quintin's Friday ther- apy and had been at work for half the shift at this point when I got a call from Bobby. He said, "Did you talk to Bri?" I said no. He said, "Well, you'd better call her." I knew by the sound in his voice this was important. I am an optimist, so I didn't think anything bad could be going on, but I left the nurse's station to make the call. She answered the phone. "Mom." I said, "Yea?" I was waiting to hear what she needed when it hit me like a ton of bricks. "I'm injured." I paused and said, "Okay." This was one of those moments when I tried to connect to Sabria and be the listening ear. *Surely*, I thought, *she just needs a little advice or encouragement.* She said more crushing words, and I felt more bricks hitting me, "It's my knee." This was something I never wanted to hear coming from Sabria. She had a few friends who suffered knee injuries, and we worked so hard to prevent this! Even though her and I had talked in length about this potential injury over Thanksgiving and how we, unfortunately, saw this coming, still, I was in denial and didn't ask what happened or why she felt she was injured because I really didn't want this to be real and surely there was no way she could be seriously hurt as my son had ACL surgery just a few days ago and this would be just too terrible to be true. I just knew God couldn't have expected us to go through this. I said, "Okay, honey, I'm sure you're fine." She said, "It's bad, Mom. They think it's my ACL. I'm getting an MRI as soon as they can schedule it." I knew that Sabria had the capabilities of assessing the situation and seeing the reality in it. I knew she wouldn't have called me for a simple injury, so I knew this was big. She had been present when people she knew had sustained this very injury on the court, and so she was familiar with the circumstances surrounding it and knew what specific moves could cause it. She knew her body. She said that she was driving toward the hoop and made a jump stop, and as the force of her body was too much for her knee, it buckled in the opposite direction, and she heard a pop. I heard this, and it crushed my soul. My heart broke at what this could mean for my daughter and my family, especially after what I had just been through with Quintin. I decided to love Sabria as I knew she loved me. We both knew this was an obstacle that was no match for us, and we would have to overcome it together with God. We would do what we knew how to do best, conquer. I told her everything would be fine, and whatever the case, we would deal with it. I honestly just realized that there was nothing I could do to change what had happened, because there was no power in that. However, I did have power over how I responded to the situation, so I decided to just keep moving along, believing that God had a plan. I got off the phone, and I went on at work as I always did. I was getting better on the transition. I took myself away from my own home and family issues and gave my full attention to my patients and their families. This was where God kept me, in the now. This was an act of faith. I left my problems in his hands. I had to, or I could not be useful to him, and being of no use was not an option.

This would be a good place to talk about my life early on with Sabria. On my journey as Sabria's mom, I have been many places and through many obstacles, but it always ended well. She grew into a very tall and muscular girl, beefy. When most people stood next to her, they felt small, and most felt weak when competing with her on the court. She was often called a "beast," tall, lean, yet thick and very athletic. I took on many roles as her mom. Whether it was going on Dunkin runs, doing late-evening workouts in the gym, just simply hanging out, or chasing away the boys, it was an honorable job. When she was young, this job was very different. As a baby, the hardest part was leaving her to go to school or work. I just wanted to be near her. I remembered holding her in my arms and pacing the kitchen at 3:00 a.m. in my parents' home that I had grown up in. I had gotten pregnant when I was a senior in high school. I was eighteen years old. As class president; captain of the basketball, softball, and volleyball teams; student council member; and NHS participant, I was held to a high standard. After finding out I was pregnant, I chose to try to hide this fact from the world, even to my own mind. If the Christian school found out, I would be forced to leave and would have to finish my senior year somewhere else. I was in denial for a while until the springtime, when I finally told my parents what was going on. We did not tell the school and decided to deal with the situation privately as this would be my best chance at graduating. I had to give up my spot on the softball team because by now I was about four months along, and the doctor advised me to give up the sport as it was not safe for my baby. I let down my peers and teammates as they did not understand my situation because, of course, they did not know of my pregnancy; and this left them to feel abandoned since I was the one with the most experience in softball there. I had played since I was five years old, and I was responsible to help develop the first girls' softball team at our school and taught all the girls how to play fast-pitch from scratch, as many of them had no experience playing the game previously. When I told them I wasn't playing that last season, they were confused, let down, and upset about my decision. I felt ashamed and really wanted to give up on life. I cried every night before going to bed, and as morning approached, I woke up into the feeling of complete dread about what was in store for me that day. Hiding my belly, dealing with morning sickness, giving up sports, and living a complete lie were just the beginning. You may wonder what my dad's reaction to this was. I have told the story of my father to many, and I describe him as a saint. The day I had told my parents of my pregnancy is forever etched in my memory. I was alone with my mom in the basement of our house and told her of my secret. She screamed bloody murder and ran away from me as she called for my dad. She ran to her room and slammed the door, and my relationship with her ceased for many months other than a snarl or talk about how I should give the baby up for adoption because I could certainly not raise a child myself. She let me know how she was embarrassed of me and this was all she could see me as, an embarrassment. I understood. I was raised in a family where the bar was set high. My immigrant ancestors came legally to America and built their own homes with bricks they laid with their own hands. They made their own food from scratch, even building their own brick pizza oven in their backyard to feed the neighborhood, and never asked for handouts. My great-grandma told us of how she was a wet nurse, offering to breastfeed the babies in their neighborhood during the Great Depression. My dad expected the world from me. This was the man who told me that I could do anything. After my mom ran away from me and left me to my pile of tears and complete emptiness and despair, my dad came up to me. My dad heard the screaming for him, and as my mom had passed him on her way to her bedroom, she screeched, "She's pregnant!" My dad slowed his pace after running to the emergency of my mom's screams and then realized what was going on. I felt him pause after hearing the news and then gently approached me. He wrapped his arms around me as I crumbled into his chest. I was wailing over the disappointment I had just laid on the two people I loved most in my life. I could not breathe. I just moaned as he held me. I don't remember anything that happened directly after that moment. I'm sure I told him I was sorry, and I'm sure he told me it was okay. He is my hero and has never made me feel like trash. I was still his treasure, and there was a lot of work for me to do, and he would not let me face that battle alone. He helped me believe that everyone makes mistakes and that we are all broken. These are the people God fixes, the broken. My dad helped me see the light of tomorrow, and to God, I was worth fixing.

As other people still wanted to make sure I got a beating for my behavior, I learned to face the music. I had decided to keep the baby and to not have an abortion or give her up for adoption. This decision came with much consideration, and I told God I would take on the job of motherhood because he had asked me to, and I knew if he asked me to do such a task, it would be worth my efforts. I could not see this working out well for me or my baby but believed that somehow it would be good because I loved that baby and God loved me. I just had faith to keep moving and to keep trusting. At commencement, as I walked down the hallway of the school alone and thankful for the school year to be over but resented how it ended, a well-respected teacher came up to me. She stopped me and whispered in my ear, "I want you to know that I know you are going to be okay." I smiled and said thank-you and realized that she and, I'm sure, many others at the Christian school knew of my situation. As I walked into the gym trying to stand tall and look presentable to make my presidential speech that I was not worthy to make, I felt very ashamed of who I was and very unqualified to be representing my class. I reluctantly made my speech to inspire and encourage the group to believe in a bright future and to be proud of a job well done and hoped they could take the message from someone such as me, a nothing, who's shaking in my boots as my baby, whom I didn't deserve, moved around and grew strong in my womb. As we celebrated and left the gym, I walked past my senior picture. It was blown up to a large size and hanging on the wall alongside my classmates' pictures. I thought the picture was nice. It was a professionally taken picture that was taken before my pregnancy when I was still a nonpregnant, skinny, athletic, pretty fake—you know, the one who fits in. As long as nobody knew of my sins, everyone loved me and held me to a high standard, but as soon as they realized I wasn't perfect, I was hated. I walked up to the picture, and as I got closer, the deception was revealed. Someone had drawn a picture on this hanging portrait. It was a little cartoon picture of an obviously pregnant girl. There was an arrow pointing to the big belly with the caption "Bobby Jr." I was mortified as all the blood in my body, I felt, was now in my face, and I became completely flushed with embarrassment. I couldn't get out of there fast enough. I left that school feeling like the trash I believed I was and told my mom that I was sure everyone who walked past that picture only saw that little cartoon at the bottom. I told her to burn that picture that was used to disgrace me, and to this day, that picture haunts me. She, of course, told me that it was a beautiful picture and we would not burn it. I never felt so humiliated as I did that day. My mom had the hardest time dealing with my pregnancy, but that day, she defended me. After graduation, my pregnancy was officially made known to friends and family, and the news just made it through to all the people we knew. Eventually as the news spread, that's when phase two of the lashings began. Churchgoers and hardworking, self-righteous men and women in my life told me of their disapproval. Parents of other kids we knew told my parents how they wouldn't let their kids hang around me, because I was a bad influence. Everyone thought I ruined my life and I would not amount to anything. I was tired of hearing it really, at this point. I was trash. I knew it. I couldn't take care of a baby, right. So where does one go from here? I believed I was a bad influence. I believed I had made poor decisions. I believed I disappointed my parents and was not good enough to raise a child. This was all true.

As I confined myself in my bedroom and opened my Bible, I read a different story than what most people were telling me. I do appreciate their harshness toward me because it helped to demolish me. When I pressed in to find God that day in my bedroom, I realized my dad was right. I was still a treasure, and God was going to build me back up—not to the person I was before; but he would build me into a better version of myself—a person who was capable of raising a child. I kept reading, and I kept believing. Before too long, I was smiling again. My mom saw me laughing one day and told me that she didn't know how I could be laughing at a time like that and that I should be sad and embarrassed at the position I was in. I told her that I was seven months pregnant and I was over being sad and I wasn't wasting any more time feeling guilty. God had forgiven me, and so should she. It was time to not worry about what other people thought of me but only be concerned by what God saw in me, and he saw that I was good. My mom and I still revisited that conversation at times because she had trouble with her own self-image and wanted to put this on me. My dad came home every day and asked the same question, "Did you find a college yet? What's your plan?" He never stopped believing in me, and I drew from this hope he had in who I would become. I was big and pregnant and did not want to care about trying to plan my future, but I made sure to push hard. I chose to go to nursing school after having Sabria and seeing how the nurses placed no judgment on me. They only showed me love and compassion at a time I needed it the most. I was enrolled in school by the time Sabria was three months old, and I admit it was no easy task. Bobby had wanted to marry me; but I knew I could not be a wife, mother, and nursing student at the same time. I chose to stay focused on what God put in front of me. I decided to stay home, raise Sabria, and go to school. I told Bobby if he really loved me as he said he did, he would wait till I was ready. If he didn't want to wait for me and chose to move on, I was willing to accept that.

I spent many nights crying and studying through the night only getting maybe a nap in before going in for class or clinicals in the morning. I knew my dad believed in me, and as my mom would make hot meals every day for the family, she would leave a plate out for me for when I came home late. When I contemplated giving up and I would ask my mom if I could quit, she would say, "If you want to quit, go ahead." I knew she was giving me an out, but I knew my mom needed me to continue because I was the strong version of herself. She couldn't have an excuse to be weak in life if her daughter was willing to be strong, so this was when I chose to find grit. I wasn't going to give my mom a reason to say she was right about me failing to be good enough, when I knew I was. I wasn't gonna give her an excuse to fail at things in her own life when I could have taught her instead how to push hard to succeed. I chose to love my mom that day and give back to her for all her efforts in loving me. I was so sorry for letting her down in the past, and I didn't want her expecting fail from me.

I didn't want to lose my relationship with Sabria, so while I sat on the floor and studied for anatomy and chemistry and drew and labeled all those microorganisms for biology, she would lie on the floor next to me on her blanket and play and watch *Sesame Street*. I would suck down some ramen and head back to class, leaving Sabria home with my mom. I do find it intriguing that I had to study so hard while pacing through the house crying, even getting a tutor to pull off a B in chemistry, while Sabria ended up loving this class so much and even contemplating majoring in the subject. I was so thankful when class was over. I would rush home to my little girl to see her smiling face. I would scoop her up, kiss her soft round cheeks, and then strap her into her seat on the back of my bike; and we'd ride all over town, just me and her, through the West side of Youngstown. No boundaries, no one judging us. It was just her and me. The wind blowing in our hair, the sun shining on our skin, and the trees standing tall, proving that God was real and that he was with us. I'd take her to the corner store, Cherol's, where we'd visit with the owner, Joe, who enjoyed visiting with me when I was a small child and came into his store to buy snacks and now took joy in watching Sabria grow up too. We'd pick out our snacks and then get back on the road. She rode on the back of my bike until I couldn't possibly squeeze her into the seat anymore. Riding around town, just the two of us, was magical, electric. It was knowing I was a nothing and still God used me to create this amazing and beautiful human. It was humbling to see those soft shiny brown and gold ringlets of hair bouncing as she ran around. I watched as her little belly popped through that little faded purple shirt with the butterfly on it that she wore out but refused to let me get rid of because it was her favorite. Even though I made so many mistakes, God blessed me with this bundle of joy. So even through the terrible twos when sticky fingers and temper tantrums were everyday dramas, I enjoyed those days as she was most curious to get into anything and everything, like the one day when I dozed off and she tried to paint her own nails, leaving a giant purple stain on my parents' cream-colored Berber carpet. These were the easy days of parenting I would come to find out. The harder days would be coming, although I had no idea how God would use me in her life, but as Sabria and I grew up together, we became the very best of friends, and as I pushed and pushed, I finally made it through nursing school with good grades and passed my boards, earning my RN. Sabria was not a hindrance but, instead, my inspiration.

When I discovered that my good friend Sabria had a great talent in basketball, I knew as her parent it was my responsibility to support her and teach her all I knew. The Bible teaches that a good teacher hopes that his student will eventually pass up their teacher. Once I taught Sabria all I could, I prayed for guidance, and people to come into our lives to get her to her next level because I knew I was not worthy of such a task. I still had a role, though, and I was responsible to find out what this was as it changed over the years. I was willing to do whatever it took to be an asset to Sabria, whether it was purchasing some equipment or a program I could enroll her in or to pick up more hours at work to get needed funds to support her. There was always an honorable task God gave me to do that would support Sabria on her journey, and for this, I was thankful. I wanted to always know my limits because then I could get out of the way so Sabria could surpass her own limits and push through that ceiling of her potential, allowing for the disappearance of her boundaries. This is done through humility and knowing that you don't always know everything and that even if you don't have what your kid needs, there is someone who does and God wants everyone to work together using their gifts for the greater good. No one is better than their neighbor. After all, where would a tree be without its roots? Where do leaves get their nutrition without the branches to sustain them? As I began to understand that Sabria was out of my league, God brought Coach Carl LaRosa, Coach Carlos, Coach Andre, and Coach Dan into our lives. He brought them all at different times to direct her and get her that edge she needed. All of them had different roles, and if you got all these guys together in one room, they would all say the same thing about Sabria. She was most coachable and very hardworking. She wanted to learn. She desired to get better. She appreciated these men in her life who set the bar high for her. They set the bar high for themselves, too, as they represented what good men are to be like. They gave her the best example of how a man should treat women and especially, in her case, young female athletes. They treated her with respect, expecting nothing but her best every time she played or worked out and who were accountable, trustworthy, consistent, uplifting, and encouraging. They told her to believe in herself and the sky was the limit and to know that she was blessed and so were they for having the opportunity to work with her. I saw in these men, people who saw my daughter the way I did, and this in life is a true gift to a mother. There are very few men I have met whom I would put into the class of exceptional. These men fall into that class, and I am a better person for knowing them, and my daughter is a better person and athlete for knowing them.

As Sabria got better, I continued to see how God would use me to facilitate and encourage her growth in the sport by being humble, listening and watching and waiting for direction from God to address her needs as they arose. I was still being used to aid in her success even though her greatness surpassed mine, and for this opportunity, I was forever thankful. She would say that she felt bloated and weighted down on the court, so we'd go on some extra runs and clean up her diet a bit, maybe do a berry cleanse. She'd say that she noticed she felt weak when she'd go up for her shots, so we'd spend some extra time in the gym doing legs. This was why I was upset at her decline at West Point in the time leading up to her injury. She was noticing weaknesses there, but her self-assessments were not validated, maybe because she didn't speak up enough or maybe this weakness was expected of plebes. We didn't know why she was able to decline, but we wanted to learn, and we knew, whatever the case, she would recover and hopefully surpassing her previous level. When Sabria left Ohio on July 1 for R Day, I was confident that I was sending my daughter in the best shape of her life. I raised her, I trained her, and I knew her well. She was ready. She was a sharpened tool, ready to be used. She was smart and knew her body. She was stubborn and wouldn't settle for less than working her body to make it her slave. When she started basic training soon after getting to the academy, she was doing air squats, and she felt herself bouncing off the ground. She was jumping so fast and so high that the other kids looked at her and asked her how she was able to do it so well. She was proud of the fact that the men would even give her fist bumps on the runs as she was able to even challenge their efforts. Once the six weeks of basic training was over and basketball had started, it had been about three months since she had left Ohio. This is the time frame I refer to as "the gap."

By the time October had come, she was really beginning to notice the decline in her strength, conditioning, and her overall athleticism; and she told me she felt weak. She was telling me that she didn't understand why, because this was the army, so she expected to feel strong, but the workouts for basketball did not challenge her and there were days she didn't even sweat while working out in the strength and conditioning class. This was a huge contrast to her days back home after jump stretch when we left the class barely able to walk and sometimes had to stop to let the nausea pass before driving home. We really felt accomplished after those classes. She now had begun to lose muscle and was unsettled and began feeling like the workouts were a waste of her already limited time. She told me she desperately missed jump stretch class and how strong she felt after doing squats with the rubber bands and that nothing she had done, no workout, had ever compared to the strength and confidence she felt after working with the bands. She said she really felt nervous that she was losing her edge and was struggling without the class, losing vertical on her jumps and an overall lack of energy. I could sense the concern my daughter had, and knowing that she knew her body well, I urged her to voice her concern to the coaches. I believed that the coaches who I believed saw worth in my daughter would analyze her criticism and see it as constructive. Without a doubt, they would assess her vertical and see that it had decreased from when she started. Surely, they would see her muscle decay, fatigue, overall lack of endurance, and bad form in her running and lateral movement on the court that she was describing and I was witnessing as she played. Sure, she still had some reserve and was still able to deliver good basketball, but this could only last for so long before her stores would run out, and she would either stop performing well or, worse, get injured. I believed that the same coaches who believed she could be an asset to the team would now help her to troubleshoot the way I would help her when she was home. They could see where her weakness was and help make it strong, and they could do this for all the girls who were all having struggles. I did what I should never do, I assumed. I was naïve to think they would love my daughter the way I did. I believed they would take the baton from me and run with it, aiding Sabria to get to the next level in her sport. I knew the "beast" I delivered on July 1 was a machine built to conquer. I remember all the pull-ups that she didn't want to do but did anyway. "One more, Bri, gimme one more," I would say. I did them with her because one thing I've never been able to tolerate is a parent pushing their kid from the sideline but never toiling in the work. Doing your max wasn't enough. Give more. I went on those practice weighted rucks in Mill Creek Park with her even when I didn't want to, even after those long shifts at the hospital when all I wanted to do was go home and rest. I could remember those times when I couldn't breathe or take one more step in those woods or up those hills, but I did because she was leading me and I wouldn't dare hold her back. I would walk till my legs fell off if it meant giving Sabria the edge she wanted and worked so hard to achieve. I helped fuel her passion for greatness; and this was worth all the blood, sweat, and tears that came with the struggle. This is where my passion as a parent took me. It was the place God took me as he built me up from that broken person I was so long ago. I believed I could do anything, and I would let my lungs cave into my chest on those runs through the trails in Mill Creek Park before I would let Sabria fail to be her best and to reach her peak performance. I ran those bleachers with her at Fitch, almost losing my balance so many times and going until tasting nothing but spit and blood in my mouth to assure that she was gaining that edge. I was there watching as she pushed herself to that sweet spot in training where you should give up, where you need to give up, when you desperately desire to throw in the towel but you don't. You take one more step, do one more rep, run one more bleacher until you are right there at that edge, the edge of collapse.

That's the place you have to get to in order to end your workout. Otherwise, it's just not good enough. Sabria had that edge. She was good at getting there to the sweet spot, reaching it more often than most athletes. This was where I went with my daughter. This was where those few exceptional men had also been able to take my daughter. *How come she couldn't get there now?* I thought. I sent her to West Point in confidence that she was ready to get to the next level. She had shed lots of blood, sweat, and tears to have that confidence of being ready to serve her country and play Division 1 basketball. When she'd get nervous, I'd look at her and say, "You are ready, Sabria." I knew I could say that. God took all my doubts away because I spent that time with that girl in the reality of the passionate work and toil that she put in. She was amazing. So the call I got on December 6, 2019, about her knee being injured was unacceptable to me except that I knew a God who took the broken and made something brand-new and better out of it. To know that I watched her body deteriorate before my very eyes to the point of her having the feeling of dread, knowing she was in the zone, the zone of vulnerability, knowing injury was a real potential was devastating to me. Then to have her fears of injury become reality should have been unbearable, but we saw this devastation coming. God prepared us in the months leading up to this. We knew we were in a storm but that it would not overcome us. I knew Sabria would come out of this better. This was how I perceived the situation.

They did do an MRI four days later and waited another twenty-four hours to give her the results. Before I even got the results back, I did send an e-mail to the coach expressing my deep concern for my daughter and the weakness of the basketball program as I saw it. Sabria and I were dedicated, especially the last two years of her high school career, to the prevention of this very injury that she may had sustained. She withstood years of grueling travel, including plane rides, car rides, and train rides, to arrive and play against the best basketball players in the country. She had experience facing very good competition even before this freshman year in college and was, in fact, currently leading the Patriot league in rebounds. Only a few short months into this program, she lost vertical, muscle mass, speed, agility, flexibility, stamina, balance, and good form. This preventable injury that she possibly sustained is one that will take her off the court for nine to twelve months and could potentially destroy her entire career in basketball. I voiced these concerns to a man who represented the basketball program. He asked me if I was okay. I responded that, no, of course I wasn't okay. I was devastated. I am pretty sure he didn't know where I was coming from as Sabria's mom and couldn't possibly know of our past and our journey and what this injury meant to us or to our family. Although we were ready to battle this head-on as Sabria was invested in the program, she wanted to be an asset to the team but knew that change was needed. I told him of the decay that I saw in my daughter's body, and he didn't seem to notice these same changes. I told him if things did not change, I feared that we would see more injuries (which unfortunately did happen later in the season), and I did not want to see this for the girls. What I heard was someone telling me that because this program was expensive, I should trust it. What I heard was that because there were years of experience represented, I should trust the program. I don't trust money or résumés. I trust actions. I trust truth and results. Even though I could see that we did not see eye to eye, I was determined to let God work out the kinks as he's always done in my life and would also do this for Sabria. I asked him to please forward my informal e-mail to anyone who could help to make changes in the program. He did tell me that he was not a facilitator, so I actually don't know if he communicated my concerns to the other coaches and athletic staff. He did not personally offer any feedback concerning this. I do believe that this injury would be needed on Sabria's path. It would further lead her down her path and give her a greater passion and understanding of the body and how it works. I did not doubt that God had a plan, but I did think there were things that needed to change. The surgeon called me to talk to me about the results of Sabria's MRI. He told me that the test revealed a complete ACL tear and possible meniscus and MCL tear. The surgery would take place in one month. This whole process seemed so mechanical and strategic to me. I really understood the commonness of the situation when the doctor told me that ACL injuries were quite common at West Point for plebes (freshmen). I said, "Oh…really?" I talked to the coach again and asked him why this information wasn't revealed to us in the recruiting process since this would have been good to know so we could have maybe tried troubleshooting to try to avoid this injury. It wouldn't have changed Sabria's decision to go to West Point, because this was still, in her mind and mine, a very honorable and humbling opportunity. I could have set something up for Sabria beforehand to bridge certain obvious gaps that I saw leading to this injury. I was more intrigued and began to further investigate the situation. I asked if they measured her vertical, and he said he didn't know. I asked what kind of exercises they did specifically geared toward prevention of ACL injury since the doctor informed me of the fact that women do have a higher risk level than men for sustaining this injury and it was apparently a common injury for plebes at West Point in general. The coach said he didn't know what, if any, exercises were done to prevent this. I told him I noticed Sabria's knees were bowing in at the Brooklyn game and how she worked to correct that very specific weakness back in Ohio by doing exercises to balance the muscles on the inside and outside of the legs to promote good form, balance, and safety. He then told me that I was not like any other parent he had dealt with. He said that I seemed to have a lot of insight and I knew a lot about my daughter's body and he could tell that I spent a lot of time with her. He then said he would refer me to the athletic director to help answer some of my questions because he could not. I did express my concerns to the director and told him that from what I understood and learned from my studies of ACL injury and experience in athletics, I knew that it only takes seven pounds of pressure to tear an ACL. Sabria weighed almost two hundred pounds. One little move this way or that and it would be more than enough of weight transfer to sustain this injury. This was the thinking behind why we like to pay special attention in workouts to activate the big and small muscles surrounding the knee to make them strong enough to withstand tweaking when cutting and quick jarring movements on the court. (Sabria injured herself doing a simple jump-stop type move in practice.) Stretching, semiheavy weightlifting, conditioning using rubber bands, and circuit training to activate both small and large muscle fibers are key to prevent ACL tears. He had told me that he had looked back and discovered that Sabria tested at a high-risk level for tearing her ACL in the academy. This information intrigued me, so I asked him what kind of revisions were made in her workouts to keep them individualized to strengthen her weaknesses in this area and to get her out of the high-level risk zone, and he said he didn't know. When I later asked Sabria about this, she said they never told her that she tested at the high-risk level. They knew she was at high risk for this injury, but what good is this information if no action was taken to correct it, and why was this information not communicated to the person who would have most benefitted from this knowledge, Sabria? Even though they failed to communicate this information to her, Sabria knew she was at risk because she knew her own body. She herself didn't even need the test. But why was the communication not facilitated and preventative workouts not instituted? I wanted to understand. Why did the coach tell me that he was not a facilitator? Why would anyone resist communication concerning an athlete? Aren't we all facilitators as parents and leaders, anyway?

If I learned anything over the years and what I've already worked hard in this book to tell, it is that I am no one, except that God is found in me. He is the only one who makes me anything, so I cannot judge anyone else or even expect anything good to come from anyone except that which comes from God. This is a good way to look at any circumstance that may be troubling you in life. So, as I had found out that it had been this way for years and many girls had suffered knee injuries in the past at West Point, I had heard that other mothers were upset, too, when their daughters were hurt. Emotion by itself is worthless. I thought, *Why had no one asked the questions I was asking? Why didn't anyone else approach the situation? Or did they?* Was this even about the actual ACL injury, or were we going to learn so much more than just about an injury? There was so much I didn't know. All I knew was God called me to respond. He called me to learn, act, and move in the situation. He called me to accountability. He put this situation in my face, in my lap, on my journey, and on my conscience. I had to believe that those leading in athletics wanted change, too, and I would do whatever I could to help bring about the change I knew they wanted, even if it was only a change in my daughter because I still, as always, had a responsibility as Sabria's mom and as her friend and that bond did not end just because she was in college. Even though I didn't know how God could use me in this, I made myself available to be a tool to be used by him and by Sabria so that good could still come from a seemingly bad situation. I knew the impossible was possible. She accepted the injury as it was, a hurdle, and told me it was meant to happen or God would not have allowed it. She said that it would all work out according to his plan and if she was meant to play again, she would. She knew I had her back, and she was leading me into the battle to bounce back. Despite her substandard level of athleticism, Sabria still delivered good basketball in those first eight games she had played at West Point. That was what she had trained her body, mind, and heart to do. She would tear her body into a million pieces in order to remain obedient to her coach. Her heart drove her actions. She played how Sabria always played, and her body failed her because it was not properly cared for, whether this was her fault alone, fault of the program, both, or neither. Whatever the cause for the injury, the reality was clear that Sabria herself had to make the choice to be accountable to learn, grow, and change. No one could get her to the next level but her. God's plan would be crystal clear as the journey continued. Even though she only played the first eight games before the injury, she managed to earn, in that time, the title of Patriot League Rookie of the Week twice and was the leading rebounder in the league, even as a player coming off the bench. Her training only built her to last eight games (as I saw it), and this was sad to me, but I told Sabria I would ride this to the very end with her and she would come back stronger than ever. We would have a long hard journey ahead of us, but what else was new? I was excited as I knew God had a plan, and I was not going to let anyone tell me this was a common thing. There was nothing common about Sabria. There is nothing common about any of us. We are all made in God's image, fearfully and wonderfully made. This would be a very exciting ride, and to even try to imagine what God had in store for us was impossible. I would just have to wait and see and dare to enjoy the ride with my bundle of joy.

CHAPTER 22

SLEEP ON A ROCK IF YOU HAVE TO

S abria was now in the injured zone, unsure where her future would take her, sitting on the bench instead of playing the game she loved. As soon as she felt better, she began to work out and get as strong as she could before surgery because this was the recommendation. She came home for Christmas break, as her injury allowed the leave, and our family was together again. She and Quintin really bonded over their injuries, and even though their injuries happened in very different ways and on different legs and even in different sports, the challenges were similar. God gave them each other to lean on. Sabria was getting a dose of the reality that was coming for her, and as she saw her brother being strong, it allowed her to be brave herself. Quintin was still, at this point, going to the bathroom on the portable toilet in the living room, using the urinal, and getting sponge baths. I was still working long hours and taking him to physical therapy three times a week, and Sabria could see the struggle her family was going through; and yet thriving through the storm and staying positive and optimistic, I think she gained hope for her own situation as she watched how her family toiled. She watched as Quintin worked so hard at therapy and would have outbursts of frustration at times when he was tired of being handicapped. She felt proud of her brother for rising to the challenge of dealing with such a difficult injury, and it gave her no excuse to be weak in her own case, which was encouraging. I knew she was watching how I dealt with the situation, too, and I wanted to remain strong to be a good example of strength and love. We went to the Y to get workouts in, and she got on the elliptical as her team was getting ready to play another basketball game without her. She got her phone ready and logged into the game so she could watch her team from an uncomfortable angle but still be supportive. Before the game started, they showed the staring five players, and Sabria's picture was still there as a starter. Her heart dropped at the reality that she had made it to a place she could be proud of after working so hard; and now she was at the bottom, perhaps even lower than the bottom, the lowest she'd ever been. As the announcer began to talk about the game that would be beginning, he said that Sabria was out with an injury. He said that West Point had done a good job recruiting that year but, unfortunately, they hadn't figured out how to fix their problem with injuries. It was a hit in the gut. Everyone knew of this chronic injury problem but us, it seemed. Why was this a well-known fact that there were many injuries at this school? Why was it a fact at all? Sabria amazed me with her ability to remain hopeful and diligent to induce change. She herself would have to change through this once-again humbling experience, and she stayed motivated to come out on top to be a good example to others.

Christmas went well, and we all tried to enjoy the time together amongst the chaos. I felt like my job as nurse never ended. I was a nurse at work and one at home. I was doing workouts with Sabria, which were different from Quintin's, which were different from the other kids'. I was transitioning from this to that to the other, and it was exhausting but amazing. I wanted to be a good example to the kids that, although much is expected of you, God makes it all possible. Finally, the first week of January came, and we all got together to watch a movie in the living room before Sabria and I left for our journey back to West Point so she could have her surgery. The kids would be staying home, and I would be taking Sabria and staying with her for her surgery. I was tired at this point, beyond tired. I had only three hours of sleep after helping Sabria get packed for our journey back to the academy and then worked a twelve-hour shift. I was back home again tending to everyone's requests: "Get me water," "I want a snack," "Mom, sit with us." I finally sat down and said, "You guys, I'm so tired." They knew I had to get up early to start the drive, and they understood I was hitting the bottom of my energy store. They put the movie on, and I told them I was sorry but that I would probably fall asleep. The next thing I knew, Theresa had come up next to me, reclined my chair, and sat next to me. I laid my body against hers, and she put a blanket over me, making sure to cover my feet and then put her arms around me, and the kids told me I needed to sleep. I asked her, "How did you know I was cold?" The kids just knew me. She then started to stroke my arms, head, and even around my ears in a soft and rhythmic fashion as an obvious attempt to nurture her mom. Suddenly, I felt my body calm down. I was so warm and comfortable. This is the kind of precious comfort that should be wrapped up and sent out as presents at Christmastime. My body just melted into Theresa's arms like soft butter getting spread onto warm bread. I fell asleep and had a wonderful nap during the movie. The kids didn't mind, and we were together. That moment with Theresa was a little preview of heaven, and she is a loving little girl.

Sabria and I left early in the morning as planned. I was beginning to really feel small in the situation, but God told me he was made strong in me. I drove for forever and made it to New York, through the mountains, all the way to West Point. I parked the car and walked with Sabria as far as I was allowed toward the building that housed her barracks. She then left me and walked with her stuff toward her room. She had a large laundry basket and three duffle bags to carry with that injured knee, but she did it even up the five flights of stairs. She humored me by turning around for a quick picture before turning briskly back toward that beautiful stone building, never looking back. I watched her disappear into Sally Way before turning around to go back to my car. Leaving her hit me hard every single time. Even though I was only leaving her for the night and I would be back the next day to take her for her presurgery workup, it was still hard because of the circumstances and the fact that her surgery was less than two days away. I hoped I would even find my car because the whole way there to that building, I was just watching Sabria and taking in the opportunity to be in the moment with her, knowing in a couple of days I'd be leaving her to recover alone there. As I was walking back to my car, I looked down at my feet to see the new boots Sabria had bought me for Christmas. She had some money in her bank account and knew I needed winter boots. I had passed them up in the store because they weren't on sale. Sabria went to three different stores to find the exact ones I wanted, in my size, and surprised me on Christmas Day with them. This was who Sabria was. I was able to walk to my car feeling confident that the unconditional love I always tried to show to Sabria, she also showed back to me, and this was what kept us strong through the tough times of being apart and going through challenges of life. I was never really leaving her at West Point. We were intertwined. We went with each other everywhere even if we were physically apart. This was through the Spirit of God.

This first semester, Sabria had been through the perfect storm to tear her ACL. I had to make this drive so I could help her see the rainbow that comes after the storm. This was my thinking as I was in my car driving to my hotel. I looked at the sky and was starting to feel sad. I noticed that the sun was shining so bright that I almost couldn't stand it. I put my visor down and still had a hard time seeing. Then I looked to the side, and there in the sky was the most beautiful splash of colors I'd ever seen in the sky. It was a rainbow. I was in shock, and I just smiled as this was God's way of telling me he was there and I would, in fact, help Sabria see her rainbow after the storm. I looked and saw a second rainbow bigger than the first. God was telling me to be confident on my journey and to remember that he was by my side always. This reminded me of the feelings I had before leaving for this trip. I was standing in my kitchen before deciding then to go and sit with the kids and watch the movie and take that much-needed nap next to Theresa. I was anxious as I would be dealing with the third major surgery with my kids in the last four months. I was overwhelmed and tired but still hopeful. I knew I needed to be strong, so I looked outside the window to find the trees to tell myself to be strong like the trees. By now it was dark, so as I looked outside, all I saw was my own desperate face reflected in the glass. I started crying, thinking that was the last person I wanted to see myself—the one who was desperate for a break, tired, anxious. I thought, *Oh, God, help me get through this.* I couldn't call anyone at that point. They wouldn't hear me through my tears, anyway. I dried my face so my kids didn't know I was crying and went to sit with them. It wasn't until my drive that next day after leaving Sabria and driving to my hotel and looking at those rainbows that God explained that he was found in me. He said that when I need him, all I need to do is look inside myself, that's where he is. He said when I was looking for the trees and, instead, I caught my own reflection in the glass of that window the night before that I was actually looking at him. His Spirit lives in me, so I don't ever have to look far to find him. He said he is always with me. I realized that as God was taking things like time and energy out of my life and actually making it more complicated, I was becoming stronger and more focused than ever; and I have realized this was because when I am weak, God is made strong in me and he wants to be closer to me. This is what I want to share with others so that people can believe there is a better life than the one they are living on their own strength.

In the last six months, my mom had been in and out of the ICU awaiting a liver transplant. My uncle who had a big impact on my life passed away after battling ALS, and three of my six kids would have had major surgery, with two of them also needing extended therapy to follow. Through this, I'd still been able to get the kids to sporting events and school. I maintained the house and yard and held down a strenuous job and rigorous work schedule, found time to fit in workouts for myself, and somehow found passion and joy throughout that time. Then as my latest project approached, my meeting in person with the athletic director at West Point after Sabria's surgery, I was more motivated than ever to discuss my concerns and help to possibly promote change. People had begun to say things to me like, "I don't know how you are doing what you are doing. It seems like so much, and yet you are surviving, thriving, and still happy and smiling all the time." This is why I chose to tell my story of God's great love and power in my life. As my husband is rarely found with me and the kids, I have chosen to look to God for guidance, love, companionship, friendship, strength, and help in time of need. I've always found it. Don't ever think that you need anyone else to depend on. God will provide people, help, money, sleep, endurance, and any other thing you may need in this life. Never believe there is no hope for you. Anyone can be happy in good times, but bring the fire, and see how many people will still be smiling. Only God can teach that kind of happiness and joy.

On my drive to my hotel, I decided to stop at Walmart because Sabria had a long list of essentials that she needed to move into her new barracks. They moved a lot at West Point, I've come to realize. Sabria's surgery would be in two days from that day we arrived, so the plan was for me to get her needed supplies and then be ready for her call to take her to the army hospital on base to get all her presurgery workups done. I went in to Walmart and immediately knew I was not on a good side of town. Growing up in Youngstown and as the daughter of a police officer, I did have some good instincts. I felt someone watching me in the clothes section, so I got out of there and moved over to the Keurig section as this was something on the list. All the boxes were broken and dented, and I knew I was just wasting time in that store as it was starting to get late. I was spooked at all the obnoxious and rude people. The atmosphere was giving me a true panic attack, so I headed for the door. As I was rushing out the door, I managed to go out the wrong way and set off an alarm. Since when does Walmart have an alarm system just for going out certain doors? After that trip to Walmart, I decided I would give up for the day and figured I would find another Walmart in the morning after I had gotten some rest. I was planning to check out of my hotel early anyway and go to stay with Sabria's sponsor family to try to save some money and have some support that I desperately needed. They had offered a room to me at their house, so I figured this would be a big help the following day. I finally made it to the hotel, which was about a half hour from Sabria. I was starving at this point, so I stopped at a restaurant that was right next to the hotel. I went in, and this was literally the only time I ever remembered eating at a restaurant alone. I sat down and ordered a chicken salad. I looked down at my plate and ate as fast as I could as the loneliness I felt was too much to bear. I missed the kids and was worried about Sabria. I just needed to go to bed. Finally, I made it to the hotel alone and settled into my bed thanking God for a break, finally. I drank my organic sleep tea in hopes to get a few good hours of sleep to be rested for Sabria and my meeting with the athletic rep.

The next morning, I checked out early, cleaned the snow off my car, and headed back to West Point to be there by 7:00 a.m.

for her pre-op appointment. We went from one department to the next—admissions, lab, physical therapy. We made all the stops, and she was all ready for her surgery the next morning. I dropped her off and made plans to go to another Walmart to finish the task of getting Sabria's list of essentials when my phone rang. It was Bobby. I knew he was in a panic and upset about something, so I pulled back into the parking lot to handle whatever he had going on at home. This day was to be Quintin's first day back to school following his ACL surgery. He had been homeschooling for about five weeks now, and he was ready to go back. This was the first week in January 2020. Sabria and Quintin's surgeries would end up being almost exactly five weeks apart, which, to me, is mind-blowing. I do believe God sets up time and place and only he could have put these two major events together the way he did. I figured being in New York with Sabria was the harder of the two situations, so that's where I went. Bobby was to stay home, and he took vacation from work to take care of the kids while I was away. After I had called the school and made arrangements with the nurse in advance, I figured Bobby could handle getting Quintin back and forth to school. He still could not take the bus. I even had Bobby's brother on board to come to the house every day to check up on things and keep the peace there as sometimes our home could be challenging, and Bobby has never indulged in family affairs, so he is weak in dealing with the activities of daily living in our home and gets easily overwhelmed when challenges arise. Bobby did not know that his brother Codey and I had this arrangement, but I knew he would be glad to see Codey when he came by to visit and help out while I was gone. I really took special care to make good plans before I left to make Bobby's job easy, but still he was calling me upset, so I listened as he told me what was going on. He never knew how to respond appropriately when he met resistance or any kind or confrontation. So when he met resistance at the school with Quintin returning, he could not troubleshoot.

Troubleshooting is a tool that comes with experience. Bobby has no experience with issues with the kids, because he always stays away from the responsibilities associated with raising the kids and just allows me to handle the work. I knew it wasn't going to be a smooth transition for Quintin to go back, because nothing with the school has ever been smooth; there are always kinks. This was why I tried to plan as much as possible but left some trouble-shooting up to Bobby, which I hoped he would do by rising to the occasion so he could grow and change, but he chose to sabotage the opportunity and instead put the situation in my lap. Bobby has trouble responding to questions that he can't answer, and really he doesn't know much about what his kids go through, so he can't answer questions about them when asked. When he had tried to call me and couldn't get me to answer, because I was in the hospital with Sabria with no signal, he got angry because he couldn't use me to respond to the school as he was used to. The problem started when the school questioned him about the elevator pass *again*, a note from the doctor to return to school, and then yelled at Bobby for being in the hallway himself without a pass (all parents are screened before coming into the school, but no one had been at the desk to screen him). Instead of the school being courteous, caring, and helpful, they were rude, obnoxious, and not helpful. Instead of Bobby politely asking the school for a list of missing things Quintin needed to return to school and then Bobby getting those things for the school, he rudely left the building and told the school that Quintin would not return to school that day. Bobby was telling me he was upset, that all this was not done already by me, and that I did not answer the phone when he called me, which further upset him. I reminded him that this was why he took vacation time, so he could help Quintin get back to school calmly and without added stress as this was a challenging time for our son and I couldn't be there because I had to be with Sabria. I told him that even though arrangements were made, kinks would be expected and, as I cannot see the future, these kinks needed to be worked out then with him. I explained to Bobby that although the school was abrasive toward him, he should have used his aggression as a tool and been a strong advocate for his son, instead of just storming out of the school, going back home, and getting nothing accomplished. He should have asked for help in getting the paperwork together, and I'm sure they would have sent him in the right direction. Bobby said he understood, and I agreed to take care of matters with Quintin and the school right there in that New York parking lot because God taught me I could do anything. Bobby, at that point, had shut down and worked himself up over nothing and was now unable or unwilling to get back on track to make any progress that day. I called the nurse at the school, spoke with the front desk, and talked to Quintin's surgeon's office. I had proper papers faxed, and all was set up for him to return to school that week on a Wednesday. I called Bobby back and told him the new plan, and he was relieved. I told him that I've learned a lot over the years about troubleshooting when things don't go the way I think they will and he will never learn this if he doesn't learn how to talk to people with curtesy and this is necessary in being a good parent to kids. You have to remember that this is how we get molded but also our kids get molded by watching us and how we handle situations and troubleshoot in good ways when things don't go as planned. Our kids are worth us coming out of our comfort zones to be good examples to them.

I ended up finding a good Walmart and got everything Sabria needed. Then I headed to her sponsor's house to have a place to wait until I was able to see Sabria. She had to be at the hospital at 8:00 p.m. to stay overnight for surgery in the morning. They made dinner, and I ate with these wonderful God-fearing people. Their house was located on base and across the street from the hospital, which was very convenient. They made me feel comfortable at a time in my life that was not so comfortable, and for this I was so thankful. I don't like people having to make a fuss over me, and I feel I am called to serve and not be served, but I needed the help that day, and they knew it. They let me wash two loads of Sabria's clothes, which was awesome because I did not want to hunt down a Laundromat and sit there for two hours washing clothes and Sabria really needed them done. The dinner that was made was so refreshing. It was homemade vegetable spaghetti. I was very impressed at this little family and how energized I was when I left their home. I felt like a traveler, and I wasn't one by nature, but as I came out of my comfort zone, God was providing people and resources along my journey that I would need. I just needed the faith to keep moving. I was at their house for about five hours, and then I headed to get Sabria. It was very cold there in New York in early January. Getting all of Sabria's clean clothes and all the bags from Walmart, including a big box that housed the Keurig, was no easy task. I helped her as much as I could, but then she was on her own. She got the stuff to her barracks and then came back out to meet me, and we headed to the hospital, which was up the street from her barracks. We got to Sabria's hospital room to get checked in, and we met her nurse. She was a very kind lady with a New Jersey accent, very good bedside manner, and old-school nursing practice that I appreciated. I had asked if it would be okay if I stayed overnight with Sabria in her room as this was a better option than leaving and coming back. They didn't know exactly what time they'd be taking her in the morning for surgery, and that time could even change at any time. I didn't want to miss the opportunity to see her off to surgery and wanted to spend as much time as I could with her. They told me I could stay in that room with her, and I was so very relieved. Up to this point, no one was sure if this would be allowed, so I was really hoping I could stay with her. I told her sponsor mom I wouldn't need her room, and she was very happy knowing I wanted to be with my daughter, and she wanted that for us too.

There was a small sofa chair in the corner of the room. I didn't know at the time that it folded out into a small bed, and I just thought, *How am I going to sleep in that?* As long as I could stay with Sabria, I didn't care. I would have slept on a rock if it meant being with her. I was reluctant, though, as I could feel myself staring off in a daze. Sabria noticed and asked, "What are you thinking about, Mom?" I was thinking, *How in the world am I going to sleep in that chair?* But I didn't say that, of course. I probably mentioned that I was just getting tired. After only sleeping for about eleven hours total in the past four days combined, I was really hitting a wall and finding it hard to focus. I'm sure with being that tired, I could have easily fallen asleep in that chair, but I was actually wondering how much longer my body could hold up after the beatdown it was getting. I just wanted to make sure I could complete my mission there, which was to support Sabria through this surgery and help her to see the rainbow after the storm and to have a meeting with the athletic rep, hoping to shed some light on the subject of change and then drive home. This was a lot actually, so I wanted to be prepared. God tells me to only deal with today, and this was always where he kept me. It was only possible for me to stay in today, thinking about tomorrow was too much to ask, and he never asked me to do that. "Let's work on today, Tina." That's what he always says to me. So that's what I did. I don't like to look back at the past, except to be able to tell my testimony of how much God had brought me through so much so others can find him in their time of need. I reminded myself of how much I'd gone through this far and surely I could do whatever God asked of me because he always pulled me through. The nurse looked at me and I'm sure saw that my eyes and heart were heavy even though I hadn't talked to her about my journey; she just knew. She has compassion on me. I had gone out to my car to get my things, and when I made it back to the room, I was stopped in my tracks by what I saw as I entered the room. Sabria looked at me with a big smile and said, "The nurse did it. She made a bed up for you, Mom." I looked on with complete amazement and relief. She had pulled the chair out into a bed. She had dressed it with sheets, pillows, and blankets and had turned it all down for me. I was only gone a few minutes, and she did all that. She was my hero. *What a nurse!* I thought. I thanked her, and even though there was no way she could have known how much this meant to me, I'm sure she knew. I pray God blessed this woman as I could never repay her for her good deed. I got *amazing* sleep in that little pullout chair bed that night.

In the morning, Sabria was taken to surgery. We said our goodbyes, and I waited and prayed while she was gone, hoping that everything went according to God's will. She was brought back to the room and said, "Hi, Mom." With a big smile on her face, she lay on that cart with that ever-familiar black full-leg ACL brace that I was tired of seeing in my world. It was a long day. They had picked her up at 10:00 a.m., and she was back into her room at 4:00 p.m. I was so happy for that part of the journey to be done. She said she woke up from anesthesia and asked, "When can I see my mom?" She was in a lot of pain, but this was expected. She was visited by some very respected staff at West Point who offered her support and made sure she had their phone numbers. She held the highest respect for these individuals. One of them told her that Sabria brought the most beautiful basketball to the court that she'd ever seen and she could not wait to see her back on the court. She told Sabria she compared watching her on the court to having some delicious dessert. That it was so refreshing to watch her play and that it was a real treat. She told her to get back on the court so she could have her dessert again. This made Sabria laugh, and she was delighted to hear how her work on the court brought happiness to another person, especially someone she highly respected and someone she thought the world of. I had been in contact with the athletic director, and he offered to put off the meeting since I had a long day and Sabria had just gotten out of surgery and surely I needed to just relax and spend time with her. I would not agree to that. I absolutely was still quite willing to have the meeting that I myself requested to have in the first place because God held me accountable as Sabria's parent. He did agree to meet me and asked where I wanted to go. I guessed I would then be calling the shots. I had expected to be told to go to some unfamiliar office where I would get lost three times before panicking and then finding the room. Instead, I got to choose, so I told him to meet me at the Starbucks, which was the only place on base that I knew I could get to easily and which was right next to the hospital. I got ready to go, making sure to put on the outfit Sabria had gotten me for Christmas so I could remember my mission and whom I was there for. I wanted to look nice, put together, organized, and confident. I didn't want to show up looking the way I felt, exhausted, disheveled, and apprehensive. I figured I would look the way God saw me, not the way I saw myself. Sabria looked at me and said, "Aww, you look cute. You don't look like a mom." This was exciting to me because I live my life to try to represent what I feel all moms are, fearfully and wonderfully made. I hope to always remain the opposite of weakness and push against the grain to let moms know they can and should be different as they are found to be in God's likeness. This means that I want to change what the recent image of a mom is. I told Sabria to wish me luck, and she told me that there wasn't luck, only blessings. I smiled at her and told her she was right.

I made it to Starbucks and figured this man thought of me as an angry mom from Ohio with a chip on her shoulder with no business there, but that's not who I was. I was driven and purposeful, and I wanted change. The meeting started out interesting. I bought himself and myself a coffee and one to bring back for Sabria for when we were finished. When I offered him the coffee, he looked at me and said that he didn't drink coffee and that he was caffeine-free. I was impressed at how he could snub a woman offering him a drink, but I knew I could handle the rejection and let him know by my getting right down to business that his rudeness, in fact, did not faze me. My offering him coffee was simply a nice gesture. Surely, he could have taken the simple coffee I offered him and dumped it out privately after we left the meeting. This action of his was familiar and told me that he did not find my presence worth the offering of reverence or even simple respect. I just prayed in my mind that God would smooth out the mood and that this man and I could talk out this situation and that some kind of good would come from this encounter. I told him the story of Sabria, and we talked about jump stretch and her history at home with the measures she took to prevent an ACL tear through her time spent in this program. He said he had never heard of the program, so I then pulled out my notes and research I had done and gave him a couple of DVDs. These videos were from Coach Carl. I explained that I saw a lot of potential in my daughter and I was passionate about the situation she was in. I told him that Sabria was known in our area as a beast. She had a twenty-four-inch vertical and could finish her shots with three girls hanging on her arms. She was strong and efficient at running forward, backward, and laterally; and she got this way by performing rubber band squats against hundreds of pounds of pressure for time and reps and by running and jumping against the resistance of the rubber bands during the intense circuit training class. She did these hour-long workouts twice a week for the last couple of years, which I did believe kept her legs strong enough and balanced to withstand all the hard basketball she played without sustaining any major injury. I explained that the problem I saw after Sabria coming to West Point was that from the time beast was over to the time of the first basketball game was a total of twelve weeks. This was a substantial amount of time for a player to either gain and build their athleticism or lose it. Beast or basic training was six weeks long.

During that time, the kids were not doing athletic training, to my understanding. Sure they were doing soldier and physical training, but that does not take the place of athletic training in a Division 1 sport. It is completely different. After their week or two of rest and getting reorganized after beast, they would then have twelve weeks before their first game, and this is actually enough time to get athletic and conditioned to play at that Division 1 level. As long as the training then extended and continued throughout the basketball season, they would remain in shape the whole season. Of course, the intensity of the training would lessen a bit, but that would be appropriate as long as the results were still seen in the athletes and their physical needs throughout the season were met as would be evidenced by their good form in running and cutting and their energy levels were maintained. If not, troubleshooting would be necessary. I asked him if he was aware that after only two weeks of ending a specific workout program, one loses 50 percent of whatever was gained during that time. He agreed this was true. Those twelve weeks between beast and the first game of basketball was a critical time for a freshman (plebe) because, athletically, they would be severely out of shape after those eight weeks, and I really was concerned about what kind of conditioning and ACL prevention was being done during the time they were preparing to go onto the court and play games. He did let me know that there was a communication issue concerning this and an injury issue and that they did not have an ACL-prevention program in place. The athletic director told me that one of their trainers had trained people in the Olympics so this should be of comfort to me. I am only impressed with results, and he knew I was not impressed with the result I was there to talk about that day. Sometimes people want credit from either a degree or an experience, but what are the results of the program? Are you producing good conditioned athletes or not? Are you keeping your kids from injury or not? What was the fruit of their labor? This is the same way you measure any other action in life. I will say that in the Bible, James 2:14–17 says, "What good is it, my brothers and sisters, if someone claims to have faith but has no deeds? Can such faith save them? Suppose a brother or sister is without clothes and daily food. If one of you says to them, 'Go in peace; keep warm and well fed,' but does nothing about their physical needs, what good is it? In the same way, faith by itself, if not accompanied by action is dead."

The talented girls they recruited that year had done the work to succeed this far, using God's gift of talent and appreciating it enough to feed it and do what it took to make it grow. Now was the time for the coaches and whoever else was involved in this athletic program to respect the talent they were gifted in those athletes and to respond to the faith they had in the girls by building a program that met the athletes where they were and could be a tool to help them to reach to that next level and one that would keep them safe while performing. The director said he had only been there for a few months and was still learning of the deficits but did know there was a weakness in communication and that they did have a too many sustained injuries. He understood that I was only interested in helping my daughter and the other girls to be healthy and that I saw some very big gaps and deficits in the athletic program and I really felt that there was a lot they could do and were obligated to do to bridge that gap and make necessary changes. I asked for Sabria and the other girls to have individual training available so they could train in the best way for their own individual bodies in relationship to their own personal positions on the court. This would be expected at any college, and we even do this in jump stretch and even with multiple different sports represented in one class. Just doing different moves and exercises that will activate certain muscles that are more used by an athlete in a specific sport and by doing exercises that mimic moves expected to be done by the athlete during competition. He said this was a good idea. He agreed that this was necessary. I asked why this wasn't done already

and why the girls' concerns about their bodies and lack of athleticism weren't noticed by anyone. He explained that it's because
most kids who come into that program don't have a routine that
works and they need the leadership, instruction, and direction of
the coaches. He said most girls weren't like Sabria. I appreciated
that he was saying that Sabria was special, but I disagreed in this
idea that the girls didn't know their own bodies and didn't have
good info to share about what exercises worked for them. Girls
who come to West Point are not common girls, and they should
be treated with more respect in the area of athletics. They should
be encouraged to take responsibility for their own bodies but to be
led to do this by their coaches they trusted at the next level. This
was a time that Sabria thought she could grow athletically through
the West Point program, not decline. Now that she was injured,
she was looking even harder at the situation to be accountable for
herself. She was growing passion through her toiling. She was very
dedicated to obedience and respected those in authority but now
felt urged to be responsible for herself and to be accountable to
be a leader in a new way. She would learn through this ways to be
outgoing, of better voicing her concerns, and ways to be her own
advocate—which were tools needed in leadership that she apparently lacked at the West Point level. She saw ways she could grow,
and this was encouraging and birthed a new motivation in her.

A good parent raises their child in hopes of one day getting
out of the way and letting the kid lead their own selves. A parent, while teaching, even before teaching should be able to see the
strengths in the child to be able to highlight these strengths while
they raise them and aid to turn their weaknesses into strengths.
This is what Coach Carlos did concerning Sabria. Before he even
took Sabria onto the court, he consulted with us, her parents, to
ask what we felt her strengths were and then also what she hoped
to get better at. He needed these bench markers as a coach so he
could help Sabria be built into the athlete she believed she could

become. He gained our trust as he never went offtrack with this and always stayed in a place that yielded growth. To yield growth in the athlete, you must have a plan, and that plan should be built with the athlete, so there is no confusion, and there must be open communication throughout the process. I told this man at West Point that Sabria had knowledge and experience that yielded good growth in her and this should be used to help her make a routine for herself in a way that could further the process. Her request from him was that she felt like she lost her way after getting out of shape there and she needed a point of reference. She wanted bench markers. Numbers to look at. A plan to follow. She wanted good communication and standards set with accountability that produced positive results. I would see in the future if they would help her or if she would have to reach inside herself and find true grit and self-empowerment to be successful and to be the athlete she truly desired to be. She knew exactly what was missing in her workouts but would those in charge lead her or still tell her to be taught. Both, in fact, would be needed. I knew she couldn't have trust in the program now, because, although God allowed the injury to take Sabria on an inspirational journey, there were still obvious issues that led to the injury. If Sabria was going to be taught and trained, there had to be something there to be of good use to yield growth. What would that be? I couldn't help but to be excited to see what was to come, because, as God is my witness, when there is a will, there is a way; and Sabria was willing, and God was always faithful. Even after being injured, she was willing to be used by God and to be a soldier. She was motivated and thankful for whatever was to come. She wanted to be obedient but knew that there was no growth in her body as a result of her obedience thus far concerning athletics. Still, she would remain confident that God would remove obstacles and allow humility to rise up in the program to clear vision to see where the deficits were. Otherwise, no gains would be made, and this was what I was fighting against. If ever you see any success that is built with pride, it is short-lived, or it is fake, having no quality and deemed worthless. This is true in any school and on any team. This lesson is taught in Matthew 7:24–27. It is the story about building your house on a firm foundation, and the facts hold true in athletic training as well.

> Everyone who hears these words of mine and does them will be like a wise man who built his house on the rock. And the rain fell, and the floods came, and the winds blew and beat on that house, it did not fall, because it had been founded on the rock. And everyone who hears these words of mine and does not do them will be like a foolish man who built his house on the sand. And the rain fell and the floods came, and the winds blew and blew against that house, and it fell, and great was the fall of it.

Sabria was being asked to spray a hose full of kinks, and she cannot expect to get water out of that hose. It cannot happen... I believed that, whether or not changes would be made for Sabria, she would find a way through the storm because God was there and he would lead the way. He was her firm foundation, and she knew if she trusted him, he would provide what she needed to train hard and right to be safe and to get to the next level.

I left our meeting feeling refreshed because I knew I did what God asked me to do, and that was how the pressure was taken off my conscience. I knew I was engaged. I knew God could use this man, and I sensed that this man had compassion enough for my daughter and the other athletes by his willingness to meet with me that day and to hear what I had to say. He admitted that he knew there needed to be changes made and was going to look into the situation to see what needed done to prevent more injuries. I understood his apprehension and abrasiveness at the beginning of our meeting because we both would be talking about, something we didn't want to discuss but both felt obligated and pushed by our conscience to reveal it as a problem. I hoped he could see that, even though I was not an expert per se, I was knowledgeable and had a very good reason to be concerned for my daughter and the other girls and I was just acting on my duty to be an advocate for Sabria and athletics based on that knowledge. I knew this man had a lot on his plate and did not envy his position but did thank him for his efforts that I did believe he would use to further investigate and make changes. I didn't know how, but I knew Sabria would be on course because she was on mission to heal and succeed, and with God by her side, there was no way to fail. It was simply trust and obey. God would see her through the storm. The athletic director did end up following through with my request of calling Coach Carl to understand better the jump stretch program Sabria had been doing so that he could better serve her as an athlete, as he was open to the idea of possibly incorporating some of the exercises there at West Point she was used to doing in her career prior to this and that she knew kept her safe and athletic. I will tell you as a sidenote that, interesting enough, about thirteen days after our meeting in that Starbucks, the athletic director was forced out of his position at West Point. I thanked him for his attempts and did not lose hope in the situation. My anchor holds firm, and my hope remains that there will be change.

Therapy was scheduled for the next day. This was a hard day. Sabria was having a lot of pain, but how she dealt with her recovery and her example to others through this experience would be very important. Going through this recovery with honor and learning how to get better under pressure was not going to be easy. Athletics at every level has a large platform. At the college and professional level, the stage is big and bright. Many young people, and even those who are older, look up to athletes as a ray of hope. We need to do a better job of helping those athletes to see their responsibility while in such a spotlight. They need to be more careful of what they are representing in their behavior. It is everyone's job to make people see their worth as we set the standards higher. I believe good character which is displayed by a player's respect of others, self-discipline, love toward the players and fans, selflessness, and diligence should be what are seen by others when watching sports. If a player does not have these qualities, they are, in fact, not an athlete at all and should not be granted the privilege of playing on the field or court. Being an athlete should highlight your life; it should not be your life. There are many players in sports I could talk of who do not display good character, and this should be looked at. Sure everyone deserves second chances, but to live a life of this behavior should not be encouraged by others. I believe I am also thinking back to my younger days and not being a good example to others. I do believe that I longed to have someone hold me to a higher standard. I wanted to be held accountable for my actions and really would have benefitted from someone to see that my deeds did not match my faith and called me out on it to help steer me in the right direction. People do great things in the world of sports, but not having the good character to go with the physical talent means that you are not truly successful, and your career will not go as far as it should go. In other words, you will not produce any good fruit. In essence, I am saying that we will, unfortunately, never see the highest point of these athletes' potential, because they are distracted by their desire to be reckless with their attitudes and heart. It is well-known that women's sports are not given the respect of men's sports, but God gives the same respect to both, so we as women are never really at a loss. My concern for Sabria's case is just that she would be loved and that attention would be paid to fixing obvious problems in the training of young athletes. I do hope, and even expect, to change the world's view of women's sports versus men's. I am very focused, though, to just make a change where I am because there is power in that. We as parents do have the opportunity to change the world, and it starts in our own home and with our own kids. This is where I am called to action. I do know God has a plan and it will prosper despite the hardships and prejudice that have come our way. These are stumbling blocks but no worse than what we all face every day. These are common problems, according to 1 Corinthians 10:13, which tells us that no temptation has overtaken us except what is common to mankind... Our response should not be common, though, as referenced in Romans 12:2, which tells us not to be conformed to the pattern of this world but to be transformed by the renewal of our mind. People must believe that they bring the difference. This is where change can occur. Even if the change is within ourselves for the sake of others. Prejudice is only in the mind of the beholder. It only has power if the one it is meant for accepts the hate, instead of denying it. We are who God says we are, and he says we are all equal.

CHAPTER 23

I LOOKED UP AND SAW THE MOON, MY WITNESS

A s I sat bedside with Sabria after her second therapy of the day, we began to talk about the experience we were in. I told her it was nice that her basketball friend came to visit her and talked about her own experience tearing both of her ACLs there at West Point. One injury involved the meniscus, and one did not. She was explaining to us that the leg that had no meniscus involvement had substantially less pain and recovery time was reduced dramatically. With no meniscus involvement, you may start weight-bearing and running much sooner. This was exciting to Sabria, and I know she was thanking God for what she was dealing with knowing that it could have been worse. She believes that, according to the MRI, the meniscus was torn and also the MCL. After a month's time once the surgery took place, the doctor saw that only the ACL was torn. The MCL had time to heal, which was the hope and often the case with this particular ligament after rest and rehab; and the meniscus did not show injury and did not need repaired. Sabria and I believe that God healed her meniscus over that month. She accepted the challenge of going through this injury and was willing to be a light. God met her there. He always meets us where we are in our faith and doesn't give us more than we can bear. I believe he knew it was not necessary for Sabria to have the injury be worse in order to get a good spiritual growth out of the situation for her, her family, and those around her; so God spared her the extra struggle. She had faith in him, and he showed her who he was in the situation. This also built her trust in him. She told me in that hospital bed that our sufferings were a sweet fragrance to God if we give the glory back to him. She said that she trusted God when she got injured and knew he would see her through. She didn't completely understand why this happened, but she didn't need the full understanding to follow as he led. She just continued to be a witness of his power and grace even through a tough situation. We believe he performed the miracle of healing her meniscus to show that he had everything under control. He could have healed the entire knee, but this was not the plan. We knew the plan he had in store was even better than we could have imagined. The tear on the ACL was clear-cut and was able to be repaired in such a way that it could actually end up being stronger, with more support than before the injury. They used additional support from the IT band, and this particular part of the procedure was done with the thought that it would protect the knee during pivoting moves, specifically. Sabria told me that she thought of her knee as an accessary to aid in her journey to potential greatness. I could see her love for life and basketball as she talked to me and was still smiling through the pain and a future filled with unknown blessings. She was seeing the rainbow. Maybe I was the one who needed to see the rainbow after the storm and Sabria was showing me as we could see God's existence and position in this situation as he was teaching us so much.

The two nights in the army hospital spent with Sabria are times I will never forget. I helped her as much as I could and was thankful that she didn't have to be there alone, although I do know God never leaves her side. I was honored to be able to show her love that she could learn and show to others and to just feel the love and compassion that one can have for another is good medicine. The doctor was considering having her stay another night because her pain was so bad; but being that she was who she was and wanted to face the music and get on with life, plus the fact that I had to leave and go back to Ohio and would not be staying another night, she decided to be discharged and go back to her barracks. I walked out to my car that evening to pack up our things before leaving the hospital, and as soon I got out to the dark parking lot, I started to feel the pressure of leaving my girl again. Letting my guard down, I began to cry. I told myself to be strong and kept walking, feeling my feet taking my body to the car as I became stoic. A blankness came over me. I looked around at the beautiful crooked trees and the shadows that were made from the beautiful lighting at West Point and, as I looked up, saw the moon, full of light. *There it is*, I thought. *My witness. Evidence that God is with me and his light never goes out and is always leading me to my next task.* I remembered my mission, my purpose.

I had a flashback to my senior year in high school. I saw myself standing in the driveway of one of the houses Bobby had lived in with his mom in the ghetto. I had just come from inside after taking a pregnancy test that revealed the reality I had been afraid of. I looked around at all the unkempt landscaping and the run-down nature of that little old house in the ghetto, and I began to panic. How would I explain myself to my parents, coaches, friends, and church? *No, this can't be true*, I thought. *Let's go back. Let's rewind time.* Reality told me this wasn't possible, so I thought, *How can I just make this thing I'm going through disappear?* My life flashed before my eyes, and I knew that I had to go through this with dignity and honor. I had to do what was right. All my options went through my head at lightning speed, but the only one that made sense to me was to love the baby that was inside me. No matter the devastation this situation would have on my senior year. No matter the disappointment it would bring to my family and friends. I was vulnerable, weak, confused. The one thing I still had was that little glimmer of light that was inside me. Jesus told me to keep moving. I flushed the option of abortion out of my mind because my actions were not the child's fault and this was, even in, a desperate situation, against what I believed. Adoption, maybe. Raising the child myself, possibly. That day, I saw myself as broken, disappointing, ugly, and reckless. God told me I was made in his image. He told me I was fearfully and wonderfully made. He taught me to see with his eyes because his vision brings power. This power provides passion, motivation, strength, endurance, wisdom, and encouragement. I didn't, on that day, completely believe what he was telling me; but all I needed was a little faith and to take one little step at a time, and this was where I was at that point. Everything will work out for the good because he is good and he is in me. He is a way maker, a mountain mover, a storm calmer. He would lead the way to loving that baby I later called Sabria. Every move I made after that moment, in that driveway, in the ghetto, that day was made to love Sabria. Sure, I failed. Over and over again, I failed, but I never lost hope, and God never left me. Even after my mom shunned me, my peers gossiped and found nothing good about me. My love for Sabria forced me to ignore my morning sickness enough to allow my body to push itself out of that bed and get to school, a place that highlighted my sin and indignant behavior. I decided over time to realize what I was for Sabria. I was a vessel. I had told God during the pregnancy that I had enough wisdom to know that I was not worthy of the task of being this baby's mother and I put that child in God's hands. I would be the vessel used to bring the child into the world, and

God would raise her through me. This was how it was meant to be for all of us as parents. It took the pressure off me, and I became as light as a feather. Sabria always inspired me to be better, to do better. The transformation that happened inside my heart because of this baby was a true miracle, and I was never the same after God showed me that truth. So as I walked to my car looking at the moon and thinking how amazing it was that I was at West Point and Sabria was the same age at that point that I was when I delivered her, I was overwhelmed with shear amazement at where God had brought us nineteen years later after standing in that driveway in the ghetto and feeling hopeless. I was recharged in that parking lot remembering where Sabria and I had been together and how God had brought us through so many storms together.

I knew right then that God was behind me with his hand cupping my back, leading me forward as I continued loving Sabria. His light shined from the moon as evidence of the light in my heart, casting away all shadows of doubt. I smiled and joy filled my heart. I was happy to take Sabria back to the barracks. This was my mission. Not to take her home with me or to stay with her another day. My mission was to love her, and that meant taking her back to her room at the barracks and let her live her life and to be her own vessel for God. I was thankful for where God had brought us and thankful for his faithfulness in never leaving us. I needed this encouragement to go back to Sabria's hospital room. I went back to her room to escort her to the car, and I could see in her face that she was apprehensive. She'd been so tough up to this point but now was having an intense moment of pain; and knowing what was coming in her hard life at the academy, she asked me, "Mom, am I gonna be okay? Can I do this?" After thinking of what God had just showed me in the parking lot, I looked at her in complete confidence and said, "Yes, you can do this. Let's go. You're ready." We made it to the car, the same car I had tried to get Quintin into after leaving the hospital in Akron after his ACL surgery a month earlier, and I knew this would be a struggle. Trying to maneuver her six-foot-one, 190-pound body into that car was torture. I helped as much as I could, but she was in serious pain. Thankfully, I had done this with Quintin, so I knew how to elevate her leg after getting her in, but it was not easy. Tears streamed down her face, my stomach was in knots, but I told her tomorrow would be better and she could do it. We drove that snowy night down the street for about three minutes to her barracks, and every bump or slight swerve of the car was brutal, and she was yelling at me the whole way. She moaned and cried; and I just gripped the wheel, drove as smooth as possible, and told her I was sorry and that things would get better. Finally, we made it. I got her laundry basket out of the trunk that housed her ice machine and odds and ends—things that she had to take back with her. It would be a long haul from that parking lot to her room, and I did not know how she would make it on crutches. We started the walk into the cold, blistery New York winter night. The fierce wind was blowing. My ears were on fire from the bitter cold. She wasn't saying much; she just kept crutching fast, and I could tell she was focused. I looked over at her and could see that her ears were beet red, but, of course, she didn't complain. There was a busload of cadets who had just gotten back from a game and were getting back to their rooms. I knew it was hard to watch all the other athletes scurry past us with no trouble as I imagined she struggled to hold back tears from the pain. I couldn't believe the distance she would have to go and only one day after surgery. This was a feat, and with every step she took, I was admiring her. We finally made it. I counted four hundred crutch strides to get from the car to the place where I'd leave her. I told her she was a champion. I was surprised she did not faint or vomit on the trip, but she was so determined that this would not hold her back. I was amazed at this young lady. We said goodbye, and thankfully, one of her leaders met her to carry her basket to her room since she was on crutches. I watched her walk away until once again she disappeared through Sally Way toward that beautiful brick building that would house my precious pearl. I turned around and walked through the cold night back to my car, thinking of how passionate I was about preventing this injury from happening to anyone else as it did to my daughter and my son. I do believe all things happen for a reason, but I am not comfortable with just taking this injury and not looking for the responsibility of everyone to do all they can to promote health and safety to athletes. I saw how everyone's life was just going on as normal, but for Sabria, she had to go down this other road. Soldiers were marching, running, walking, playing. Coaches would continue their schedules as normal. The basketball team was on their way back that night from an away game and had to the opportunity to visit the Pentagon while on that trip. Sabria would have enjoyed that opportunity to visit the Pentagon and was really bummed that she, instead, was recovering from surgery. Her entire next year of her life was rerouted as a result of this injury, and I do believe this needs to be looked at so preventative programs are put in place and utilized to keep athletes safe and to also prevent the loss of other opportunities and training. My family was willing to go through the struggles that came along with this setback, but did anyone ever look at the pressure that is put on cadets and their families when these kinds of things happen? My husband taking a vacation from work and us splitting up to meet the needs of our family, the financial strain of taking an unexpected trip to New York and the strain that put on our other kids, Sabria being taken away from the sport she loved—these were all very good reasons to look into the situation and find better ways to train to prevent injury and to not just look at these kids as statistics and to say this was a common problem but to look deeper and see if anything could change for the better and, once again, gain perspective.

CHAPTER 24

THE PERFECT STORM

I left West Point that night and headed home. I started out a little apprehensive for a few reasons. I was starting out later than expected, and if there was anything I hated, it was driving in the dark…in the winter…through the night. There I was, facing my fear. I had just witnessed Sabria being so brave, and I knew I had to be, too, in order to complete the mission and to be a good example. It began as a nice drive. The roads were clear. I was wide awake and had a full tank of gas. Before I left home, I had done all the checks. I got a membership with AAA since I would be traveling alone, and my dad had gotten me a brand-new tire to put in my trunk in case I needed a spare since my car was a model that did not come with spares and he did not think this was safe. I made arrangements for Quintin and the other kids and had gotten shifts covered at work. I had done all I could to be responsible to make this trip alone, and my dad made sure to tell me before I left that I was ready, just like I tell Sabria when she needs a boost of confidence. I knew there may be some kinks along the way, but surely I would be able to overcome the obstacle, and I felt I was responsible for planning as much as I could, and I left the rest up to God. As I was on the freeway, heading home and feeling accomplished in all that had happened those last three days, I was proud of being brave and trusting in God. I was making good time thus far. There was no traffic, and I was thinking, *Well, this isn't so bads after all.* It was about an hour into my drive when I looked to the right and saw a big mound of snow. *Hmm, this area must have gotten hit with a lot of snow. I'm so glad it's not snowing now. Thank God, it's not snowing now. That would be terrible!* I thought. Just then I started to see some flurries. I thought, *Okay, this is fine. I can deal with some flurries. No problem.* Then it started to get really dark all of the sudden. I put my wipers on to try to help somehow to see better, and then it hit. All of the sudden and straight out of nowhere, a complete whiteout! Big, white snow. That's all I saw coming from every direction. I saw nothing but white on my windshield. I looked to my side—nothing. I looked to the other side—nothing. I tried to look to the ground—nothing. White everywhere! I saw nothing but snow against the darkness. I gasped and slowed my speed. I couldn't see cars ahead of me or behind. No signs were visible. I couldn't pull over, because I could not see any lines on the road. I knew I was still in the mountains and that there were cliffs surrounding me, but at this point, I had no direction, whatsoever. I thought of exiting the freeway but couldn't see exit signs and knew there were semis on this route and was afraid if I stopped, they would not have time to stop after seeing me in front of them. I had no point of reference, no bench markers, no compass. There was nothing to tell me that I was staying on course. I had no idea what to do next or where to go from there. I did wonder if I would make it through that storm alive. I gripped the steering wheel with my sweaty palms and felt my legs trembling. My whole body began to shake as I felt the fear of death that could be coming. I prayed as my jaw was clenched and my teeth, chattering. My stomach was in knots, and I began to feel nauseous. I could see a dim light from the car in front of me that I was approaching, so I knew I was still driving straight, but then it would disappear, and I didn't know if that car sped up or if I slowed down or if the snow came harder. I just knew the light was gone. Once in a while, there would be a streetlight, and this would illuminate enough for me to see cars or an exit sign, but then it went dark again. My body began to shake all over like it did every time after giving birth to my kids. It was that feeling of no control. I clung tight to the wheel and started saying, "God, please take the snow. God, please take the snow." I prayed what I thought could be my last prayers on earth, knowing this storm could very well end my life. Just then I remembered a story that my childhood friend's mom, Monica, had recently told me of a time when she was on the way to visit her mom in the hospital in a blizzard and she couldn't see anything. She couldn't see a way through on the road, but all of the sudden, out of nowhere, a way opened, and there was a perfect path for her to drive through. It was like God just paved a path for her. It was like he just took the snow and moved it right out of the way for her! I believed God could do this for me, so I just kept asking him to take the snow as I knew it came from him anyway and he had complete control over this situation. I drove in this stormy whiteout for what felt like forever, but I believe it lasted about forty minutes. Sure enough, after the situation nearly annihilated me, the snowed cleared; just like that, I could see again. All of the snow was gone, and the roads were clear and dry. I was so relieved that I could see again and thanked God for getting me through that storm.

I really felt like I stared death in the face and ultimately realizing it wasn't my time to go, knowing that God had complete control over life and death and he chooses when it is time. It wasn't until later that I connected the dots. I wondered why this happened. Why did I have to face one of my biggest fears and then be shook to my core by facing that fear with no direction, no vision, and the feeling of complete helplessness and vulnerability? Why did I survive that drive? So many people have died as a result of

accidents on the road involving ice and snow in similar circumstances to what I had just encountered. Why was I safe? Why did
I make it home to my family when so many others don't? Why
even ask why? I immediately knew the answer. God revealed to me
that what I was experiencing on the road that day in that whiteout
was what Sabria was experiencing at West Point. I had a complete
vision of what she was experiencing and was up against—she was
being tested by being away from home and after giving all she had
to the academy that she allowed to break her down, followed by
having the thing she loved most in life possibly taken away from
her, and now trying to bounce back without really knowing what
to expect or what was even going to come of her efforts. Sabria
had told me that right before her injury she didn't know her body
anymore like she once had. She said that she couldn't even tell how
far gone she was athletically, because she had no bench markers
and no point of reference. Her compass was gone, and she did not
know where to go from there. This was what I was feeling on the
road. God gave me perspective and vision to see what Sabria was
really dealing with. It is what we all deal with on a daily basis in
our own lives and struggles. He also showed me that even though
I could not see where to go, he still carried me through. Sometimes
he leads, but sometimes he must carry us through our storms. I
knew that this experience of surgery was refreshing for Sabria. She
was able to tap into God's grace and mercy and find power in
hope. She had vision to see that God would carry her when she
did not know her way, and this was where he had us both. Seeing
the rainbow after the storms and seeing hope for the future. As
I dropped her off, she was walking back into West Point with a
beat-up spirit, and she was weary, but nothing could keep her away
from the fight for greatness. Even as she crutched her way back
in only able to walk on one leg, she would not give up. I knew she
did not know what was coming, but we never do anyway. She did
know that God was carrying her, and that was enough to keep her

going forward. That knowledge of hope in God was enough for her to leave her mom once again and never look back.

These battles we go through are for our own spiritual growth as well as the growth in others. These are faith building blocks. Even when we don't completely understand the situation, we can still be faithful and keep moving even blindly. Even when we can't move, we can let God carry us. Eventually, when the time is right, the snow gets lifted, and we can see again. I know that God took me through that storm so I could be a help to my daughter, so I could have vision and passion to help her in her time of need, and so I could understand her fear and face my own. What an honor and true gift of grace to go through that storm and learn on a new level how to trust God. I knew that whether the basketball program made changes or not, God would make Sabria game ready. He would be her compass, her point of reference, her benchmark, her direction. Sabria was confident that, no matter the obstacle, she would be complete again and would be better than before because God had changed her and was, in fact, molding her into a beautiful stone, smooth and solid. She would be strong and would be ready to play basketball again without fear and without anyone or anything holding her back. We both knew that there was nothing separating us from God's love. This was where she would smack the ground and get mad like she did in the Army/Air Force game right before halftime. This was where she decided that she was coming out second half ready to slay and take care of her team and make her coaches proud, with her family cheering her on and nothing holding her back from winning the game after a huge deficit when the other team thought they had the game in the bag. This was where Sabria was most comfortable. She needed a reason to try hard and a reason to shine, and this was it. The target was in range. Her mission was in view. She was locked and loaded and ready to fire. I was confident that I would see some amazing things from Sabria, and I couldn't wait for what was to come. I made it home from that long drive, and I was never the same. I walked in the house into the kitchen in the middle of the night, when everyone was in bed; and as I turned around, I caught a glimpse of my reflection in that window, the same window I looked in before I left to take Sabria back. Only this time, I saw confidence, beauty, and strength. I saw him. My body was in shock over what it just went through, and I was still jittery. I was really just so excited to have this moment knowing I was in God's hands, and nothing could take away that moment of competing with self-doubt and winning that battle. That is where you want to go with God. Go through experiences giving everything you have and getting pushed to your limits. Anything less than that is just not worth doing. Thinking about all the little details associated with this life on earth can seem petty after going through big storms, but God helps to see the importance of these details and how to remain focused on it all. So many times, I see people measure worth by how much something costs or how long they themselves worked to get where they are at in life; but along that route, they become self-righteous, unable to truly see anymore.

As a nurse, would I love my patients any more if I had a higher degree than just my simple diploma? Surely not, but this is the agenda pushed by hospitals and society today. The higher degree you have, the more valuable you are. Sometimes I see this chase for success ending up with empty knowledge, as it never really helps a person become any better or do greater work, so I wonder sometimes, what is the point in all the toil? I have not needed to go down this route yet of pursuing a higher degree, but I will only go down that route if it is God inspired so as to not waste my time in empty study and research, chasing after a prize that yields no worth. I have learned over the years (without extra college) how to love my patients better. I have learned how to walk into a room and actually look at them and their families to see how I can help them on their journey in life. Whether my patient is a thirteen-year-old girl, one whose baby was a product of rape, or a woman who had several losses and finally had a healthy-term baby to take home. Then there is the patient who thinks I'm going to judge her or think anything less of her because she's been a drug addict for several years and, as a result, her baby is sick or the prostitute who cannot wait to be discharged after delivering her tenth child so she can leave the baby and get back to the streets for her next fix. How would more college teach me how to better love the mother who had a scheduled C-section for Monday to deliver her full-term baby, only to find out the baby died over the weekend and no one can explain why? Would more college help me explain to this mother how to do the impossible and transition her heart and mind to, instead of planning for the new arrival of her sweet baby, plan for the funeral and say goodbye to the child she never got to meet? Would more schooling teach me how to help this mom go home to her fully prepared nursery and to return all those gifts she got from her baby shower or take down that crib that she no longer needs? Certainly not. This is why I am so concerned with our society that has us wasting so much time "learning" when I'm left wondering when people are going to start using the brain and heart God gave them and use his wisdom and guidance to help the people of this world. Did I go to school to learn how to fix those old plaster walls in my old starter house that was built in 1920? No. I learned how by remembering things my dad taught me when I was young—being brave, thinking outside the box, and searching for tips while being eager to learn. I couldn't afford to hire anyone to do the work, and the job seemed too big, but that's why I prayed first and then got to work. Did I back down from fixing the kitchen after the broken pipes ruined the ceiling? No. I prayed first and then got to work. Am I any less of a mother because I can't afford to buy my family a $400,000 house to live in to have more space, or are my kids content in the small $80,000 house they grew up in? I remember a paper that Sabria wrote in high school. She wrote about how her heart was heavy thinking about how she would miss her time spent in our old house and how she appreciated that it was small because her family all gathered in the living room where there was more space. This is the place we would all talk about our day and unwind together as a family, and that closeness is what she would miss at West Point more than anything else. This closeness we shared led to strong family bonds as we learned from each other over the years, helping each other through good times and bad. We don't need all those extra things, more space, or extra schooling to have great experiences with God and to give our kids all they need in life. I'm telling this to those who wonder how to have God's richest blessing in your life; it's free. So as your kids are struggling through situations alone or getting into trouble while you are chasing that degree and your family is falling apart because you have to make one more dollar for that dream house, that boat, new truck, or camper, remember in the end, it is worthless. Be careful that the storms you are in are the ones God led you into and not ones you led yourself into. Sometimes we create our own problems and then blame God for the result. There is nothing he cannot help you overcome, but this life is full of distractions that can keep you far away from the truth on your journey. Even if you think you know it all, try to learn what God wants to teach you. Even if your life is in shambles and you don't think it can be fixed, know there is always hope in the one who made you. You may be surprised at the good life you could be living that you are, in fact, missing out on. God led me to write this as he and I both know I have learned from many mistakes over the years, and I don't even deserve to be writing these stories, but that grace was sufficient for me, and it is for you also.

CHAPTER 25

SEEING SPORTS AS
A PRIVILEGE

It makes me sad to hear about kids who once loved a sport but allowed the discouragement of poor coaching or teammates who didn't respect the game and didn't see the act of playing sports as a privilege, a special right. Only those who are honorable should be granted the opportunity to play. Of course, sports is a tool used to teach honor, but if this is not learned and shown by the athlete, this should be recognized by the coach who can then troubleshoot to help direct or redirect the athlete. None of us deserve to play on such a big platform. We all play sports in grace. Sports can be a way to rise to our greatest potential in life and can also serve as therapy, motivation, and accountability when we fall offtrack. I've seen the passion to play sports stolen from kids so many times, and this is a true tragedy. Coaches may sometimes have their own selfish agendas when they decide to take the position as coach. Coaches, teachers, and parents are very weighted positions that are held in high honors by God, so taking these jobs lightly is a risky move. As James 3:1 teaches us, "Not many of you should become teachers, my fellow believers, because you know that we who teach will be judged more strictly." It seems that people are pushing themselves into these positions but they don't always truly appreciate the sacrifice, passion, and fierce willingness to push against the grain that it takes to be a good coach. They must really care about kids and even adults who may have grown up continuing their journey in athletics but never learning how to have good character. Good coaches are not consumed with climbing the social status ladder, just simply needing something to do in the evening, wanting something to go on their résumé, or simply desiring to stay connected to a sport they enjoy. These are worthless reasons to be a coach, and yet these are all reasons some will give as to why they chose to be a coach.

I will tell about a situation I experienced with my son Dylan and how he is learning the value in good coaching and how playing the sport you enjoy is a privilege. I had watched Dylan's basketball team play and was impressed with how the coach really watched the boys and demanded discipline. The team really looked like they played together well, and there was good chemistry established on the court. The boys were focused on making plays running them through and making good passes instead of driving in and flopping to get the foul called. Every now and then, you'd see one of them doing this in their weakness, as it was still in their nature as young boys to be selfish. The coach was on top of it, though, constantly reeling the boys back in to team play and really keeping that self-centered play to a minimum. I appreciated this as I watched and wanted my son, who was a freshman, to learn discipline and respect for his neighbor while playing the game of basketball and to see others before himself. Dylan had a rough year thus far as he suffered from severe acne and was on a harsh medication called Accutane. Taking this drug may cause certain side effects such as back pain, mood swings, dry skin, and nosebleeds, which he did experience. He had to be regularly monitored by the doctor while on this drug. Dylan struggled while on this medicine for six months to rid himself of the terrible acne that haunted him and caused him pain. Dylan was not much of a complainer and was rather humbled through this experience, being thankful for the said cure that he hoped would deliver him from the condition. I watched as he would get made fun of by his peers and people he didn't even know would make jokes about his face. He pushed through lifting at the gym for football, despite the terrible back pain he endured. He never wanted to stand out or have a spectacle made of him or to make it seem like he was making excuses to not give his best, so he just pushed through hoping his efforts to be strong and vigilant would bring him clear skin in the end without making gaps in his football and basketball training. He continued to tell the doctor on office visits that he felt okay and that he was willing to continue the treatment as long as it was recommended, but he would always later ask me, in private, when this would finally be over for him. I encouraged my son after his lifts in the gym and helped him clean up after his nosebleeds, praying that God would protect my son and keep him in his hands while he battled through this as it did seem to consume our lives. Dylan and I believed that God would eventually deliver him from this when it was time. He was a shy kid and just wanted to look normal and wanted the physical and emotional pain of the acne to be gone. Those nosebleeds brought back to mind his younger days in school when his so-called friends were bullying him. They would push his face up against trees and hit him in the face with the zippers from their jackets. Amazingly enough, the teachers who were on duty during recess when these episodes took place never witnessed this activity. I only found out later when Dylan started having random nosebleeds at home, and after investigating the situation, we found out of the abuse. He didn't want to get those boys whom he considered his friends in trouble. I had to explain to Dylan that this was not behavior that came from friends and he needed to stand up for himself and for what was right.

Over the years, Dylan has had many encounters with people who have pretended to care about him; and he had to learn that not everyone is loving, kind, and honorable. God does not promise that we will never be confronted with this kind of sin but wants us to be a light so those around us can know the right way to be a friend. He is still learning now at the age of fifteen but has become a good judge of character through the situations he has encountered in life. So now as he was dealing with the acne and all the side effects that he had been dealing with behind the scenes, he learned to really appreciate his close friends who never judged his face or made him feel different. Before we began the treatment, Dylan was diligent in following directions to try to keep his face clear, and he worked harder than I could have even expected of a boy his age but to no avail. So this medicine brought much hope for him, as nothing else worked. I knew he was learning discipline, perseverance, and diligence; but I hoped he wouldn't lose his sweetness through this and would not lose hope and become depressed, as some kids do, while on this particular treatment regimen. This is what I asked of God: to keep my son connected to him while facing the battles in his life. He remained focused and dedicated. He knew some kids were just mean, and this was a way for Dylan to gain perspective and to learn how to treat others with love and to not make them feel the way he was made to feel when he was made fun of for the thing he hated most about himself. We began to see a light at the end of the tunnel after several months and continued the therapy for about a total of seven months. We did see some scarring from the acne, but I told Dylan we would deal with it if we needed to, no big deal. He really wasn't concerned as he was not a vain kid and didn't mind the imperfections. He was a handsome kid and was rather relieved that the condition of his acne was disappearing and his skin was clear and pain-free. I figured if the scarring ended up being bad enough that Dylan wanted to fix it, we would; otherwise, we left well enough alone. I wanted to teach him how to troubleshoot when situations came up in our lives and, even though we may not want to deal with things that are hard, we could go through it, gain confidence, and have success as we are challenged.

During this time on Accutane, Dylan also encountered the episode of appendicitis and found an answer to the chronic head-aches he was having, which we found was due to vision problems that he noticed while reading. I took him for an eye exam and got him fitted for glasses. He was learning accountability, and I was proud of his eagerness to be responsible for himself through all these situations. This span of time was from about June and went through Christmastime in 2019. This was a crazy year for my family with all the surgeries and medical issues as well as Sabria going off to the academy. By Christmas, my whole family had been through a lot, but I never wanted anyone to feel they took a back-seat, ever. Dylan knew of the family's financial strain and never asked for much of anything. He only had a few outfits but was thankful and wore those outfits many times over, rarely asking for new clothes. He was always so content. I knew he wanted a pair of Apple AirPods for Christmas and decided he deserved a reward for all he had went through and was still battling. I made sure this was one of the first items I bought when I started my Christmas shopping. He deserved those and so much more, but that was his main present that year as they were an expensive purchase for us. About three weeks after Christmas, Dylan texted me after basket-ball practice and told me that someone stole his new AirPods out of his locker. He had them in his locker, tucked and hidden under some of his clothes. I told Dylan to go tell the coach right away so they could be found and returned. He told me that he was in the lifting room and would go after. Dylan was very careful to respect authority, and this came before his stolen item, so he didn't want to cause a stir or disrupt the session. I gave Dylan the permission to leave lifting and go to the coach. Once he met up with the coach, he showed him his cell phone, and the coach could see the AirPods were pinging somewhere close by in the gym. The thief was crafty and managed to pair the AirPods to their own cell phone, and Dylan and the coach lost the signal and ended their search. A report was made with the police officer, and I asked the coach to call me so we could discuss the matter and touch base on the situation. The varsity and freshman coaches both called me collectively to discuss the issue. First of all, the underlining fact that I knew they would bring up first was the fact that all the kids were to have locks on their lockers and were told this at the beginning of the year. Sure enough, this was what they brought up to me, which was a petty issue, so I decided to humor them and responded by saying that, yes, my son did not listen when told to get a lock on his locker and should be held accountable, yet this does not excuse a young boy for stealing a $150 item from his teammate committing, in fact, a misdemeanor. I was not so concerned with the item but with the abusive and criminal boldness that was displayed by a child at that school and more than likely an athlete. I was dismayed by this. Dylan deserves to be punished for not having a lock on his locker because this was an act of disobedience, but to have his Christmas present taken away forever and to be violated by a schoolmate was not an appropriate punishment in my mind. I made many suggestions to the coaches on the phone including calling the boys' parents and telling them what happened so they could check with their boys to see if anyone had brand-new Apple AirPods that were recently paired to their phones so they could be questioned about how they got them. Surely, any good parent would know if their child had a new $150 device that they couldn't have paid for on their own. The coaches said no way would they be contacting the parents of the boys. They told me that many people had access to that locker room, and they would not admit or assume it could ever be a boy on their team—even though at the time the item was stolen, their team was in the locker room. They said they wouldn't dare call out any of their boys and accuse them of stealing if they had no proof.

It then made sense to me, after years of wondering why the GPA requirement to play sports at that school was a 2.0. I wouldn't dream of setting the bar that low for my son or any of my kids, and they would not even be permitted by me to walk on the court with a 2.0 grade point average. The standard is set low, and this is a disgrace for any so-called athlete to be allowed to play a sport with a 2.0 GPA. Athletes are looked up to. They are to be the elite. They are to be standouts. I believe that leaders are too afraid to make a change and demand excellence because this rising to a higher standard would be expected by the leader as well. A C average in grades is an unacceptable grade for any athlete. Stealing is an unacceptable action for any athlete. Authority should be strict. People should be taught when they are very young to keep their hands off other people's things. This is a simple thing. I was told that this was not a personal crime against Dylan and that it was a random act. Dylan's name was above his locker, and the perpetrator had to search through his personal items and clothes in order to find the item to steal. This tells me whoever took the item knew what they were looking for and knew who had what they wanted and this is as personal as it gets. The coach told me that he was a counselor. I believe he divulged this information to prove him being qualified and having the expertise to handle this appropriately without my help or advice, but as I have said before, I am impressed with action, not titles or degrees or bios or experience. I want to see good results from those around me. I don't trust empty words or promises. I match what is said to me with truth of action and results. He told me to let him handle the issue. He also reassured me that the police were on the case so they, too, would be of good help. I told him okay, which meant, "We'll see if what you say is followed by action and good results." The coach ended the phone call with an authoritative tone telling me that he'd been doing this for twenty-five years so he would be talking to the boys the way he needed to and sarcastically asked if that was okay with me. Of course, I said yes and thanked him for calling me. I got off the phone and began to think about what was discussed. Politically speaking, I take no sides in parties. I am what I guess you would call an Independent party supporter, but I do tend to agree more with Republican views. This coach said something on the phone that stood out to me. He said that he would take a Democratic stand while dealing with this situation, which I understood as meaning that he was favoring social equality in the situation. Now why he had to make this thing a political issue was intriguing to me since I could not seem to get away from politics at this school system. Everything is tweaked based on whom you know, how much money you give, or how much volunteer time you provide. Basically, if you make yourself popular and you support the agenda that is presented, you will go far, or your kid will go far.

I am very familiar with the boasting of the value of certain sports and school programs that end up not yielding good results in the kids. There are also those situations where support and opportunities are given to those thought of as less fortunate, only to gain some kind of popularity for the supporters themselves as they dabble in the act of hypocrisy and self-righteousness. I'm guessing what the coach meant by the statement of keeping it democratic was that he wanted to make things fair across the board his way. I knew that this would result in an injustice for my son, as it did with Quintin in second grade and Sabria in ninth grade. I believe that everyone involved in the raising of kids should have the same agenda which is God inspired. The agenda of raising kids to become leaders who are strong, humble, loving, and passionate about leading a purpose-driven life in Christ. If you spend your time just focusing on pushing social equality—instead of giving the kids the ingredients and the recipe to learn to love others as themselves and to see others as God sees us, as all being equal—

you will be wasting your time. Supporting any selfish and superficial agenda to promote social equality is just keeping you running in a hamster wheel, serving no real purpose and never reaching any destination. The coach wanted to treat everyone equally, which was evidenced by his actions courtside, letting everyone have equal playing time and dishing out good discipline when it was needed and keeping the boys in check. This is all good, right? Teaching good body mechanics is beneficial. It does promote discipline in the body. Spiritual issues, however, need to be dealt with spiritually. You cannot face spiritual issues with only physical mechanics. When I was young, I remember getting spanked when I needed punished for my disobedience. What was far worse was the hour-long lecture that came from my dad afterward when he told me that he disciplined me out of love and that his heart was broke over my disobedience. This was what urged me to change and be responsible and accountable for my actions and to learn the value of listening to my conscience. Discipline is only of value when it comes with spiritual growth, and spiritual growth comes from teaching and the willingness of the student to learn. Now if you've ever heard a Democrat talk, you will notice they often do not have a rationale for why they believe something to be a good idea. They believe in what they believe in because they were most often raised in a Democratic home. They themselves have no idea why they even support certain issues. They just say that was how they were raised, so they take the stand out of what's comfortable and even habitual. It's a stand that's comfortable. Even if it's wrong, it feels good because it's familiar and simple. This may be an okay strategy for a freshman basketball game because it's a mechanical situation—run the play, shoot the ball, pass the ball, set the pick. The mechanics are simple—habitual.

This reminds me of the situation after Sabria tore her ACL. The mechanics were simple—ice, crutches, MRI, doctor visits, surgery. But if you take the situation deeper, that's where you must

reveal the problems that led to the situation or a rationale supporting your actions. That's where you can get to the good stuff and
grow and change. This is where you can obtain attributes of heart.
This is uncomfortable. This will be new and hard and unfamiliar,
but that's where you need to go to teach and learn passion, compassion, love, trust, humility, good sportsmanship, self-control, diligence, humility, and perseverance. Using the experience with the
AirPods would be an opportunity for Dylan's coach to go deeper
with the boys to teach in a spiritual way that would build up good
character and teach good morals, values, and virtue. By remaining Democratic, it keeps things superficial because that's what is
comfortable, familiar, and in the scope of practice that the coach
reportedly had twenty-five years' experience in. This approach
may help the boys organize their thoughts and actions but wasn't
going to train up passionate men of good character. In fact, it may
not even be enough to keep these boys out of jail. Dylan felt bad
because he always had his friends' backs and was proud and eager
to do this. He always played for the team and not himself. He took
pride in being on the team and having the boys around him. He
mentioned to me that his plate was above his locker, and this told
him that this move was a personal violation against him. People
who don't learn how to be personal are capable of unimaginable
evil, never attaching the reality of their actions to a person, soul,
friend, or neighbor. They are mechanical. God says to love your
neighbor at all times. That means all your neighbors. This means
any actions you do to another person is personal because you are
to love everyone, all the time, even people you don't know. Reality
is, truth is, that all of our actions are personal whether intentional
or not. Remaining mechanical is to remain in darkness and in a
fantasy world. When you choose to leave other people's property
alone, you are acting with intent; it's personal. You know to leave
other people's property alone, so you act on what you know is right.

The opposite is true too. If you take from another person, you commit a crime against that person. It's personal.

This living in fantasy is a deep-seated problem in America. This is why Disney is so popular. Everyone is wanting to escape reality and live in a fantasy. You can believe you are a princess or a frog or a pixie because anything is possible in Disney world. I understand the concept and the fun surrounding it; but it is a waste of time and, if taken too far, can grow into a distorted view of God's plan for us. I tell my kids they are, in fact, royalty, but this is because they are kids to the King of kings, and this is reality that brings responsibility and much reason to act with intent and to be personal. Keeping your kids in reality is far more fun and rewarding than living in fantasy where there is nothing of value in the end. I find it intriguing that parents are quick to spend their hard-earned money on and will take much of their time planning their prized vacation to Disney but would never even think to put as much effort into cracking open the Bible on their child's behalf and praying to see how they can be utilized in their child's journey through the reality of life. So many kids are shortchanged because their parents are afraid of the very reality that they are expected to show to their kids. They themselves would rather live in fantasy where nothing is expected of them, except to act and move in their minds. Sabria is getting challenged to her core at West Point. It is a school that challenges an individual to search inside and find their spiritual, physical, and mental grit, striving to respond to the challenge of becoming the absolute best real version of themselves. Many people do get weeded out of the system after it has become obvious that they do not want to live their best life. Witnessing people fail and choosing a life of selfishness does not mean as parents, leaders, and coaches we are excused from making it our mission to encourage and promote the striving of those around us to live a life of honor. No one is perfect; no school system is perfect. The battle of teaching each other and our children doesn't end when you send your kid off to college, even a military college. People still have to make choices in life, and we need to help others make good decisions, and when they fail to make a good decision, we need to help them maneuver through that. Brushing things under the carpet and not dealing with them leads to decay, and that is an ugly place to be. We as parents need to be aggressive to help our kids maneuver through a world that is careless and reckless as a result of only living superficially. I will raise my kids to mimic the good behavior they see in school and to be better than the character that is displayed in those who choose to be selfish and to appreciate all the more those leaders who desire to be the best version of themselves for the sake of others. To rise above the sin. I will raise my kids to have their things stolen right out of their locker and still manage to love their neighbor.

Dylan did get a lock on that locker because he chose to man up and right his wrong, knowing this would not get his Christmas present back and even knowing he had nothing else of value to be taken. He followed instruction and chose to be obedient. Did his AirPods ever get found or returned? *No.* The kids, not the coaches but the kids, did have a suspect in mind. Even though the coaches believed they instilled trust in the kids and believed the kids knew to turn in any information they may have on the perpetrators, the kids would never tell them. They did, in fact, not trust them. There was a boy on the older basketball team who walked around with brand-new AirPods the day after Dylan's were stolen. This boy was on Dylan's football team since they were just young boys, maybe seven years in total. Dylan and the other boys did not want to confront the boy or tell the coaches for fear of retaliation, but they did believe this was the boy who took them. I told Dylan that even though things could very well be as they seemed, only God knew for sure. He should not love the boy any less but learn how to act around others, knowing that not all will act in love. I agreed to just leave it alone and take a lesson from the situation. Dylan was in awe that this kid he considered a friend could have done such a thing. I explained to Dylan that he needed to remember how that felt, so he made sure to never do anything like that to anyone else and to cherish his good friends. I waited a few days, and sure enough, the coaches never followed up on any of this. Where was the democracy for my son in this? How was it fair to him that the situation was never rectified? Social equality? What is the value of social equality or democracy if those who get violated don't see justice but those who violate are free to continue violating? This is not something I believe in. I believe that if God's word is not at the heart of your ambitions and on the forefront of your journey as you strive for democracy, you will never find it or instill it on your team as a coach or in your kids as parents or in the world as leaders. God is not one who tolerates talk with no action, and if you want good results, you must go deeper. Dylan really had learned a lot over that last seven months and was truly becoming a respectable young man, and this was what I cared about. God would reveal his true love for Dylan, and this would be enough to help my son through his own storms in life.

Coaches should be willing to go through the fire with their boy and girl athletes to refine them as young men and women. This means getting uncomfortable. Coach Carlos was willing to go out onto the court to meet Sabria, look at her in the face, and confront her by asking her when she was going to grow up and start acting like a f——king woman. This was a fine approach to me because Carlos knew what would get Sabria's attention and what would prompt her to act. He was not just calling her out in her actions on the court but in life as well. He knew how to light her fire and fuel her passion. He had to push Sabria to go deeper and loved her enough to act. These kids want to have accountability. They want to know that people expect something better out of them than just an average C on their report card and a misdemeanor charge on their record. A few days after the dust settled with Dylan, I was in the stands at one of Theresa's sixth-grade games. Theresa's team was not expected to win that game and was losing against a bigger and better team who was skillful and tough defensively. Theresa's team was down, and she was caught up in a passionate fight for the ball with her opponent when a jump ball was called. Theresa, being skinny and who appeared smaller and weaker than the other girls, reached down and pulled her opponent off the floor and padded her back for encouragement. Even as Theresa's team was losing, she loved her opponent. I was in awe at her commitment to good sportsmanship even when her team was losing. Her attitude remained positively consistent throughout the game. My heart was full. I teach my kids to be personal and to act with intent, treating others how they want to be treated. Let the game of basketball be a tool that helps you teach love, patience, and self-control to others while learning them yourself. She showed that day that you can show love to others, even your opponents and even while losing a game if you keep it personal. Theresa's team actually ended up winning that game as the underdogs, and I told Theresa I was proud of her hard work and good sportsmanship and proving that playing with heart weighed heavier than skill and muscle alone. Coaches play an important role in kids' lives, but God must remain the rudder. As character builds, passion forms. As parents, we need to find ways to fuel that passion, and that job never goes away for us. A child should never lose their passion for a sport because of bad coaching. The struggle is just a battle in the war in life. It's an experience some will go through and must learn to manipulate through the vast jungle of hardships which will, no doubt, prepare them for future feats. They should not give up. They should not expect social equality because oftentimes they will not find it, but more importantly God is in control, and as God's kids, we can teach and be a light as to how to treat others fairly and with respect. Sabria's freshman year in basketball nearly put her fire out for the sport. She was broken down from every angle, but what the school and friends and bad coach broke down, God built back up. She had to be broken down to her core, exposing her weaknesses and the reality of her downfalls, because only then could she gain perspective, drive, and confidence. It all came after learning humility and being brought down to her lowest point. These experiences were needed for her future at West Point, but she couldn't have known that then. Don't underestimate the good that can come from having a bad coach in your child's life. It will prepare the child to appreciate the good one and will allow the opportunity for the parent to be the child's advocate if they, too, are willing to go through the fire with the child, thus building passion while learning to strive to succeed under pressure. Romans 8:28 says, "And we know that God causes all things to work together for good to those that love God, to those that were called according to His purpose."

CHAPTER 26

DIG DEEPER

For six weeks, Quintin had been working diligently to get stronger and recover and make gains at therapy. Finally, we had our appointment with the surgeon for his six-week checkup. We were expecting the doctor to be blown away at his progress and completely impressed at how hard he had worked. Thinking of how I had constantly been switching schedules and Quintin continued to push through the pain, we were ready for the doctor to come in, smile, and tell us we did a good job. He came in and looked at Quintin's leg. He checked his bending. He pushed hard and then harder. Quintin let out a scream that I think the whole office heard. He started crying, big tears streaming down his cheeks. We were both shocked, and my stomach flipped. The doctor turned and looked at me and said with a disappointed look on his face that he was very concerned for Quintin's leg. I was shocked and asked, "What? Why?" He told us that Quintin had developed scar tissue and that if we didn't take care of it then, he would never regain full range of motion in that knee. My heart sank, and I was completely discouraged, but I just transitioned my mind to be able to even hear what the doctor was saying to me. He said we needed to increase therapy to three times a week and add in swimming two to three times a week. This was our chance to get a better degree of range of motion, and if significant progress wasn't made in a few weeks, he would have to put Quintin under anesthesia and manipulate that knee to break up the scar tissue. Quintin was devastated. All the work he did and it wasn't enough. Homeschooling, bathroom breaks in the living room, urinals, sponge baths by Mom, therapy several times a week, and now bad news. We asked, "Why is this happening to us?" But we were determined to fight. We expected to get good news that day and we could finally relax; but God said it wasn't yet time to relax, it was still time to fight. This would be like overtime in a game that you put all your heart and energy into and were completely spent only to get a tie and then realize you must still play another quarter. That's when you find the strength that is there; you just have to tap into it. You are confident that all the blood, sweat, and tears from training are remembered; and you find that grit. The doctor reminded us that this was a very tough injury for such a young boy, and Quintin told me he didn't want to go back under the knife. I told him that I didn't want that either and I would help him but that he was gonna have to work hard and do what the doctor said and pray to God that his efforts would be blessed.

Since Quintin had the meniscus involvement, he had a resting period that we had to follow, and during that time, he wasn't allowed to bend the knee too far or put weight on it. That made time for the scar tissue to develop, so the therapist said it was just collateral damage, basically. Unavoidable. He had many restrictions on his range of motion, but now that those restrictions were lifted, they could start really working the knee to get it to bend more. Now he would need to push through the pain and break that tough scar tissue that prevented his knee from bending. Another mountain yet to climb. The doctor told Quintin if we didn't get this under control that his leg, in that condition, would not be compatible with playing sports and his dream of playing football again and all sports he loved would not come true. We had no choice but to give everything we had. We knew there was a reason for the struggle. God was molding Quintin, teaching him how to strive. We added the extra day of therapy every week and also went to the YMCA to swim. I took the other kids too. I had a responsibility to them, too, and wanted to include them in the opportunity to learn and grow in this challenge. They encouraged Quintin and knew his struggle. This therapy was so involved, and I wanted to keep our family bond and be what I needed to still be for the other kids. It was so cold going in and out of the Y in the dead of winter, but we did it. After work or before work, whenever I could fit these swimming sessions in, I did. Three days a week, we went to the Y and did full-length laps in the lap pool and exercises that the therapist gave us a list of: butt kicks, sidesteps, and squats in the water. I became Quintin's therapist on those days, and that was okay because that was what God called me to be. The water was so refreshing and acted as a shock absorber, taking the pressure off Quintin's leg, so he could do more activities than he could out of the water. The water also dulled the pain he felt in bending the knee; and if he went under the water and bent the knee, he could actually hear the scar tissue cracking apart, releasing more tension for movement. He was intrigued, and so was I. This gave Quintin hope and encouraged the drive to keep going. Before long, Quintin was becoming more active and learning his limits, which, in the pool, seemed less strict. I watched as he began to play with his siblings like a normal boy again, laughing and smiling and moving. This was more than physical therapy. It was spiritual and emotional therapy, too, for all of us. It was fun. We continued to be disciplined with this plan, even in the sixteen-degree Ohio winter. We were diligent. We would drag ourselves to the pool and force ourselves into the water, knowing it was going to pay off because our faith would not let us believe anything else. Once we were there, we ended up having fun and making the best of it and were thankful we didn't cave and give up when it was tough to do what was right. Quintin was learning to do what was right and not just indulging in what felt right. He was learning to let his heart lead his body, instead of letting his body be in charge. Your body will show weakness, but your heart is guarded by God, who has more strength than we could ever need. Always make up your mind to follow your heart in facing battles that seem too hard for you. This is how you will find God's strength, which is necessary to get to your highest potential.

As Sabria learned of Quintin's struggle and hardships, she was feeling connected to him, understanding his toil and perseverance. I sent her a video of him on the stationary bike and pictures of him in the pool. She did know how hard we were working to get progress, and she appreciated this determination she saw in her family, her team back home. It was contagious. She also had to push hard, crutching her way through the New York winter from one class to the next, making sure not to slip on the ice and slush as she was forced to rush here and there. We appreciated FaceTime, and this really helped us stay close and feel connected while being so far away during tough times. Then one day at therapy, instead of just rocking the pedal back and forth, Quintin was able, that day, to make a full rotation. We celebrated as this was a big deal for Quintin. I sent Sabria the video of Quintin's progress on the bike; and the next day, she, too, made a full rotation on the bike. The two were connecting and competing from four hundred miles away. Quintin's surgery was almost five weeks before Sabria's, but because Quintin tore his meniscus as well as ACL, he had that extra six weeks of recovery and was forced to wait on certain things in therapy. Sabria was a week ahead in her therapy because, of course, she is a beast, a hard worker, and was challenged by Quintin. This meant they were actually in the exact same place in the progress of physical therapy—pushing each other to get the work in and comparing exercises over the phone. This is proof to me that God sets up time and place, because there was no way that these two situations with my kids could have been coincidence, and these types of things are the main reason for me choosing to write this book.

God was so evident in our lives that I had to be obedient to him and share these stories with the world. I could not keep them all to myself, because this is how God moves in our lives here on earth, and we need to connect with that to grow in him. If Sabria's meniscus would have been torn as they thought it was, she would have needed that repaired, too, which would have added six weeks of recovery time, and she and Quintin would not have been on the same path. I believe God healed her meniscus during the month between her MRI and her surgery. No other explanation makes sense to me. Now as Quintin and Sabria were connected and had a deeper bond, they encouraged each other. Even if they didn't speak all the time and even being so far apart, their actions and discipline spoke for them, and they were connected on that spiritual level that is the strongest bond to have. I tried to be a facilitator of positivity. When Quintin had a hard day, I would tell him to remember that Sabria was working hard, too, at West Point doing her therapy and he needed to stay the course because she fed off his strength. I would then tell Sabria that Quintin depended on her to be strong to lead him to be strong and dedicated. I prayed that my kids would be bonded even through Sabria's journey through West Point and that we wouldn't lose touch. This was God answering my prayers, even if it wasn't exactly how I imagined. Quintin and I were doing five to six days a week of therapy; and I watched as he reached 90, 110, and 120 degrees of flexion on that knee. He made gains every single week. The therapist told him to keep working hard so he could impress the doctor with the results of his work. We were confident that day, a few weeks later when we went in to see the doctor. We knew we grinded, and there was no way Quintin was going back under the knife or missing out on his dream to play sports again one day, we made sure. The doctor walked in and bent Quintin's knee, and we all smiled as he measured and made it all the way to that sweet spot on the measuring tool. He extended his arm and shook my son's hand and said, "Great job, young man." We celebrated in the office that day as my eyes welled up at what we had just accomplished. I thanked that doctor. He was so hard on us because he wanted to see success for Quintin. He is an amazing man, and I think very highly of him as he was a good example to my son of how to raise the bar high to get good results. I really was inspired to learn all I could concerning preventing ACL injury after all we were going through, even to get certified myself to teach the program. I grew passionate in the field and wanted to learn all I could to keep my kids and anyone and everyone safe in athletics. In February of 2020, just a week before getting my certification, Steve Saunders, Baltimore Ravens' head strength and conditioning coach, visited the YMCA in Youngstown to meet with Coach Carl and Coach Hartzell to share ideas and concepts. The Ravens had experienced a large number of injuries for years, and their coach wanted to improve this situation after they reportedly led the NFL in injuries in 2017. Coach Saunders himself was trained by Hartzell and was familiar with the jump-stretch program. After he decided to implement similar exercise techniques as those in jump stretch into the training for the Ravens, he noticed a big improvement. The injury level decreased in the football players, and they had much better success on the field as a result. This was encouraging to me that there was hope for teams who have a history of a high number of injuries and that there is a program that has worked to keep the body safe and more resilient. The pattern of injury on teams can change, but it takes effort and willingness to learn of what works, and if the players and coaches work together, positive change can occur for the team as a whole.

CHAPTER 27

VALUE OTHERS ABOVE YOURSELVES

As playoffs began for women's basketball at West Point, Sabria informed me that she may be able, after all, to come home for spring break in April. She wouldn't know when because she was committed to staying with the team as long as they were winning and advancing further in the playoffs. Even though she wasn't playing on the court, she supported her team from the sidelines. I ran and told the kids, "Sabria's coming home!" We didn't know exactly when, but this was getting to be normal for us to just find out last minute, as this was how it worked at West Point. We knew it would be in a few weeks, so we decided to do what we had wanted to do for a long time, paint Sabria's room. Her sisters asked her what color she would want it to be, and she picked her favorite color, yellow. We chose a pretty pale yellow for the walls. All the Hunter girls shared a bedroom, and Sabria's sisters wanted to welcome her home, so they decided to do the room up how she would like it. This idea to indulge in their sister's homecoming was inspired by the verse in Philippians 2:3: "Do nothing out of selfish ambition or vain conceit. Rather, in humility value others above yourselves." We headed to Home Depot, prepared the walls, cleaned and organized, moved beds and dressers, went back to Home Depot, and after a few days we were pretty tired. This was a big job, between all my shifts at work and painting, cleaning, putting the paint away, and then getting it back out when I had some time. It was crazy. A couple of weeks went by, and we finally saw the thing coming together. We had gotten new blinds and picked out new pillows for the beds that matched the walls. It started to look good. My dad saw all the work being done and, of course, got involved. He said, "How about that TV on the wall?" I told him I had taken it down because it no longer worked, and I didn't have any more money to replace it at that time. He said, "They have a sale at Walmart right now on TVs. Let's go!" So we went to Walmart to buy the girls a TV to go on the wall in their room. I wasn't sure if I would have time before Sabria came home to get the cable guy out to hook up cable in that room, but while we were in line at Walmart, the cashier told us there was a better TV there for the same price, and it was a smart TV, so no cable needed hooked up, after all. Knowing how much my girls love Netflix and Disney Plus, this would be perfect for Sabria's time at home to bond with her sisters. We were all excited, and my son Dylan scurried back to the TV section and grabbed the other one and brought it to the register for his sister. We came home and got that new TV hooked up. My dad always found ways to add excitement to any project and situation. Then, during the time we were doing this work at home, Sabria called and said, "Mom, can I ask you a question?" I said, "Of course," and I wondered what this could be about, knowing it was big, because I could tell by her tone. She said, "Could Kam come home with me too?" Kam was Sabria's best friend at the academy and was from California. With the travel time and time change, she would never be able to get home during their short spring break and would have to stay at the academy. I didn't hesitate, and surely Sabria knew that my response would be, "Yes, of course, she could come home with you." I told her to let Kam know that our house was comfortably chaotic and small and to let her know we would feed her well and that the only bathroom in the house was very functional but not pretty as it was under construction. Sabria told me that Kam was happy to come spend time with our family and to get out of the academy and she would appreciate our house as Sabria did. I always indulged in the opportunity to love another person despite the fact that we didn't ever have a lot of money or a big house to offer.

God always provided the resources to make loving others a possibility for me, and I appreciated that by walking in faith, being humble and trusting him. The kids were excited to spend time with both Sabria and Kam, whom they met over Thanksgiving when we had taken the trip to see Sabria and ended up having the opportunity to have Kam join us for that weekend and knowing she was coming home with Sabria fueled our ambitions even more to prepare for their homecoming. I figured this would help Sabria with her homesickness because if Kam came home with her and their friendship could grow and she could connect with our family more, it would be like Sabria was able to take someone from home back to West Point with her. Sometimes after being home for a while, she was able to fulfill the need to be with her family, but then she would miss her friends at West Point, so this way she could have both her family and friend and be able to just rest and enjoy her time. Also, this could allow her friend to understand why Sabria missed home so much, and this could deepen their bond as friends. We really worked to make the house inviting. Looking in the girls' room, I needed to be creative in deciding how to fit five girls in there comfortably. They had a bunk bed that fit four of them comfortably, so I thought, *What could I add?* I knew Theresa wanted a beanbag chair, but this would not be big enough to sleep on. I searched the Internet and found the perfect addition to that room. It was a two-hundred-pound memory foam bean bag chair called Big Joe on Amazon. It was huge and perfect. It was like a beanbag chair but big enough to fit two large adults on it comfortably, and I knew this would be the perfect thing for Sabria and Kam to relax on and watch movies with the girls. Since it was filled with memory foam instead of beads, it could also be used as an actual bed! There would not be enough room for another actual bed, but this bag was soft and pliable. It could be utilized perfectly in that small room. I ordered it to be delivered to the house. This meant if it all worked out that I had accomplished my goal and actually made comfortable sleeping space for all five girls, with even extra room for others in case other friends came over or if we decided to do a movie night in there with the girls. This is to tell that where there is a will, there is a way and that it is very beneficial to become resourceful; and I learned this over the years, to learn to use what I had to work with and make it nice and accommodating to those around me. God blessed me as I did this over the years, so I learned as he inspired me. I never tried to buy a bigger house because as I listened, God showed me how to maximize space so I could use my money instead to love people by inspiring, teaching, leading, and caring.

Sabria had called, and as she was busy with finals that week, she forgot to tell me that she had the opportunity to come home in just a few days, so I needed to be ready to go pick them up. I hoped the beanbag bed would come before she came home. It did! We found it was just as we expected, huge and comfortable, like you were lying on a cloud. It took all of Bobby, the girls, and me to roll it up the stairs together, and after much effort, we got it in the room. It had a spot at the bottom of the girls' bed, fitting snugly between the bed and the wall, taking up that whole corner of the room, creating the perfect little comfy space and where the TV was in perfect view. Theresa picked out a pillow that said, "My happy place," and placed it in front of the other pillows on the bed. We looked at all the work we did in that room and said, "Sabria will love this!" She did not know of all the work we did. We only told her we were painting. So the transformation would be a surprise to her. We hung up some pictures she liked and replaced some hardware. It was all ready for our hero to come home. I had crock pot plans for the week and filled the fridge and cupboard with all our favorite foods. We were gearing up to celebrate. Once again, I wanted Sabria to know that while she was away and working so hard to do well in school, keeping her grades up, and staying motivated through her recovery after ACL surgery, as well as supporting her team and coaches while the season continued, we were still thinking of her at home. We had everything planned. I had to cover shifts at work, and the plan was to meet Sabria after she got home from the game in Baltimore. We would be there at 0500, which was the earliest she would be allowed to leave the academy. This was only pending their loss in Baltimore. We listened intently to the game on the radio broadcast. My whole family was invested. We, of course, wanted the team to do well, but they were not expected to win against the team they were playing, and we wanted our girl to come home so badly that we banked on the loss. The more games they won and continued on in the playoffs, the shorter the spring break would be and could potentially end up being no spring break at all. We expected the break as our hearts couldn't imagine the alternative, and realistically, West Point had many injuries on the team so they weren't expected to make it far in the playoffs. I was actually cleaning our car out during this game knowing I would have to head straight to New York right after the game ended to meet the girls if they lost that game. Dylan and Bobby were giving me updates, and as the game came closer to ending, the suspense was building. I was not prepared to reroute myself if they won. I prayed that God would prepare me if this happened. Much to my surprise, West Point won that game in the last few minutes. I imagined my daughter sitting on the sidelines conflicted by wanting her team to win but wanting to come home so bad. I knew she was dealing with a lot of emotions, and I felt helpless to help her.

This is just one of those situations that makes you grow up. I had been so busy nesting for my daughter to come home that I never actually imagined it not happening on that day. People have often told me that I seem to have a motor inside me and that never seems to stop. That night, my motor stopped. The reality set in that my daughter would not be coming home that day, and I just started crying, and that was all I could do. I knew God would provide a new plan, but all I can say is when your kid is at a military school and they have the chance to come home and then that changes, even if it's by a couple of days, it's an overwhelmingly emotional experience. I needed to reroute and work on plan B. Her spring break would be cut even shorter, but I would not dare to complain, since I would get the chance at some point to see my kid again; at least that was always my hope. The new plan came together, and that was for Bobby to drive from our house to Bucknell New York where Army would be playing next. Sabria and Kam got clearance to leave after the game with Bobby to come home to Ohio if Army lost. Bobby had to make the three-and-a-half-hour drive to Bucknell to watch the game in actual hopes that they lost so he could bring the girls home. This drive was half the distance of what he would have made to West Point, and this fit into our schedule perfectly. I couldn't do the trip, because I had to take Sophia to her first travel basketball practice with SMAC, which was forty-five minutes in the opposite direction, at Lebron James's alma mater, St. Vincent–St. Mary in Akron, Ohio. So once again, Bobby and I divided to conquer. Sabria was very proud of Sophia's brave choice to play with her old coach and friend, Andre, so she didn't mind that I couldn't be there to pick her up. It actually took pressure off to have something else going on during the game. Bobby sat in the stands and watched the game, and as he hoped he could take his daughter home, he still supported the team. They did end up losing, and he called me on the way home with two very giddy girls in the background to tell me the good news. The girls were on their way home, finally! Even if it was just for a few days, it was worth the wait. I got home first and waited up on pins and needles. They pulled in the driveway, and we met them on the front porch to greet them, hugging and smiling as our hearts were full. We showed them to their room, and Sabria was completely blown away at the transformation. Kam was delighted to see that she was offered the opportunity to take a break with her friend, and this came as much relief after their hard time at the academy and since they were both suffering from knee injuries and needed time to rejuvenate. During the girls' time with us, we made sure to introduce Kam to some hometown staples like Mill Creek Park and Wedgewood pizza. We enjoyed our family time together. We were all learning to trust God, and as he was teaching us how to maneuver through hardships and struggles, we would need this teaching more than ever soon. What we didn't know was what was coming. We had gotten word after about a week of the girls being home that there was a sickness caused by a virus that had recently become a problem. The academy was extending spring break, and this meant that Kameron could make arrangements after all to go see her own family in California. We were so excited for her and assisted as she made plans and ultimately got a flight booked out of Pittsburgh that very weekend. We took her to Pittsburgh and said our goodbyes, sending her away with our love.

After that very night of her leaving Ohio, cadets were banned from traveling, and we had just made it through the window of opportunity for Kam to get home to her family. The coronavirus had shown its ugly face and this was the beginning of the most widespread epidemic our country had seen in many years, contributing reportedly to hundreds of thousands of deaths having millions of reported cases. Covid-19 brought along with it a level of fear that would be responsible for rerouting the next several months of our lives, and even changing lives forever. We could not imagine what God had in store for us, the Hunter family, as the circumstances surrounding the virus would change our lives at home, school, and work and in sports; but as we never lost hope, God would remain faithful in leading us through yet another storm. What I had encountered throughout 2019 would prepare me for whatever was to come. From July 2019 to April 2020, our family grew from Sabria's send-off to West Point, and we thought this would be enough to keep us busy, but we would find there would be much more to be added to our plate. Quintin's football injury in September; Dylan's appendicitis and surgery in October; Quintin's surgery in December; Sabria's injury in December and then surgery in January; my meeting with the athletic director at West Point, Quintin's intense physical therapy; and then in April, Sabria's return home, which turned into an unplanned extended leave until further notice while plans were made concerning coronavirus. These were just some of our battles and blessings over a very crazy ten months, and I know God will continue to lead my family. I hope these stories and more to come will bring anyone who hears them hope and perspective. May you be encouraged to find joy in the toil as God always shows he is faithful. Please find it in your hearts to be a true advocate for what is right as God stirs your conscience and leads you on unimaginable journeys.

ABOUT THE AUTHOR

Christina "Tina" Hunter has been a registered nurse for seventeen years, working in the fields of critical care and postpartum. She is a mother of six and is passionate about spending time with her kids while teaching them the value of knowing God's love for them. In the fall of 2019, her son tore his ACL during a football game, at the age of nine; and only about a month later, her daughter, a freshman at West Point Military Academy, tore her ACL during a basketball practice. She vowed to learn all she could to help prevent all athletes from succumbing to this devastating injury. She became certified in the dynamic rubber-band circuit training class called jump stretch and encourages her kids to learn the value of being their own advocate, using their voice to keep them safe, and that discipline, humility, honor, and accountability are most important in the building process of a true athlete. She hopes to inspire parents, coaches, teachers, and athletes to learn the power of love, to live passionately, and to be purposeful in their actions. She hopes to raise the bar in the world of athletics by instilling in others a deeper respect for sports and to understand it is a privilege to play the game. She enjoys living in Austintown, Ohio.